D1202387

THE BALTIC STATES

THE
BALTIC
STATES

THE YEARS OF INDEPENDENCE

Estonia, Latvia, Lithuania

1917–1940

by

GEORG VON RAUCH

translated from the German by
GERALD ONN

C. HURST & COMPANY, LONDON
UNIVERSITY OF CALIFORNIA PRESS
BERKELEY AND LOS ANGELES

Published in the United Kingdom by
C. Hurst & Co. (Publishers) Ltd.,
38 King Street, London WC2E 8JT,
and in the United States of America by
University of California Press,
Berkeley and Los Angeles.
This translation © 1974 C. Hurst & Co. (Publishers) Ltd.

First published 1974
Second Impression 1987

ISBNs
Hurst 0-903983-00-1
California: 0-520-02600-4

German edition *Die Geschichte der baltischen Staaten*
© 1970 W. Kohlhammer GmbH, Stuttgart, Berlin, Köln, Mainz

Printed in England

CONTENTS

APPENDICES

MAP

> Those who approach the past
> with astonishment, with humility
> and a touch of sadness will also
> show a proper sense of respect
> for the mysterious character of
> freedom, and the enigma of the
> future; and they will not deny
> their readers the right to hope.
>
> – GOLO MANN

INTRODUCTION

In the precise sense of the term, a history of the Baltic States must necessarily be restricted to the relatively brief period between the two world wars, in which the peoples of Estonia, Latvia and Lithuania were able to assert and maintain their independence. Both the acquisition, and the loss, of this independence were closely linked with the great political events of the epoch, and can only be properly understood within an international context. In 1917–19, as in 1939–40, the Baltic question constituted one specific aspect of the great developments which made those periods turning points in word history. During the final collapse of the Teutonic Order (1558–61), and the disintegration of Sweden's *Dominium Maris Baltici* (1710–21), the Baltic territories were an important factor in international affairs; so too were the Baltic States during the period 1917–40. The history of the Baltic peoples in these years is a part of world history.

Inevitably, the fate of the Baltic peoples has been dealt with only at a very superficial level by the authors of general histories. A number of native Baltic historians, on the other hand, have produced comprehensive accounts, in which they have recorded the political and social life of their individual territories from the earliest times right through to the modern period. Many of these books have been translated into western languages and are, therefore, readily accessible. But since they deal with historical development on a strictly national basis, works of this kind presuppose a somewhat narrower view; not infrequently, the history of a particular people, when recorded by a native historian, appears as an emanation of the national character of that people. This kind of approach is, of course, a product of the nationalist era. However, since it does not, in itself, preclude the possibility of critical reflection and objective assessment, it is a perfectly legitimate method, and one which can clearly be applied in the historical appreciation of all nations, both large and small. Today, of course, attitudes have changed, and historians are now very much concerned, and rightly so, with the need to avoid the subjectivism that was such a frequent concomitant of the nationalist ethos. Not that this new approach is unproblematical. On the contrary, we now run the risk of what might best be described as ideological rigorism. The method adopted by the Baltic historians prior to 1940 was based on purely national assessments; and so, no matter how objective they tried to be, they were bound to restrict the scope of their enquiries, and so were unable to furnish an integrated account of events in the whole of the Baltic area.

Between the two world wars, however, a pan-Baltic approach was adopted by a number of politicians and journalists, who published articles in which they discussed the economic affairs of the territory at some length, and commented on Baltic history and folk traditions in rather greater detail than the authors of contemporary guide-books. Thus, the western reader was able to acquire some insight into this remote corner of Europe, which bordered on the completely different world of the Soviet Union.

Although there was no lack of native scholars with the requisite historical and linguistic knowledge, it would have been unreasonable to expect an Estonian or Latvian historian to produce a comprehensive 'Baltic History' even in the traditional sense of that term, i.e. a history of the old Russian provinces on the Baltic. And in fact we find that the standard work on the history of the 'Baltic territories of Livonia, Estonia and Courland' is the *Baltische Geschichte* of R. Wittram, which first appeared in 1944 and was reissued in a revised form in 1954. In the original edition of this work, which covers the entire period from the end of the twelfth century to the emergence of the independent Baltic States in 1918, Wittram concentrated on the development of the German ethnic group while in the revised edition he sought to provide a history of the whole territory, including the Estonian and Latvian peoples.

Today the independence of the Baltic States is a thing of the past. Consequently, it is incumbent on the contemporary historian to investigate, and to try to assess, this whole period, which came to an end a generation ago. Sufficient time has elapsed for reflection. Sufficient documents – although by no means all – have been collected. There are certain research problems, it is true; but they are of a different order.

When I came to consider this period, I decided to extend the traditional borders of the Baltic territories southwards by combining the history of Lithuania with that of Estonia and Latvia. This decision may well appear surprising at first sight, for despite their linguistic and racial affinities with the Latvians, the Lithuanians undoubtedly followed a very different line of development, and formed very different political associations, during the major part of their history. These differences will be discussed in Chapter I of this book. But the essential fact remains that, for a variety of reasons, the Lithuanians did not renew their old bonds with Poland, preferring to throw in their lot with the Latvians and Estonians. This led to the formation of a new and enlarged community, which became more and more closely knit throughout the twenty years of Baltic independence. The sense of identity inspired by that community is still a force to be reckoned with today, and is likely to remain so in the future.

Before the collapse of the Russian Empire there were no close ties between the three Baltic territories. All they really had in common at that time was their membership of the Russian Empire, and their subservience to the Tsar and his officials. On the other hand, they underwent similar experiences and were faced with similar problems. For example, all three peoples awoke to a sense of their national identity during the second half of the nineteenth century, and all three suffered

A*

the same privations during the First World War (when parts of Lithuania and Latvia were actually amalgamated into a single administrative unit under the German occupation). They all later seceded from the Russian Empire and fought to establish their independence. And although these undertakings were mostly pursued independently of one another, they none the less laid the foundations for a closer *rapprochement* during the period of independence, and even led to the establishment of administrative and institutional links, which reached their apogee with the conclusion of the 'Baltic Entente'. Finally, there was the fact that all three Baltic States became caught up in the great-power politics of their totalitarian neighbours, Germany and Russia, and consequently lost their independence in the Second World War.

In view of their considerable historic achievements in the inter-war years, the peoples of the Baltic States did not deserve this tragic fate, to which they are still forced to submit. Neighbouring Finland regained her freedom following the German capitulation; the Baltic States did not. Of course, the fact that all three territories have continued to suffer under this common yoke strengthens the case for a comprehensive analysis of their history, although in adopting such an approach we must be careful not to oversimplify the relations between them between 1918 and 1940 or suppress any peculiarities in their earlier backgrounds.

If we are to avoid these pitfalls, then we must reject a purely additive account, in which the history of each of these three states would be analysed in turn. This would not only constitute an oversimplification of what is actually a highly complex issue, but would also fail to exploit the very special opportunity offered to the researcher in this particular instance. It seemed to me, therefore, that an integrated approach would be preferable in so far as it would facilitate comparisons, and would highlight both the similarities and the differences between the three territories. And there is, I think, a certain fascination in discussing the agrarian reforms and the problems of the minority groups, the relations of the Baltic States to the Soviet Union, the emergence in those states of authoritarian tendencies, and, finally, their involvement in the power politics of their two great neighbours, in terms of a corporate community rather than on a purely individual basis.

This history of the Baltic States will doubtless reveal many shortcomings, and may well finish up by pleasing nobody. In my judgements, and even in my choice of materials, I can hardly expect to meet with general approval: there are bound to be many shades of opinion on these matters among historians of different nationalities. Some, no doubt will, argue that an anthology consisting of a series of articles contributed by historians representing each of the different Baltic territories would have been more appropriate, although a work of this kind would have lacked the synoptic quality which I find so desirable. It could also be argued that in a synoptic work such as mine – written, after all, by an outsider – the assessments of the various Baltic peoples could not possibly be as authentic or profound as those made by indigenous historians. But the outsider also has a certain advantage, for he is perhaps less likely to be partisan in his judgements. As a Baltic German, I can possibly claim to write with an insight not shared by other outsiders, but this is not total; it seldom extends beyond Estonia and Latvia to Lithuania, where the language barrier creates serious difficulties. So we see that even when the historian is at pains to identify interrelated factors and to eliminate subjective impressions, the validity of his statements must still depend on the validity of his basic viewpoint, which will always have the defects of its virtues. Fortunately, the period which has elapsed since the 1920s and 1930s serves as a filter which helps us to clarify precipitate, modish or affective judgements, and so acquire a clearer view of past events. For my own part, I confess that I was greatly encouraged to undertake this study by the friendly relations and meetings which I have had with Estonian, Latvian and Lithuanian colleagues in recent years.

In writing this history of the Baltic States and their peoples I have probably dealt in somewhat greater detail than is customary among Baltic historians with the different minorities, and – for the simple reason that prior to 1917–18 it played a more important historical role than the other indigenous communities – I have also paid rather more attention to the Baltic–German ethnic group than to any other.

Since I wished to concentrate as far as possible on the brief period of Baltic independence in the main body of the text, I have dealt briefly with the wider historical background in an introductory chapter. To have embarked on a more ambitious treatment of this early period would, in any case, have been impossible in a one-volume work. But although the events immediately preceding the establishment of Baltic independence are well documented and have already been analysed at length by other authors, who have described both the struggle of the Baltic peoples to assert their right to self-determination and the military and political role played in that struggle by the great powers, I none the less found it necessary to consider those events in rather greater detail in Chapter I. For the period following the armistices I based my account on two earlier studies of mine, which appeared in 1954 and 1967 respectively. I was also able to draw on a number of significant new specialist studies, whose authors have adopted a synoptic approach to the Baltic States, treating all three territories as a corporate whole. In this respect I would like to draw attention to the work of U. Germanis, J. von Hehn, M. Hellmann, B. Meissner, A. Mägi, H. von Rimscha, Stuart R. Schram, A. E. Senn, A. N. Tarulis, A. von Taube, H. Uustalu and W. Wachtsmuth, which I have consulted.

All dates prior to 1 February 1918 are based on the Julian Calendar, all later dates on the new Gregorian Calendar. Bibliographical notes and, where necessary, end notes have been provided for each chapter.

I would like to express my sincere gratitude to Dr. O. Angelus, Dr. J. von Hehn and Frau K. Mrongowius for their many helpful suggestions, and for having undertaken the onerous task of checking the completed text in manuscript form. I would also like to thank my colleagues Herr P. Dybowski, Dr. Phil. M. Garleff, cand. phil. J. Pagel and W. Toerner, M.A., for assistance with the research, for proof-reading, and for preparing an index. Finally I wish to express my sincere thanks to the publishers, C. Hurst and Co., for the great understanding they have brought to the translation and editing, and indeed to the subject of this work.

THE AUTHOR

FOREWORD TO THE ENGLISH EDITION

At certain periods British politicians have taken an active interest in the Baltic and the Baltic territories. This happened during the Crimean War of 1854–6 and the Russian Civil War of 1917–20, and during the twenty years of independence, when the United States also turned their attention to the Baltic area.

The interest taken by the western powers in Baltic sovereignty was of crucial importance, for it provided a counterpoise to the aggressive policies pursued by the Russians and Germans, first in competition, and subsequently in collaboration, with each other. It also led to the development of an extremely active trading relationship between Britain and the Baltic States, which naturally had political implications.

In view of this strong western involvement in Baltic politics during the inter-war years it is perhaps not unreasonable to assume that a survey of this period might be of interest to English-speaking readers. And then, of course, there are the numerous Baltic emigrants to be considered, many of whom have settled in the U.S.A., Canada, Britain and Australia. The majority of these emigrants fled from their homes in the Baltic area during the Second World War, although as far as the Lithuanians are concerned there was by then already a long tradition of emigration to the U.S.A. dating from the closing years of the nineteenth century. Consequently, there now exist large expatriate Baltic communities, many of whose members were born in exile, and it was felt that they too might welcome a synoptic account of the twenty years of Baltic independence.

The terminology of Baltic history is not without its pitfalls, and at this point I would like to deal very briefly with this aspect of the subject, and outline the method I have employed in my study.

It was during the rule of the Teutonic Order (1201–1561) that the Latin names of Estonia, Livonia and Curonia (Courland) were first used to describe the three Baltic provinces, which were occupied by the Estonians (Estonia and Northern Livonia) and the Latvians (Southern Livonia and Courland), the smaller Livonian and Courlander communities having been assimilated by these two majority groups.

Meanwhile, the whole of the territory ruled over by the Teutonic Order was also frequently referred to as 'Livonia', which consequently acquired both a general and a specific meaning. Later, after the collapse of the Order, the three Baltic provinces came, first under Swedish and Polish, and eventually under Russian, control. But throughout the whole of this period they retained their original names.

It was only after the War of Liberation that the three Baltic provinces were replaced by the twin states of Estonia (which was composed of the old province of Estonia together with parts of Northern Livonia) and Latvia (which embraced Southern Livonia and Courland). The third Baltic State, Lithuania, was a completely separate entity up to 1917, but from then onwards began to establish close ties with its northern neighbours.

Because the Baltic Germans had played such a dominant role in the historical development of Estonia and Latvia, German place-names were used in both countries for all official purposes prior to their liberation. Not surprisingly, German historians have continued to use these German place-names (I did so myself in the German edition of this book). But there is no good reason why they should be retained in the English translation. On the contrary, the Estonian, Latvian and Lithuanian place-names are far more appropriate, if only on account of the expatriate Baltic communities now living in English-speaking countries. It is, of course, true that German place-names have been employed by British historians in the past (we are told, for example, that Edward VII visited Reval [Estonian Tallinn] in 1908), and for this reason the German form of each place-name has been added in brackets on its first appearance. Bilingual lists of the most important place-names appear at the end of the book.

Russian names have been transcribed in accordance with English phonetic practice (i.e. Trotsky for Trockij). Russian towns which have changed their name have been referred to by the name in use at the time in question (thus, St. Petersburg for the period 1703 to 1914, but Petrograd from 1915 to 1924, and Leningrad from 1925 onwards). One final point that should perhaps be mentioned is the distinction that has to be made between the White Russians (or Byelorussians) as an ethnographic concept and the 'White' Russians (or 'White' Armies) as a political concept denoting the forces opposed to the 'Red' Bolsheviks.

The Baltic States 1917–1940

CHAPTER I

HISTORICAL BACKGROUND

1. *The Baltic Peoples*

Not all the Baltic peoples speak Baltic languages, nor are the Baltic languages the prerogative of Baltic tribes. The Estonians, Latvians and Lithuanians belong to different ethnic and linguistic groups. The Baltic languages embrace the dialects spoken by the Old Prussian, Lithuanian and Latvian tribes, who broke away from an original Slavo-Baltic community to form an ethnic group in prehistoric times. During the historical period the Baltic languages and the Baltic peoples have been quite independent of one another, and the tribes have been completely segregated from the Teutons in the west and the Slavs in the east.

The Old Prussians, Lithuanians and Latvians were all confronted, in one form or another, with the missionary and colonising zeal of the Teutonic Order. As a result of this confrontation the great majority of the Old Prussians were absorbed into the Germanic community; the few small groups who refused to conform withdrew to the areas settled by the Lithuanians. The Lithuanians and Latvians, on the other hand, were able to preserve their national identity.

The Estonians fall into a quite different category. Together with the west Finnic tribes – the Finns proper, the Karelians, the Ingrians, the Votes and the Livonians – they belong to the Finno-Ugrian language group, which also embraces the Hungarians and the primitive Finnic tribes of Northern Russia. After establishing itself in Livonia the German missionary and colonisation movement passed on into Estonia, where it came up against a similar movement launched in the thirteenth century by the Danes, who ruled over the Estonians for more than a hundred years (1219–1346). Meanwhile, the Finns were overrun, on the other side of the Gulf of Finland, by the Swedes, whose expansionist policies in the east halted Russian activity in this area, which had been a sphere of Russian influence ever since the eleventh century.

As a result of the expansionist policies pursued by their more powerful neighbours, the Latvians (together with the Livonians whom they gradually assimilated) and the Estonians were incorporated into the Christian order of western Europe before they had a chance to develop a political system of their own. But within this new order, which had been established by the two foremost authorities of western Christianity, the Emperor and the Pope, they were nonetheless able to preserve their ethnic character. And they were far from being mere pawns of their western overlords, for they played an active part in the economic life of their territory, and defended it against external enemies, which means, of course, that they also defended its political system.

The Livonian state established by the Order of the Brothers of the Sword and subsequently by the Teutonic Order in 1346 embraced the whole area occupied by the Baltic peoples (here understood in the narrow sense of that term, i.e. the Estonians and Latvians). This state continued to exist as a political entity for some two hundred years until it was finally dismembered in the sixteenth century. The northern part, Estonia, became a province of the Swedish Empire in 1561, while the southern part, Livonia and Courland, was incorporated into the Jagiellonic kingdom, i.e. the Polish–Lithuanian Union: Livonia as a province and Courland as a duchy with a German dynasty under Polish sovereignty. In 1622 Livonia too passed to Sweden. Then, in the Great Northern War, Peter the Great pressed forward to the Baltic coast, and in 1721 Estonia and Livonia were transferred to Russia under the provisions of the Treaty of Nystad, thus facilitating Russia's entry into the European community of nations. Finally, with the third and last partition of Poland in 1795, Courland also passed to Russia. Thus the three sister provinces were reunited, and the old Baltic territories again became a corporate entity.

The administrative boundaries of the Russian Baltic provinces did not correspond to the local ethnic boundaries. Livonia, the central province, contained a northern area, occupied by Estonians, and a southern area, occupied by

Latvians. This state of affairs persisted until 1917–18, when these two peoples were finally able to establish themselves as separate nations. With the collapse of the tsarist regime following the Russian Revolution, the three Baltic provinces of Estonia, Livonia and Courland were replaced by the two Baltic States of Estonia (Essti) and Latvia (Latvija).

Unlike her northern neighbours, Lithuania was able to look back on a period of national independence in the Middle Ages. When the princes of the Gedymin dynasty joined forces at the end of the thirteenth century their country became a powerful adversary of the Teutonic Order, by which it was confronted both in the west (Prussia), and in the north (Livonia). But the repeated attempts of the Teutonic Order to conquer Lithuania, and so unite its territories, were unsuccessful. Far from being subjugated, Lithuania was able to extend her frontiers in both the east and the south during this period. Moreover, once the Kiev state of Ancient Russia had collapsed, and the Tartars had asserted their authority, a process of disintegration began in Russia which prompted a number of territories in the west and south-west to align themselves with Lithuania. But in 1386, when Prince Jagiello married into the Polish royal family, a nominal union was established between Lithuania and Poland, which was followed by an act of union in the sixteenth century. In the Jagiellonic state, which extended from the Baltic almost to the Black Sea, and was one of the largest national territories in Europe at that time, the Lithuanian upper classes identified more and more with their Polish counterparts, because Lithuania was less developed and the social structure of Poland was older and more firmly established. By the time Lithuania was annexed by the Russians as a result of the Polish partitions in the eighteenth century this process of assimilation had been carried to such lengths that virtually all memory of the country's former independence and greatness had disappeared and the written language, which had been evolved in a rudimentary form by earlier generations, had been abandoned.

The difference between the early political structure of Estonia and Latvia on the one hand and that of Lithuania on the other was matched by the difference between their social and cultural structures. By the thirteenth century Livonia was a Christian state, in which the teachings and the policies of the Roman Church were implemented by a religious order of knighthood, while Lithuania was still a pagan land. Subsequently, the Lithuanians also embraced Christianity and because of their close links with the Poles, they then kept faith with the Roman Church. The Estonians and Latvians, on the other hand, became early adherents of the Reformation and – apart from the inhabitants of Latgale (Lettgallen) – quickly rejected the Counter-Reformation once their brief period of subservience to Warsaw had passed. This opposition between Protestantism and Catholicism left its mark on the social and cultural life of these territories and remained a crucial factor right down to the modern period.

Clearly, the historical development of these two territories, from the thirteenth through to the twentieth centuries, was fundamentally different. Nonetheless, there were certain points of contact which should not be overlooked.

The first of these was established following the dissolution of the Teutonic Order, when Livonia and subsequently Riga swore allegiance to the Polish crown which, primarily for geographical reasons, incorporated this new province into the Lithuanian part of the Union. Sixty to seventy years later, when Livonia was conquered by Gustavus Adolphus, Latgale, a remote district known as 'Polish Livonia', did not pass to Sweden, and remained part of the Polish–Lithuanian Union until Poland was partitioned. As a result, Latgale acquired a quite distinct character, which it retained even within the framework of the Latvian Republic. A further point of contact was provided by the long frontier between Lithuania and Courland (which was ruled by the members of the Kettler dynasty as vassals of Poland). This long frontier was conducive to the development of close ties between the two territories. For example, many noble familes in Courland acquired estates in Lithuania; there was heavy trading across the frontier, and numerous links were established between the common people on either side. It is also quite evident that despite the presence of different national minorities, the social stratification in the various territories revealed marked similarities. Thus the structure of the Russo–Polish upper class in Lithuania resembled that of the Baltic German upper class in Estonia, Livonia and Courland.

Moreover, there was a certain cultural and linguistic link between the Latvians and Lithuanians, which also made for interaction. The linguistic link between these two peoples was, admittedly, less pronounced than that between the different Scandinavian nations. But it was, and still is, much easier for Latvians and Lithuanians to make themselves understood to one another than to the members of any other linguistic group, including the Slavs. Of course, the cultural and linguistic affinity between the Finns and the Estonians was very strong, and contributed to the development of many common interests despite the natural barrier created by the Gulf of Finland.

Finally, there was the fact that both Lithuania and her northern neighbours found themselves in the same political situation, which became particularly important in the first half of the twentieth century. In both world wars it was made perfectly clear that the existence of independent states in the Baltic area depended primarily on the policies pursued by Germany and Russia. True, the western powers and the Republic of Poland played a part in both the emergence and, indirectly, the disappearance of the Baltic States. But their influence was only marginal compared with that wielded by Germany and Russia. In the 1920s and 1930s the one really crucial question for Estonia, Latvia and Lithuania was whether their two great neighbours wanted co-operation or confrontation.

And when the Baltic States lost their sovereignty in the Second World War, both their own peoples, and the peoples of the world, were forcibly reminded by this common fate of the essential unity of these three territories. That unity may be observed to this day among the six million and more inhabitants of the Baltic area in the U.S.S.R., although the Soviet Government considered it politic to administer the Baltic peoples separately. It may also be observed among the million and more people of the Baltic States now living in exile, who are by no means prepared to renounce their countries' right to self-determination.

2. *The Emergence of Nationalism*

On the path which led them to independence the Baltic peoples passed through specific phases of social development comparable to those in other European countries. The gradual process of agrarian reform in nineteenth-century Europe was prompted in the first instance by the ideas evolved during the Age of the Enlightenment towards the end of the eighteenth century, which were publicised, sometimes in an extremely radical form, by a group of German clerics and political journalists. In the Baltic provinces the first practical step towards such reform was taken by a number of progressive estate owners, who voluntarily granted certain rights to the peasants on their estates. This eventually led to the abolition of serfdom in Estonia (1816), Livonia (1819) and Courland (1817), a measure which brought the Estonian and Latvian peasants their personal freedom but deprived them of their economic security. This security was eventually restored, between 1840 and 1860, as a result of the agrarian reforms introduced by the Baltic barons, who were responsible for local and provincial government at that time and who acted in this particular instance at the instigation of the Livonian provincial marshal Hamilkar von Fölkersahm. Under these reforms the system of servile tenure was abolished, and tenancies were granted against payment of rent. From then onwards the peasants were gradually able to consolidate their position, with the result that by 1917–18, when the independent republics of Estonia and Latvia came into being, the Estonian peasants held 57·4 per cent of all agricultural land and the Lativan peasants 63·5 per cent.

It was only after this second phase of agrarian reform had been completed that the peoples of the Baltic territories were able to concern themselves with their spiritual and intellectual emancipation. The first visible sign of this concern was the cultivation of Estonian and Latvian folk art by a group of Baltic German clerics. Inspired by J. G. Herder, a native of East Prussia who had been assistant pastor at Riga in his younger years, these clerics continued the investigations first instituted by seventeenth- and eighteenth-century researchers with a sense of dedication that was entirely new in

Baltic scholarship. One of their number was Pastor August Bielenstein (1826–1907), a pastor in Courland and the foremost Latvian philologist of his day, who became the leading light in the 'Latvian Literary Society'. Thanks primarily to Bielenstein, this society, which had been founded in 1824, became one of the focal points of Latvian cultural life in the second half of the nineteenth century. The Latvian journalist Krišjānis Barons (1835–1923) also made a major contribution by producing a comprehensive anthology of Latvian folk songs. Meanwhile, the 'Estonian Learned Society', a sister society of the 'Latvian Literary Society', had been founded in 1838 in Tartu (Dorpat), where it flourished under the guidance of F. R. Fählmann, an Estonian doctor. F. R. Kreutzwald, another Estonian doctor who was a friend of Fählmann's and medical officer of health for the town of Võru (Werro), edited the Estonian folk epos *Kalevipoeg* (The Son of Kalev). This work, which revived popular memories of the early pre-German period of Estonian history, gave a boost to the nationalist movement, whose effects were still felt during the war of liberation in the twentieth century.

In the course of this nationalist movement, which was promoted with mounting fervour in Estonia and Latvia from the 1850s onwards, the inhabitants of these territories came to think of themselves as peoples in their own right with a just claim to an independent culture. Such ideas would previously have been dismissed out of hand. True, social advancement had been possible in individual cases ever since the Reformation, and there had been a number of Estonian and Latvian clerics as early as the sixteenth century. But there was never any question of an indigenous élite, since those who secured advancement were almost invariably assimilated into the German upper class. Not that the Germans consciously sought to promote this process of 'germanisation'! It simply happened, and was regarded by all concerned as part of the natural order. Moreover, only a minority of Estonians and Latvians would have held out much hope for the development of a literary language. Even as late as 1869, when Dr. Georg Schultz-Bertram maintained that within fifty years the Estonians would be producing their own university lecturers, his optimism was shared by very few people. In fact, this prediction was completely accurate.

Other positive results of the new nationalist movement included the founding of various cultural and agricultural associations, credit institutions, newspapers and periodicals. The Latvian newspaper *Péterburgas Avīzes*, which was launched by Krišjānis Valdemārs (1825–91) in Petrograd in 1863, was a particularly significant innovation.

The centre of the nationalist movement in Estonia was Tartu, the town in which Woldemar Jannsen (1819–90) launched the newspaper *Eesti Postimees* in 1864 and founded the *Vanemuine* choral society. The first Estonian choral festival was also held in Tartu in 1869, and was quickly followed by similar festivals in other Estonian towns. These choral festivals were an important development, for they acquired a supraregional significance which influenced the development of the whole territory. It was said at the time, and with some justification, that the Estonians had sung their way to freedom. The nationalist movement launched by the Estonians received an additional impetus from their contacts with the Finns on the other side of the Gulf of Finland who were, of course, ancient kinsmen. Meanwhile, the Latvian movement influenced events in Lithuania.

The special position enjoyed by the Baltic provinces within the Russian Empire was first threatened in the 1840s when the Russian Orthodox Church, backed by the secular authorities, tried to gain a foothold in the Protestant areas by launching a 'conversion campaign'. By holding out the prospect of economic advantages, the Orthodox Church was able to make some headway with this campaign, especially in Estonia; as a result, small-scale peasant disturbances broke out in a number of localities. Then, in the 1860s, the first steps were taken towards the 'russification' of the Baltic provinces. But this new policy, which was designed to promote the use of the Russian language within the provinces and to bring their administrative and educational services into line with the rest of the Empire, was introduced very gradually, and it was not until the 1890s that it was recognised for what it was. Meanwhile, due to the initial effect of this policy, the nationalist movements of the Estonian and Lettish peoples became much more radical, and a number of the popular leaders in both territories began to look upon the German upper class as the common enemy and the Russian nationalists as their natural allies. In Latvia, Valdemārs was the principal advocate of collaboration with the Russians, while in Estonia Carl Robert Jakobson (1841–82) led the radical wing, which attacked the German provincial administration with mounting passion and bitterness. It was only later, when Russian was prescribed as the official language for use in primary schools, and the russification policy began to affect more and more areas of public life, that the danger of collaborating with the Russian nationalists was recognised; and even then there were those who refused to acknowledge this threat to their own nationalist movement.

In addition to the agrarian and nationalist movements, there was a further movement towards constitutional reform in the local and provincial administration of the Baltic territories. As partly autonomous provinces, they had not been affected by the Russian reforms of 1864. But both the Baltic barons and the Baltic German urban bourgeoisie feared that the Russians might decide to withdraw their special privileges and bring their territories into line with the rest of Russia. This prompted the more liberal members of these classes to consider the advisability of allowing representatives of the peasants to participate in the administration. As a result of these deliberations, a reform of the local administration was carried out in Livonia in 1870, whereby the parish councils were enlarged to give equal representation to the noble estates and the peasant communities.

The early years of the twentieth century brought important changes in the social structure of the Estonian and Latvian people. The growth of industry and the expansion of the railway system gave added impetus to the drift away from the land, while the abolition of compulsory guild membership for urban craftsmen, and the introduction of a new law granting every citizen the right to pursue a trade, freed the Estonians and Latvians from the restrictions which had previously been imposed on them, and paved the way for the emergence of an indigenous middle class composed of businessmen and craftsmen. The number of Estonians and Latvians who owned their own houses (mostly in suburban areas at first) began to increase. At the same time the material requirements – and the purchasing power – of the peasant population also increased, thus providing a larger home market for industrial products.

Meanwhile, the proportion of Estonians and Latvians living in the towns went up by leaps and bounds. For example: in Tallinn (Reval) the Estonian community increased from 51·8 per cent in 1871 to 88·7 per cent in 1897 (or from 15,097 in 1871 to 83,113 in 1913) and in Tartu from 46·3 per cent in 1867 to 70·8 per cent in 1897. In Riga there were 24,199 Latvians (out of a total population of 102,590) in 1867; 106,541 (out of a total population of 255,879) in 1897; and 209,839 (out of a total population of 497,586) in 1913.

The 1890s saw a marked increase in political activity amongst the members of the nationalist movement, due primarily to the initiative of a few leading personalities. In Dorpat the newspaper *Postimees* gave considerable impetus to nationalist aspirations when the young lawyer Jaan Tõnisson (1868–19—)* became its editor in 1896. In Tallinn the newspaper *Teataja*, which was also edited by a young lawyer, Konstantin Päts (1874–1955), exerted a comparable influence from 1901 onwards. Both these newspapers sought to promote the economic emancipation of the Estonian community. The *Teataja* tended to concentrate on articles attacking the German upper class, while the *Postimees* concerned itself more with the educational needs of the indigenous population.

Tõnisson and Päts, who first entered the scene in the 1890s, were to influence the development of the Estonian people for nearly half a century. Both came from peasant backgrounds in Southern Estonia (Tõnisson from the Viljandi [Fellin] area, Päts from the district of Pärnu [Pernau]); both studied law in Tartu; and both acquired political influence as newspaper editors. But, although their careers were similar, they were completely different from one another in their psychological make-up and external appearance. Tõnisson was intellectually flexible, an emotional man and a clever orator and debater. Päts, on the other hand, was a tough, cautious and self-sufficient politician, occasionally headstrong, but a hard worker who never lost sight of his goal. To some extent these two thought of themselves as antithetical figures. Certainly,

* It has not always been possible to establish the year of death of those Baltic politicians who were transported to the Russian interior in 1940.

the political opposition which developed later between their
two parties had its origins in the polemics of their journalistic
period.

The early years of the twentieth century also brought
changes in Latvia, where the early nationalists of the 'Latvian
Association', an organisation founded in Riga in 1868, found
themselves confronted by the 'New Wave' (*Jauna strāva*),
which had adopted a number of socialist ideas. The mouth-
piece of this new group was the *Dienas Lapa*, and its leaders
included the poet and author Jānis Rainis (1865–1929) and
his brother-in-law Pēteris Stučka, a lawyer. These new-style
radical nationalists were constantly harassed by the tsarist
police, and many of them were obliged to seek refuge abroad.
They formed expatriate groups in London and Zurich. The
Zurich group, which was founded by Mikelis Valters (1874–
1968) and his associates in 1903, adopted a Social Democratic
platform, and advocated the secession of Latvia from the
Russian Empire, an unusual slogan at that time. Meanwhile,
the Latvian Social Democrats in Germany made personal
contact with the leaders of the German working-class movement. As a result, August Bebel began to take a keen interest
in Baltic affairs and, more particularly, the development of
Social Democracy in Latvia.

The Latvian Social Democrats attached great importance to
these contacts, and it has been suggested that, together with
similar contacts established with contemporary German
intellectuals, they were the principal reason for the relatively
high standard of literacy in the Latvian working-class movement. Certainly, the Latvian workers (although not their
leaders) were far better equipped in this respect than their
Russian counterparts.

In the new economic climate of the early twentieth century
it was possible for members of the indigenous communities to
think of competing for public office. The first big success
came in 1901 in Valga/Valka (Walk), a town in the heart of
Livonia at the point where the Latvian and Estonian population merged. This was, therefore, a joint success on the part
of an Estonian–Latvian front. Then in 1904 the Estonians
gained a majority in the municipal council in Tallinn following
a fierce election battle. This was the first major Baltic town

to be administered by representatives of one of the Baltic peoples. Meanwhile, in two smaller towns – Rakvere (Wesenberg) and Võru (Werro) – the Estonians also won a majority in the local elections. But in Riga, which was transformed into a modern metropolis during this period under the guidance of an outstanding mayor of British extraction, Georg Armitstead (in office 1901–12), the Germans still held fifty-one of the eighty seats on the council in 1913. As for the Latvians, they gained control of Valmiera (Wolmar), Tukums (Tuckum), Kandava (Kandau) and Cēsis (Wenden) between 1897 and 1960.

Although the principal protagonists in the First Russian Revolution of 1905 were the Radicals on the one hand and the Constitutional Liberals on the other, the National Revolutionaries also played a part, and nowhere more prominently than in the Baltic provinces.

The social abuses prevailing throughout the whole of Russia towards the end of the nineteenth century led to strike action in the industrial centres of the Baltic provinces in the late 1890s. At the same time, due to the progressive radicalisation of the nationalist movement in Latvia and Estonia, the different socialist organisations in the two territories began to combine, and even established a liaison with Russian organisations. Thus, when Lenin visited Riga in 1901, he had discussions with the Latvian Social Democrats; in 1904 various local committees joined forces to form a 'Latvian Social Democratic Party.' (*Latviešu Socialdemokratiska strādnieku partija*); and later the same year this new party established a Workers' Association in conjunction with the Jewish Workers' League.

Two years later, in 1906, the Latvian Social Democratic Party entered into an affiliation with the Russian Social Democratic Workers' Party, and from then onwards played an active part in the struggle between the Bolsheviks and Mensheviks, who had split the party in 1903. In the years that followed their affiliation, the Latvian Social Democrats came to outnumber the pro-Leninists in the Russian party. But they too were divided, for while Stučka sided with Lenin and the Bolsheviks, Rainis, M. Skujenieks, P. P. Kalniņš and F. Cielēns supported the Mensheviks.

In Estonia, Tallinn became the chief centre of Socialist agitation; and between 1901 and 1904, when he was employed as an industrial worker in the 'Volta' Metal Factory, M. I. Kalinin, who later became Chairman of the Supreme Soviet and, as such, head of the Soviet state, played a leading part in the subversive activities that were carried on in that town. In 1905, immediately after the outbreak of the First Russian Revolution, a Socialist faction seceded from the All-Russian Workers movement at its congress in Tartu, and set up an independent Estonian Social Democratic Party. The leading figures in this party were P. Speek, who edited its newspaper *Uudised* (News), and M. Martna, who maintained contact with the German Socialist leader, A. Bebel.

In the minds of both the Estonian and the Latvian Social Democrats, nationalist and – in terms of the Empire – federalist aspirations competed with the requirements of international socialism. The Latvians had always been interested in the Marxist conception of national autonomy – even M. Valters had considered this idea – but, with the single exception of P. Zālite, nobody had formulated concrete proposals for the restructuring of the Russian Empire or stated in so many words what the future relationship of the Baltic area to the Empire ought to be; and Zālite's blueprint had prompted relatively little comment. At that time the concept of an autonomous state within some form of Russian federation evidently aroused far less enthusiasm in Latvia or, for that matter, Lithuania than in Estonia, where the members of the bourgeoisie were far more nationalist in outlook. And, of course, in Estonia the advocates of autonomy were organised into a political pressure group by Jaan Tõnisson and his associates when they founded the Estonian National Progressive Party in Tartu. This party called for the establishment of a common administration for Estonia and Northern Livonia (which was inhabited by Estonians); the extension of local self-government, coupled with the withdrawal of the special privileges – especially those relating to hunting – enjoyed by the estate owners; a more equitable distribution of the charges levied on the public – e.g. for road-building – between the peasants and the estate owners; the establishment of fixed rents for tenancies; the distribution of land to the landless; the improvement of working conditions for industrial workers; and, finally, the use of the Estonian language in schools.

The unrest which broke out in the Russian urban areas at the beginning of 1905 following the incident in St. Petersburg on 'Bloody Sunday', when the Tsar's troops had fired on peaceful demonstrators, soon spread to the towns of the Baltic territories, where the workers broke into prisons and distilleries and had bloody clashes with the police. These initial disturbances in Russia were followed by widespread strikes, which culminated in the general strike of October 1905. This also had far-reaching effects, and strike action was soon being taken by the workers of the Baltic provinces as well. At an assembly convened in the main hall of the University of Tartu (Dorpat) red flags were hung from the windows, and a number of extremely radical demands were formulated. Among other things, this assembly called for the abolition of the tsarist regime and its replacement by a democratic republic, and for the redistribution of the land.

In the final phase of the 1905 Revolution in the Baltic provinces the action passed from the towns to the countryside, where the seething discontent among the peasant population provided a perfect setting for violent attacks on German estates and Latvian and Estonian farms. Partisan groups were formed, whose members adopted revolutionary methods – in many cases, little less than criminal. At Tukums in Courland, which had been occupied by insurgent peasants from the surrounding district, a pitched battle was waged against the Russian Army at the beginning of December, which continued for two whole days. In all, 184 manor houses were burnt down, and eighty-two Baltic Germans were murdered in the Baltic provinces. A characteristic feature of this revolutionary activity was the special animosity which the insurgents bore towards the clergy, and which cost many of them their lives.

Without actually condoning these atrocities, the primary school teachers and parish councillors of the country districts, who clearly felt themselves to be rather more than mere spokesmen for the rural community, passed resolutions at specially convened mass meetings which testified to an acute political awareness on their part. Among other things, they called for a national culture, and a new administration, to be controlled by the elected representatives of the indigenous population.

The revolution in the Baltic provinces was suppressed with great harshness. Punitive expeditions, some of them led by Baltic German officers, were sent out to arrest known ringleaders and suspects, who received summary justice at the hands of field courts-martial. In the three provinces 908 persons were executed, hundreds received prison sentences, and several thousand were deported to Siberia. The number of farm houses burnt down by the punitive expeditions exceeded the number of manor houses burnt down by the insurgents.

When the tsarist autocracy was replaced by a constitutional monarchy, in which the Imperial Duma represented the interests of the people, politicians from the Baltic provinces were also able to participate in the legislative process. In the Ist and IInd Dumas the Latvians and Estonians were each represented by five delegates. Following the arbitrary alteration of the electoral law in 1907, the number of seats allocated to the non-Russian nationalities was reduced. Nonetheless, there were still four Latvians and two Estonians in the IIIrd Duma, and two Latvians and two Estonians in the IVth. In the IInd and IIIrd Dumas some of the Baltic delegates were members of the Social Democratic Party. When they went to St. Petersburg, the Baltic delegates were able to make contact with the delegates of the other nationalities, including the seven Lithuanian delegates to the Ist and IInd Dumas, and the four to the IIIrd and IVth. The Duma also provided a training ground for parliamentaty debate and procedure, which stood many of the non-Russian delegates in good stead at a later date. Those who benefited from such training included the Latvians J. Čakste, J. Zālītis, J. Goldmanis and A. Priedkalns, and the Estonians J. Tõnisson, J. Raamot and K. Päts. In addition to various native representatives of the Baltic peoples, a number of Baltic Germans also distinguished themselves by their work in the Duma. One such was Baron Alexander von Meyendorff, an Octobrist who was vice-president of the Duma for many years. He died in London in 1964.

The 1905 Revolution had several direct repercussions on the Baltic provinces, the most important being the partial relaxation of the ban on the use of native languages in Baltic schools. This was effected under the terms of a decree issued in 1906 authorising the foundation of private schools in which instruction was to be given in the vernacular. Later the same year a grammar school for girls, which was also the first secondary school of any kind in Estonia, was built in Tartu. Meanwhile, the whole cultural life of the provinces received a notable impetus from the founding of literary societies, publishing houses, writers' associations, public museums and theatres. In the economic sphere the Latvian and Estonian craftsmen, entrepreneurs and co-operative societies were also given every encouragement. The expansion of the co-operative system was particularly important, for it not only helped the craftsmen and entrepreneurs but also strengthened the people's sense of national identity.

All too soon, the spirit of nationalism was revived in Russia, and this led to a further russification campaign among the non-Russian minorities. According to contemporary observers, a systematic attempt was made, in the period immediately preceding the outbreak of the First World War, to obliterate all trace of national identity among the peoples of the Baltic provinces. Restrictions were imposed on the political activities of the Estonian, Latvian and Lithuanian communities, whose position had already been greatly undermined by the enforced emigration of many of their leaders following the Revolution of 1905: K. Ulmanis had gone to the U.S.A., M. Skujenieks to England, and Päts – who had been sentenced to death – to Switzerland.

As for the relations between the German upper class and the indigenous peoples, the Revolution tended to emphasise the differences between them. The Baltic German bourgeoisie, landed nobility and, above all, professional classes and intellectuals ('Literaten') had also received an impetus to their sense of national identity, which had the effect of undermining not only the rigid class barriers which had existed previously, but also their relationship to their Baltic homeland and their sense of solidarity with the local population. This change of attitude found expression in various ways. In Courland and Livonia, for example, a new settlement programme for German farmers was pushed through, which must have alienated the local population, especially the Latvians.

On the other hand, numerous attempts were made to strike a balance between the two communities. Following the 1905

Revolution the leader of the Baltic nobility in Estonia, Baron Eduard von Dellingshausen, tried yet again to settle the local government issue by recommending, at a conference called to consider the affairs of all three provinces and attended by Latvian and Estonian representatives, that the big German landowners on the one hand and the small Estonian and Latvian landowners on the other should be given equal representation at district level. This recommendation, which was rejected by the Russian Government, would have constituted an important first step towards the establishment of a multinational administration. In 1906 the Baltic barons in Livonia actually implemented a conciliatory measure when they renounced their right to bestow patronage, which had become a particularly sore point with both the Estonian and Latvian rural communities.

If measures of this kind had been taken earlier, they could well have proved effective. But by 1905–6 it was probably too late for peaceful evolution. There are no historical grounds for assuming that from 1905 onwards the German upper class was seriously thinking of subjecting the essentially aristocratic constitution of the Baltic territories to a complete overhaul along democratic lines. And yet, after the abortive but extremely violent revolution of 1905, they must have known just how ardent was the popular desire for greater participation in government. But in 1914 war was declared, and by 1917 everything had changed.

The social, political and religious structure of Lithuania in the period preceding its liberation differed considerably, in many respects, from that of the Baltic provinces. Consequently, although it passed through comparable phases of development, it is possible to draw a parallel between Lithuania and its northern neighbours only in very broad terms.

Agrarian reform in Lithuania followed the Russian and not the Baltic pattern. The emancipation of the serfs did not take place until 1861 (by which time the process of reform in the Baltic provinces had entered its second phase); and even then the Lithuanian peasants were still tied to their estates, and the great estate owners still retained their economic predominance. There were, of course, regional variations. In 1795 the Suwalki district in the south-west of Lithuania had passed,

B

not to Russia but to Prussia, which was obliged to cede it to the Duchy of Warsaw in 1807. In the Duchy agrarian matters came under the *Code Napoléon*, with the result that the peasants received their personal freedom and were no longer tied to their estates, although they were still required to perform menial services. During the early period of Tsar Alexander I's reign, when liberal hopes ran high in Russia, many attempts were made, starting with a campaign mounted at the University of Vilnius (Wilna), to obtain personal freedom for the serfs in the rest of Lithuania. Nothing, however, came of these initiatives, and the Suwalki district – which, incidentally, has particularly fertile soil – maintained its pre-eminence in the agricultural sphere. And it may well be significant that many of the leading members of the nationalist movement in Lithuania came from this district.

But the movement did not originate there. The emergence of a new sense of national identity called for a more cultured setting, and this it found in the university town of Vilnius. M. Hellmann has pointed out in this connection that, under the influence of Herder and the Romantics, the early endeavours to improve the educational and cultural standards of the masses, which had been inspired in the first instance by the philosophers of the Enlightenment, were subsequently combined with an attempt to discover intellectual and spiritual values in the hitherto despised language and folk art of the peasants. But before this project could be implemented in Lithuania, the indigenous gentry living in the central part of the territory, most of whom had been assimilated by the Poles in the seventeenth and eighteenth centuries, had to be won over. This task was undertaken primarily by the Catholic clergy, who – from the Bishop of Vilnius down to the parish priests in remote villages – devoted themselves wholeheartedly to the cultivation of the Lithuanian language and the maintenance of primary school education. But the study and cultivation of the language could not be carried on in a vacuum. Guidance was needed, and this was obtained from the neighbouring state of East Prussia, where the 'Lithuanian Literary Society', which had been founded in Tilsit in 1879, had acquired great significance. The printed matter smuggled across the Russo-German border came to play a major part in the development of the nationalist movement in Lithuania, and the so-called 'book-carriers' soon became legendary figures. After the abortive Polish rising of 1830, in which Lithuania was also involved, the Russian Government changed its attitude to this territory in two ways. In the first place, it began to play off the Polish and Lithuanian communities one against the other, a tendency which acquired a certain social significance when, for example, the estates of Polish revolutionaries were confiscated and divided up among Lithuanian peasants; and in the second place it authorised the Russian Orthodox Church to implement a russification policy similar to that pursued in the Baltic provinces, the only essential difference being that in Lithuania the indigenous population was Roman Catholic rather than Protestant.

Lithuania was also involved in the Polish insurrection of 1863, and on this occasion the Lithuanian peasants were far more revolutionary than their counterparts in Poland. As a result, the Russian Governor-General, Count Murav'ev, treated them with particular severity. Thus, after banning all Lithuanian publications and introducing the Russian educational system in a large number of rural schools – especially in the district of Vilnius – and after taking reprisals against the Roman Catholic Church, he initiated a new colonisation programme, under the terms of which Lithuanian domains and estates – some of which were quite evidently confiscated on account of their strategic value – were handed over to Russian settlers. Such oppression, which set back the emancipation of the Lithuanian serfs for decades, led to an increase in emigration which reached its peak in 1884. This emigration took place on a massive scale. Even before the outbreak of the First World War, one-third of the Lithuanian people lived abroad, chiefly in the U.S.A. and Canada.

But Murav'ev's oppressive measures produced another reaction that was of far greater consequence for those who remained behind. In the closing years of the nineteenth century and the early years of the twentieth, the nationalist movement in Lithuania received an enormous boost.

After the events of 1863 the research carried out into Lithuania's early history began to bear fruit, and in this connection, the part played by the Catholic clergy cannot be

sufficiently stressed. Bishop Matthäus Valančius of Kaunas
(Kovno) (1801–75) made a particularly important contribution. Under the guidance of Valančius and his fellow-bishops,
the religious seminaries became seats of learning dedicated to
the cultivation of the Lithuanian language, and centres of
resistance to Russian policy. As the Lithuanian peasants
gradually improved their economic position, there was a
growing demand for more and better education, which was
supplied by the secondary schools and teachers' training
colleges.

The emergence of a sense of national identity in Lithuania
was a steady rather than a violent process, and as such was in
keeping with the character of the Lithuanian middle class
and the teaching fraternity, whose members had all come from
peasant stock. Nationalist feeling had found expression
initially in resistance to Russian oppression, but it later
acquired a further outlet when the Lithuanians sought to
break away from the cultural and intellectual bonds of their
Polish past. This led, among other things, to the adoption of
Lithuanian and the rejection of Polish as the language of common
speech, a step of vital importance for the development of a
sense of nationhood. In this connection it is noteworthy that
when he went to Moscow as a student Jonas Basanavičius
(1851–1927), who was one of the early champions of Lithuanian
nationalism, had a meeting with A. Valdemārs, who later
became one of the Latvian delegates to the Imperial Duma, and
a number of Valdemārs' compatriots. This would suggest that
the Lithuanian and Latvian nationalists influenced each other
from an early stage. Their situations were, of course, different
in many respects, but they had certain things in common, and
those things were important. For example, both were subjected to a russification campaign designed to destroy, not only
their growing sense of national identity, but also their con-
fessional allegiance; and both had to assert their social and
cultural independence from their Polish or, alternatively,
German overlords. But although the Polish–Lithuanian
insurrection of 1863 was certainly a factor in the peasant unrest
which subsequently broke out in Estonia and Latvia, opposition – both to the tsarist regime and to the local upper class –
undoubtedly made itself felt on the whole at an earlier stage

in the north. On the other hand, the Lithuanian nationalists possessed an historical dimension which the Estonians and Latvians lacked, for from the thirteenth to the sixteenth centuries Lithuania had been an autonomous power of some consequence; and although this period of independence had long since been forgotten, it was still there, waiting to be rediscovered. Incidentally, the limited contacts established by the Lithuanians and the Latvians remained a more or less permanent feature of their development right up to the War of Liberation, whereas contacts between the Lithuanians and Estonians were extremely rare at all times.

The literary magazine *Aušra* (Red Dawn), launched by Basanavičius in 1883 and printed in Tilsit, in East Prussia, established a nationalist trend in Lithuanian journalism, whose advocates called with growing insistence for an independent Lithuanian culture. Their ideas, which were of course completely at variance with contemporary Polish thinking, met with a mixed reception from the Lithuanian clerics who, while reacting favourably to the nationalist approach to the use of the vernacular tongue and the investigation of Lithuanian folklore and history, took less kindly to the essentially secular nature of the nationalist movement. In 1890, in response to Basanavičius' *Aušra*, the Church launched its own magazine – *The Samogitian and Lithuanian Review* – in which it occasionally advocated the establishment of a 'free Lithuanian motherland', albeit without attempting to define this concept. But in the following year the papal encyclical *Rerum Novarum* was published, and the Lithuanian Church was obliged to spell out its attitude to the modern world and, consequently, to the nationalist movement within its own territory. That attitude was generally negative. Although, as we have seen, many clerics were well disposed to the cultural objectives of the nationalist programme, the vast majority were opposed to an independent Lithuanian state. Their religious bonds with the Polish Catholics were more important.

With the formation of Marxist groups, a new element entered Lithuanian political life. In 1895 the Lithuanian Social Democratic Party was established in Vilnius with the active support of Polish Socialists, and in the following year it presented a political programme to the Lithuanian public, in which it stressed its independence from the Polish Socialist Party (P.P.S.). The members of the Social Democratic Party stood for solidarity with the Polish and Russian working classes, and favoured the establishment of an all-Russian federation. Its leaders included Kairys, Bielinis and V. Mickevičius-Kapsukas. In 1902 the liberal members of the middle class also joined forces to form the Lithuanian Demo-cratic Party, which concerned itself primarily with agrarian affairs. In the course of time, however, this party became much more radical, and in 1914 was renamed the Lithuanian People's Social Democratic Party.

The revolutionary disturbances in Lithuania in 1905 were more than a mere reaction to events in metropolitan Russia; they were also quite different from those in Estonia, Livonia and Courland. At that time there was virtually no Lithuanian industrial proletariat. Consequently, the unrest was restricted mainly to the rural areas, and consisted of spontaneous attempts to depose Russian parish clergy and country schoolteachers. The basic trend was neither anti-Polish nor anti-clerical but anti-Russian. There were only a few revolutionary excesses, all in the Mariampol district.

The peak of the revolutionary activity in Lithuania was reached in December 1905 with the convening of a provincial diet which was attended by some 2,000 delegates, including several Lithuanian politicians who had returned from exile. The chairman was Basanavičius, and E. Galvanauskas, who later became Premier of the Lithuanian Republic, played a prominent part. The diet called for national autonomy, a centralised administration for all Lithuanian territories, and the use of the Lithuanian language in schools and official departments at local level. Mickevičius-Kapsukas also pressed for an independent Lithuanian republic, but this proposal received little support. After the diet a Lithuanian Peasant League was formed which exerted considerable influence on the subsequent grouping of the political parties through its organ Ukininkas. There was also a Catholic Democratic Party, founded in 1905, which opposed the call for national autonomy and urged the formation of a joint community of Lithuanians, Poles and White Russians. The Christian Democrats, whose political programme had been evolved by the contributors to the *Samogitian and Lithuanian Review* from 1904 onwards, were extremely influential, especially in the rural areas; at the provincial diet in Vilnius they had the support of a solid block of fifty-eight delegates, including A. Stulginskis. It was only after the February Revolution of 1917 that the Christian Democrats founded an official party.

The ban on the publication of Lithuanian works in Roman script was rescinded in 1904, and the revolution of the following year led to a relaxation of the laws governing the use of the Lithuanian language, both in pamphlets and in schools, and to the removal of the restrictions relating to land ownership, the right of assembly and association, and the right to change religions.

In the Russian Imperial Duma the Lithuanians achieved very little. By entering into an alliance with the Jews they were able to command the support of eight delegates in the Ist and IInd Dumas, an unimpressive total; and in the IIIrd and IVth Dumas – in which the number of delegates from the non-Russian minorities was reduced due to the change in the electoral law imposed by the Tsar – they could count on only five. To have joined forces with the Poles would have been pointless since they would never have supported Lithuanaian nationalism. Even the Russian Liberals were opposed to an autonomous structure for Lithuania, although this did not prevent individual Lithuanian delegates from aligning themselves with the liberal 'Cadets', the Trudoviki (*trud* means labour) or the Social Democrats. The two most important Lithuanian delegates were probably P. Leonas and M. Yčas.

Although the Russians suppressed the Lithuanian disturbances in 1905 with great severity, they executed far fewer people there than in their Baltic provinces. Moreover, the land-owning peasants in Lithuania benefited considerably from the Stolypin reforms, while in the late 1900s the Lithuanians were able to develop their press and to create numerous Lithuanian associations. They also communicated with the expatriate communities in America, and as a result of these contacts Basanavičius and Yčas visited the U.S.A. in 1913.

3. *The First World War and the Russian Revolution*

The First World War brought about fundamental changes in Eastern Europe. The most important of these was undoubtedly the collapse of the tsarist regime and its replacement by a Soviet state; but if we wish to appreciate the full extent of the transformation that took place at that time, we also have to consider the ramifications of a concomitant process: the liberation of the so-called border states. Clearly, this process was the same in all of these territories in so far as it led to their emergence as independent nations; yet it covered such diverse developments as the rebirth of Poland following the partitions, the establishment of a separate Lithuanian state, the complete segregation of Finland, first from the Swedish and subsequently from the Russian monarchy, and the founding of the new independent republics of Estonia and Latvia, whose territories had been ruled over by the Teutonic Order, and so had been dependencies of the Holy Roman Empire, in the Middle Ages.

When the First World War broke out in 1914 the Lithuanians, Latvians and Estonians tended to regard it as a conflict between the German and Russian imperialists, and it was only later that they came to realise the political significance of the Tsar's western Allies. Initially – despite opposition from leftist circles – the Latvians and Estonians gave firm support to the tsarist regime in its prosecution of the war, and the loyal assurances given by one of the Latvian delegates to the Duma, Goldmanis, accurately reflected popular feeling at the time. But then, unlike the Finns, the Estonians and Latvians were hardly likely to sympathise with the Germans, whose administrative methods were only too well known to them.

In Lithuania things were rather different. When the members of the 'Lithuanian Centre', which was formed in Vilnius in 1914, expressed their solidarity and sympathy with Russia, the Russian Premier Goremykin failed to respond, with the result that these Lithuanian politicians began to look westwards. In doing so, they took up a number of Russian war aims and adapted them to meet their own political requirements. Thus, in a memorandum sent via Sweden to the U.S.A., M. Yčas recommended that the Lithuanian provinces of Vilnius and

Kaunas should be united, not only with the province of Suwalki, but also with the eastern part of East Prussia. Others, more extreme than Yčas, went one step further by insisting that this new Lithuanian territory should be completely independent of Russia. In urging this, they were, of course, anticipating a victory for the western Allies.

The Latvians and the Estonians, on the other hand, had not even considered the possibility of setting up independent states during this initial phase of the war. All they wanted at that time was a reorganisation of their administrative system along ethnic lines. A number of Latvian delegates to the Imperial Duma called for the introduction in their territory of the Russian Zemstvo system of local self-government; and in 1916 M. Skujenieks published a memorandum on 'The National Question in Latvia', which he had written before the outbreak of the war. As for the Latvian and Estonian masses, they were interested only in local affairs. For them the question of independence simply did not arise; and the war conducted by the Russians against the Germans was decidedly popular, especially in Latvia.

However, it was not long before the Baltic territories became a theatre of war. Between March and September 1915 the whole of the area inhabited by the Lithuanian communities was occupied by German troops. The retreating Russians evacuated the local administration, and as a result large sections of the local population, faced with the total disruption of normal life, chose to follow the army into Central Russia. Meanwhile, after taking Liepaja (Libau) on 8 May, the Germans crossed the southern frontier of Courland and occupied Jelgava (Mitau) on 1 August, whereupon three-fiths of the population of Courland, including some 500,000 Latvians, also fled the country. Some were ordered to do so by the Russians, others left of their own accord. Most of the industrial installations in this area were dismantled and transported to Russia, together with some 90,000 industrial workers. All in all, over one-third of the Latvian population was uprooted. The population of Courland dropped from about 800,000 (before 1914) to about 230,000. The German advance was finally halted on the Daugava (Düna), and just short of Riga.

The Lithuanian and Latvian refugees were soon in dire

B*

straits. The Russian authorities were quite incapable of dealing with this vast influx of people, who were obliged to fend for themselves as best they could. In St. Petersburg (named Petrograd from 1915 onwards) a Lithuanian Welfare Committee was set up under the direction of M. Yčas. There were also a number of Latvian refugee associations, and at a congress held at the end of 1915 these established a Central Committee for the Welfare of the 850,000 Latvian Refugees in Russia, which was headed by Pastor V. Olav, J. Čakste and A. Berg. Although they were conceived in the first instance as purely charitable institutions, both of these organisations acquired a growing cultural and political significance as national centres.

The German occupation of Courland also led to the formation of the first Latvian army units. Goldmanis and Zālītis, the Latvian delegates to the Imperial Duma, succeeded in overcoming the misgivings of the Russian High Command, and on 1 August, 1915 General Russky, the Officer Commanding the North-West Front, authorised the formation of two Latvian light infantry battalions. Soon these were increased to eight, after which they were gradually brought up to regimental strength with an overall establishment of some 130,000 men. These units, in which all orders were given in Latvian, were deployed on the Daugava front, where they successfully defended the Russian positions until 1917. The formation of the Latvian light infantry regiments played an important part in the development of a sense of national identity.

Those parts of the Baltic provinces which had escaped occupation by the Germans also suffered from the effects of the war. This was particularly true of Livonia, for many of the refugees from Courland went to Riga, where they aggravated the already serious unemployment problem caused by the evacuation of local industry, with the result that people began to flee from Livonia into Russia, leaving the economic life of this area to grind to a halt.

In the territories inhabited by Estonians – Estonia proper and Northern Livonia – the impact of the war was less pernicious. At first, the Estonians were completely loyal to the Russians (although Laaman has rightly pointed out that their loyalty was to the Empire rather than to the Tsar), but the patriotic fervour, which seized both the Estonians and Latvians

during the initial phase of the war and made them easy game
for the Russian anti-German propagandists, soon yielded, as
far as the Estonians were concerned, to a more sober appraisal
of the situation. Unlike the Latvians, they did not press the
Russian Army Command to authorise the early formation of
indigenous regiments, for they feared that these would be
deployed on the most dangerous sections of the front, and
might therefore be prematurely decimated.

The centre of nationalist activity in Estonia was Tartu,
where as early as 1915 Jaan Tõnisson founded the Northern
Baltic Committee in order to harness the bourgeois forces in the
country in support of Estonian autonomy. The contracts
made by the Estonian and Latvian delegates to the Duma with
the Russian Radicals had also persuaded the Estonian national-
lists that the war would weaken the tsarist regime and so pave
the way for the transformation of the Empire into a federation,
in which the non-Russian peoples might expect to receive
autonomous powers. These expectations were, of course,
realised by the unexpected overthrow of the monarchy in the
February Revolution of 1917.

The setting up of the Provisional Government in Russia met
with an enthusiastic response in the Baltic provinces, whose
peoples confidently anticipated a speedy transformation of the
Empire. The Russian governors were recalled from Riga and
Tallinn, and their places were taken by Government commissars, who were supposed to maintain liaison between the
local and central governments. In both parts of the territory
these new posts were given, not to Baltic Germans, but to the
indigenous mayors: the Latvian A. Krastkalns (1869–1939)
and the Estonian J. Poska (1866–1922). Hehn has rightly
pointed out that in both Latvia and Estonia the nationalist and
revolutionary forces, which had been pent up for so long,
erupted with particular vehemence. Not surprisingly, the first
demand made by these peoples was for a new system of local
government that would embrace the whole of their respective
territories. This was completely in line with their long-standing
demand for national autonomy.

Immediately after the February Revolution, representatives
of the leading civic associations in Riga met to discuss the
general situation, and on 21 March they formed a Council of

the Social Organisations in Riga so as to be in a position to advise the newly appointed Government Commissar on matters of local concern. A few days later, on 25 and 26 March, a Provincial Assembly was convened in Valmiera on behalf of the Latvian inhabitants of Southern Livonia, at which the 440 delegates called for the establishment of a new administrative region embracing Southern Livonia, Courland and Latgale (Lettgallen), and suggested that this region should be named Latvia. The delegates also called for the establishment of a Provisional Livonian (Latvian) Provincial Council to replace the old Baronial Diet. The forty-eight members of the new Council were then duly elected.

This Provincial Council was recognised by the Russian Government, but was repudiated by the Latvian leftists. By that time, workers' and soldiers' councils, and in the country districts even councils of landless peasants, had been formed in Latvia; and these councils, which were based on Russian models, reacted to the Valmiera assembly by convening a special congress for the landless on 19 April. This was also held in Valmiera, and it set up a Provincial Council of its own, designed to provide self-government for the new territory along Socialist lines. Negotiations were then conducted by representatives of the two opposing camps, and on 16 May they combined, on a one-for-one basis, to form a new corporate body. But friction between the bourgeois and Socialist groups remained a constant threat.

On 10 May a Provincial Council was also elected for the district of Latgale at a congress held in Rezekne and attended by, among others, Meierovics and Zālītis. The membership of this Council consisted of six natives of Latgale, twelve Russians, eight Jews and three Poles. The congress also voted by a large majority in favour of union with the other Latvian territories. On 15 June, however, this recommendation was opposed at an assembly convened by the Russian inhabitants of Latgale, who asked that the district should remain part of the government of Vitebsk. It was not possible to convene an assembly in Courland at this time since the territory was still occupied by the Germans, but those Courlanders who had fled the country – nearly all of whom were members of the bourgeoisie – founded a Courland Provincial Council in Tartu on 9 May, and recommended that Čakste should be appointed Provincial Commissar following the German withdrawal. But when a group of Radical refugees from Courland met in Moscow they refused to endorse this recommendation and called for the establishment of a Socialist Provincial Council.

Meanwhile, the nationalists were also organising themselves in political parties. The members of the bourgeois parties were all Radical Democrats and, unlike their counterparts in Western Europe, all left of centre. Every one of these parties – the most important of which was the Peasants League founded in Valga on 12 May – called for Latvian autonomy within an All-Russian Republic. So too did the Latvian Socialist Revolutionary Party, which had emerged from the Union of the Latvian Social Democrats in 1913. Of all the Baltic nationalists the Latvians were the most resolute in their quest for independence, and on 20 March 1917 they ably demonstrated this quality by deposing Krastkalns, the Government Commissar appointed by the Russian Provisional Government, and replacing him by A. Priedkalns (1873–1923), the Social Democratic doctor and former Duma delegate. Priedkalns' deputy, K. Ulmanis, subsequently became one of the leaders of the Peasant League and President of the Republic of Latvia. Changes were also made in the composition of the municipal council in Riga, where G. Zemgals (1871–1939) – who also became President of the Republic – was appointed mayor.

However, the Provisional Government in Petrograd was not inclined to authorise Latvian autonomy. On the contrary, it was determined to postpone any decision on the future structure of Russia until a constituent assembly had been convened. The only concession made at that time was granted in Livonia, where the Livonian Provincial Council replaced the old aristocratic diet. But the proposed incorporation of Latgale into Latvia proper did not receive Russian approval. Nor was any allowance made for the nationalist aspirations of the Baltic peoples in the cultural sphere. Thus the Provisional Government systematically opposed the attempts to introduce Latvian as the official language for use in junior secondary schools, and the concomitant attempt to reorganise the administration of Baltic education along national lines. In Estonia the Provisional Government was still refusing to authorise the use of the

Estonian language for local government purposes as late as September 1917.

In order to establish a broader base for its political activities the Livonian Provincial Council called a conference of all Latvian organisations for 12 August in Riga, where a formal resolution was passed demanding for the Latvian people the absolute right of self-determination within their ethnological borders. Subsequently, due to the mounting difficulties encountered by the Provisional Government in Petrograd, especially after the abortive outcome of the Kerensky offensive on the western front, some Latvian politicians went even further. Thus, both the National Democrats and a group of young Latvian intellectuals in Moscow, which had formed around the newspaper *Dzimtenes Atbalss*, called for the total withdrawal of Latvia from the Russian Empire. Meanwhile, the bourgeois representatives at the Riga conference had also decided to press for Latvian independence if Riga were taken by the Germans.

In the late summer of 1917 Riga fell to the Germans. After making repeated attempts to cross the Daugava in the course of 1916 and in January 1917, German troops finally succeeded in establishing a bridgehead on the eastern bank on 19 August 1917 (1 September) and entered the town on 22 August (3 September).* A combined force of German naval and army units also occupied the Baltic islands of Saaremaa (Oesel), Muhu (Mohn) and Hiiumaa (Dagö) at the end of September, thus encroaching on Estonian territory for the first time.

In Estonia a group of prominent Estonian politicians, which has assembled in Tartu on 4 March 1917 under the leadership of Jaan Tõnisson, called for Estonian autonomy and the establishment of a new administration responsible for all sections of the Estonian community. These were precisely the same demands as those formulated by the Latvians on 12 August in respect of their territory. But where the Latvians were to meet with a blank refusal, the Estonians were completely successful. On 30 March, two days after the Estonian

---

* The dates in brackets are based on the Gregorian Calendar, which did not come into use in Russia until 1 (14) February, 1918 but which was introduced in the occupied areas of the Baltic territories at a much earlier date by the German Army.

community had staged a large-scale demonstration in support
of this policy, the former delegate to the Imperial Duma J.
Raamot (1873–1927) persuaded the Russian Premier Prince
Lvov to accede to his demands. As a result, all territories
occupied by Estonians – the former government of Estonia,
the northern part of Livonia, and the islands on the Baltic –
were formed into a single administrative unit, and placed
under the juridiction of the Government Commissar, who was
to be assisted by an elective council (the *Maapäev*). The Baltic
German barons in both Estonia and Livonia were strongly
opposed to these new provisions, but their objections were
disregarded, and the decree formulated on 30 March duly
passed into law on 20 June.

The *Maapäev* first met on 1 July, but it was not until 7
September, after the fall of Riga, that the possibility of an
Estonian withdrawal from the Russian Empire was discussed
by this assembly. On that occasion Jaan Tõnisson astounded
his colleagues by advocating a Northern Union that would
embrace the Scandinavian countries, Finland, Estonia, Latvia
and Lithuania. Tõnisson argued that a large northern bloc
with a population of some 30,000,000 would be better able to
assert itself, even at an international level. But he failed to
carry the majority, which at that time still favoured an All-
Russian federation. It was in order to promote this objective
that the Estonians sent a delegation to the Congress of Russian
Peoples, which was convened in Kiev in mid-September. The
Latvians also sent delegates, including Z. Meierovics, who later
became the Latvian Foreign Minister. Of course, the possibility
of a supranational federation had also been examined by
Latvian politicians. Even before the collapse of the tsarist regime,
Rainis had considered the feasibility of a union between
Latvia and Lithuania, and in the summer of 1917 several
Moscow-based Latvian newspapers had taken up the idea
advanced by the Lithuanian American Dr. Jonas Šliupas,
who had called for a Latvian–Lithuanian Republic within an
All-Russian federation.

From this point onwards the development of events in both
Estonia and Latvia was influenced to a large extent by the
radical left-wing groups, whose power had greatly increased.
The radicalisation of Baltic politics went hand in hand with

the radicalisation of Russian politics, which gathered momentum following the February Revolution. It was not simply that the Liberal Government in St. Petersburg was replaced in May 1917 by a Liberal–Socialist coalition. Far more important was the rapid growth of Bolshevik influence in the Soviets during the late summer of 1917, a process reflected by the gradual transfer of power from the Mensheviks to the Leninists in the Latvian Social Democratic Party, whose Central Committee had been in the hands of the Bolsheviks ever since August 1914.

But in both Latvia and Estonia the moderates, i.e. the Social Revolutionaries and the Mensheviks, had retained control of the councils. In April 1917, however, the Estonian Bolsheviks held their first legally-constituted conference in Tallinn, and from then onwards their influence grew steadily. There was an extremely well-organised Bolshevik group in Tallinn, which was led by J. Anvelt, a lawyer from Narva, the first of the Baltic towns to witness the emergence of Bolshevik-controlled councils. Anvelt's group soon became a force to be reckoned with in Tallinn, but in the conflicts which broke out between the councils and the Government Commissar Poska in connection with the elections to the *Maapäev*, Poska showed that he was well able to defend his position. His representative in Tartu, Parts, was less successful, for he was arrested by the local councils and spent a short spell in prison.

The first moves in the bolshevisation of the Latvian councils were made in Moscow, where the Latvian Social Democrats held a party conference in May 1917, at which the Bolshevik-controlled Central Committee was able to persuade the delegates to support a motion endorsing the theses advanced by Lenin in April. But the Bolsheviks still had their adversaries at that time. For example, the Moscow-based Latvian newspaper *Sozialdemokrāts* would not even countenance the idea of an autonomous Latvia within an All-Russian federation, and insisted that all that was needed was a generous measure of local self-government. However, at the end of May the Central Committee of the party established itself in Riga, where it launched a systematic propaganda campaign with the active collaboration of the Latvian Bolshevik newspaper *Cīna*, which had also moved to Riga. The Central Committee wanted to strengthen the indigenous councils, and to this end it sought the support of the industrial workers and the light infantry regiments. Losses had been heavy in the Latvian army contingent, which had often been exposed to needless slaughter by the incompetent Russian High Command, and the Bolshevik propagandists found willing listeners amongst the soldiers. From the end of May onwards the General Council of the Latvian light infantry regiments adopted a hostile attitude to the policies advocated by the Latvian national bourgeoisie. But it was when they made contact with the radical groups in the countryside that the Bolsheviks really sealed the fate of the bourgeois parties. On 11 August a congress was convened in Riga, at which the representatives of the workers' and soldiers' councils joined with the representatives of the councils for landless peasants to elect an Executive Committee, which then became the principal political instrument of the revolutionary left.

It is hardly surprising that the radicalisation of the Latvian Social Democratic Party should have followed the example set by the allied process within the Russian Social Democratic Party, for the Latvian radicals were in close contact with their Russian counterparts, not only during the war but also before it. Yet the Estonians, who maintained similar contacts with the Russians, were far more reserved in their attitude to the Bolsheviks. Granted that the workers of Tallinn and Narva were extremely radical, and at a very early stage, but they were not truly representative of the Estonian people, for the major part of the workforce in these towns had been drafted in from Russia, either in the early years of the century when industry was expanding, or during the war when a new armaments industry was established. There were also other Russians in Estonia: units of the Baltic Fleet were anchored in Tallinn harbour, and Russian army contingents were stationed in the province. But although the navy and army personnel were themselves highly susceptible to Bolshevik propaganda, they do not appear to have transmitted their enthusiasm to the local population on any significant scale. Not even the relative proximity of Petrograd, where Russian revolutionary fervour was to reach its peak with the return of Lenin, made any real impression on the Estonians. Of course, the

Estonians were never in the firing line, and so had escaped the immediate horrors of the war.

The Estonian councils would have no truck with the nationalist aims pursued by the Estonian bourgeoisie, and they resisted the proposal for the creation of two Estonian regiments, even though this project had received the blessing of the Russian War Minister Kerensky. In the event, only one of these regiments was ever established. It was formed in Rakvere, and was subsequently transferred to Haapsalu, where it was brought up to divisional strength in December 1917. The extreme left also refused to take part in a national congress convened by the *Maapäev* for the representatives of the Estonian social organisations and municipal government associations. Like the first All-Russian Congress of Soviets in Petrograd, the first Congress of the Estonian Councils, held in Tallinn on 5 August, had a majority of Social Revolutionaries and Mensheviks. But when the Tallinn Workers' and Soldier's Council came out with its new slogan – 'All power to the councils' – on 18 September, the Estonians quickly embraced the Bolshevik view, which was already firmly established in Latvia and Central Russia. At the local elections the Bolsheviks won 35 per cent of the popular vote throughout the province. The figure for Tallinn was 31 per cent, and for Narva 47 per cent.

Meanwhile, in the municipal elections held in Latvia on 26 August the Bolsheviks had made even greater gains: in Riga they obtained 41 per cent of the popular vote, in Valmiera 64 per cent, and in Limbaži 70 per cent. The elections to the Livonian Provincial Assembly, which were held on 2 September and in which serving members of the army were allowed to take part, produced a similar result. The Riga district and part of the Cēsis district were of course excluded from these elections on account of the military situation. But of the forty representatives returned to the Assembly, twenty-four (60 per cent) were members of the Bolshevik-oriented Latvian Social Democratic Party, only one was a Social Revolutionary, while thirteen belonged to the Peasants' League. Incidentally, after the fall of Riga the bourgeois parties and the pro-Menshevik members of the Social Democratic Party joined forces to form a Democratic bloc. This bloc then sent a memorandum to the German High Command, in which it appealed for German recognition of the right of the Latvian people to self-determination, and passed a resolution, at the end of September or the beginning of October, calling for Latvian independence. When this was reported in the German left-wing press and subsequently brought up for discussion in the Reichstag by a group of radical delegates, a number of leading personalities were arrested in Riga.

The newly-elected Provincial Assembly was duly constituted on 17 September, and the Bolshevik O. Karkliņš was elected President. But in October the Bolshevik members of the Social Democratic Party fell out with the representatives of the bourgeois parties over the question of Latvian autonomy, the bourgeois delegates arguing in favour of a national state and the Bolsheviks insisting on international affiliations. This rift proved unbridgeable, and precluded future collaboration between the two groups. In mid-September elections were also held to set up district councils, and according to Soviet sources these produced a pro-Bolshevik vote of between 71 and 76 per cent.

The role allocated to the Baltic provinces in Lenin's plans for an armed revolt in Petrograd was by no means insignificant. In the event of large-scale military engagements the 5th and 12th Russian Armies, which were stationed in the provinces, and the sailors on the ships of the Baltic Fleet anchored in Tallinn harbour, were to protect the flank of the revolutionary force in Petrograd. And units of the Latvian light infantry regiments were attached to the 12th Army.

In order to assess the loyalty of these troops Lenin sent one of his closest collaborators, V. A. Antonov-Ovseënko (who subsequently accepted the surrender of the Provisional Government in the Winter Palace after the October Revolution), to the party conference convened by the Latvian Social Democrats in Valga on 10 October, which was guarded by Latvian troops. The impressions formed by this emissary can hardly have been unfavourable, for after the Bolshevik take-over on 25 October the soldiers and sailors stationed in the Baltic provinces were among the first to recognise the new revolutionary leadership.

After the October Revolution power passed to the councils

in the Baltic provinces. There was no open resistance to the Bolsheviks, either in Estonia or in Latvia. The bourgeois sections of both communities bided their time, hoping that the new regime would soon be swept away.

In November 1917, when the elections to set up a constituent assembly were held throughout Russia, it became apparent that the Latvians were still very much in favour of the Bolshevik programme. In the Latvian part of Livonia the pro-Bolshevik candidates gained 72 per cent of the popular vote, compared with 45 per cent in Petrograd, and only 24 per cent in the whole of Russia. At a conference convened on 29 October the pro-Bolshevik members of the Latvian Social Democratic Party gave their assent to Lenin's proposals. So too did the representatives of the Latvian light infantry regiments at a further conference held a few days later. Meanwhile, a Military Revolutionary Committee was set up by the 12th Army to implement the new proposals, and this committee ordered the Latvian regiments to occupy Cesis, Valmiera and Valga in order to prevent any movement of counter-revolutionary troops.

In Estonia the revolutionary fervour of the indigenous population also continued unabated. On 4 November the Executive Committee of the Tallinn councils set up a Military Revolutionary Committee to control all strategically important points in the town. This new committee was presided over by the Russian J. Rabchinsky; his deputy was the Estonian Bolshevik Viktor Kingissepp (1882–1922), the son of a craftsman from Saaremaa, who had taken part in the 1905 Revolution. With the possible exception of Anvelt, Kingissepp is the best known of the Estonian Communists.

The new Estonian leaders relieved the Government Commissar Poska of his post, thus leaving the bourgeoisie with virtually no spokesman. Unlike the Latvians, the Estonians had not been deprived of their capital, and it was only natural that Reval should have become the focal point of revolutionary activity. Needless to say, the Bolsheviks drew most of their support from the urban areas, while the bourgeois strongholds were in the rural areas, especially those in the south.

But although the fortunes of the bourgeois parties were at their lowest ebb in both Estonia and Latvia, following the October

Revolution, discussions were nonetheless initiated, at the instigation of the Latvian Refugee Committee in Petrograd, to promote the establishment of a Latvian National Council, in which all shades of opinion would be represented. Predictably, this project was opposed by the Bolsheviks and, less predictably, by the Mensheviks and Social Revolutionaries. But the bourgeois groups stuck to their guns, and a constituent assembly was convened in Valga, which sat from 17 to 19 November. This assembly, which was attended by twenty-six representatives from thirteen different organisations, elected as President of the National Council V. Zāmuels, who later became President of Latvia. The Council then passed a resolution calling on the Soviet Government to authorise the incorporation of Latgale into Latvia proper, and to allow the Latvian people to determine the internal administration of their territory in a referendum. The Council also issued a declaration addressed to Germany and the western powers, in which it insisted on the absolute right of the Latvian people, as members of an autonomous state, to determine their own future. It also protested against any partition of Latvian territory, and especially against the annexation of Courland by Germany.

Surprisingly, the Council of People's Commissars, which met in Petrograd on 14 December, sanctioned the incorporation of Latgale, presumably because it felt that this would strengthen the hand of the Latvian federalists. But it rejected all the other demands made by the National Council, including the demand for a Latvian Constituent Assembly, and finished up by ordering the dissolution of the Council. This order was circumvented by the Council members, who continued to run a clandestine organisation from Petrograd and established contact with the western Allies. But although this operation augured well for the future development of Latvia, the Latvian radicals were at that time undoubtedly in the ascendancy.

Six weeks after the National Council had met in Valga, the United Councils of Latvia held their second congress in Valmiera, which lasted from 19 to 31 December. At this assembly a resolution was passed vesting supreme power in the Latvian Councils, and an Executive Committee was set up under the leadership of F. Roziņš.

Before the October Revolution, there had still been some members of the Estonian bourgeoisie who wanted to maintain their traditional association with Russia in one form or another. After the Revolution there were very few. Tõnisson had long advocated complete independence and a *rapprochement* with the western Allies, and on 8 November Päts endorsed this policy in an article published in the *Teataja*. By then even the *Maapäev* was being threatened. The Bolshevik delegates had been calling for its dissolution ever since September, and on 28 November 1917, when the members of the *Maapäev* convened in Tallinn, they were driven from the assembly hall. But before this happened the *Maapäev* passed a resolution proclaiming itself the supreme authority in Estonia until such time as an Estonian Constituent Assembly could be convened, and then delegated far-reaching powers to its Praesidium and Council of Elders. Here too the bourgeois nationalists were looking to the west to espouse the cause of Baltic independence, and on 11 December the Council of Elders of the Estonian *Maapäev* sent a delegation to the neutral states and the western Allies to press for recognition of Estonia as an independent state in the hope that this would avert the threat of German annexation.

On 14 January 1918 the members of the Council of Elders and the representatives of the bourgeois parties agreed to proclaim Estonian independence in the near future. By then it was generally expected that Germany would shortly occupy the whole of Estonia, and it was important that a declaration of independence should be made before this happened in order to establish Estonian national rights under international law. Even at this late stage there were, of course, still a few who hankered after the old links with Russia, for both Estonian and Latvian delegates were present for the ceremonial opening of the Russian Constituent Assembly in Petrograd on 18 January. But after Lenin had ordered his soldiers to drive the delegates from the hall, there were no longer any waverers. From then onwards the Baltic territories were determined to go their own way.

On 3 February 1918 the elections to the Estonian Constituent Assembly began. The only reason why the Bolsheviks had agreed to these elections was that they expected their candidates

to win by a comfortable majority, and when it became apparent
that they were going to receive no more than 25 to 30 per cent
of the popular vote, the Workers' and Soldiers' Council called
off the elections on 9/10 February.

It was obvious, therefore, that the Bolsheviks were determined to maintain – and increase – their power, irrespective
of the wishes of the majority, and it was not long before the
Workers' and Soldiers' Council began to form military units.
It goes without saying that the Bolshevik-controlled councils
in both Estonia and Latvia took their lead from the Soviet
Government in Petrograd. The only respect in which they
deviated from the party line was in their attitude to the
agrarian question. Like the Russians, they intended to confiscate
all landed estates; but having done so, they proposed to set
up socialist collectives at once instead of distributing the land
amongst the peasants in the first instance. In their use of terror
tactics, however, they followed the Russians to the letter,
with the result that many of the Estonian politicians who had
advocated national independence were forced to flee the
country or go underground. This initial wave of Bolshevik
terror continued until the whole of Estonia had been occupied
by the German Army.

4. *The German Occupation*

The German occupation began in Lithuania in March 1915,
in Latvia in May 1915, and in Estonia in September 1917.
From February 1918 onwards the whole of the territory that
subsequently went to make up the Baltic States was in the
hands of the German Army, and by the time the war was
over, Lithuania, the first of the provinces to be conquered, had
been administered by the Germans for three and a half years.

Major-General M. Hoffmann, Chief of Staff to the Commander-in-Chief Eastern Front, and the members of the German
High Command incorporated each newly-conquered Lithuanian area into a single administrative unit – the *Land Ober-Ost* –
which eventually embraced the districts of Lithuania proper:
Suwalki, Vilnius, Bialystok, Grodno and Courland. This new
administration was much more than a military control
commission. The Germans completely reorganised the judicial

and educational systems; they took measures to strengthen the economy and improve communications, and set new standards for public health. They also conscripted an indigenous labour force for work on the land and in the forests to ensure that the German Army received adequate supplies of food and timber, a measure greatly resented by the Lithuanian people, and at last rescinded in September 1917. Thus, by the end of the war, Lithuania had been fully integrated into the German economic community and no longer had anything in common with the Russian economy. This development, which the Germans had planned on a permanent basis but which came to an end with the defeat of the Central Powers, contributed in a great measure to the emergence of an independent Lithuanian state.

Germ integ of Lith → contrib. to Lith indep.

For a long time, however, Lithuania's political destiny hung in the balance. Then came two events which boosted Lithuanian nationalist aspirations: the declaration by the Central Powers of November 1916 concerning the future composition of Poland, and the Russian Revolution of February 1917. The declaration of November 1916 led to positive action in the following year when the German Government and High Command decided – partly in order to oppose Polish demands for the restoration of the old Polish–Lithuanian Union – to make concessions to the Lithuanian nationalists. As a result, the Commander-in-Chief Eastern Front authorised the formation of a Lithuanian Council on 2 June 1917. A few months later, on 18 September, a conference was convened in Vilnius under the chairmanship of J. Basanavičius. This conference, which was attended by two delegates from every district and every party in the territory, called for the creation of an independent Lithuanian state. It also elected a Lithuanian Provincial Council (*Taryba*), consisting of twenty members and intended to serve as a kind of provisional government. The President of the Council was Antanas Smetona (1874–1944), a well-known lawyer, who was head of the Lithuanian Refugee Committee and who was to play a prominent part in the foundation of the Lithuanian Republic.

Smetona was born in the district of Ukmergé in Southern Lithuania, the son of a small farmer. He attended secondary school in Jelgava, and passed his university entrance examination in St. Petersburg, where he studied philosophy and law.

While in St. Petersburg he engaged in nationalist activities for which he was banished to Vilnius, but there he acquired a circle of collaborators, who grouped themselves around the magazine *Viltis* (Hope), and later called themselves the *Tautininkai* (Nationalists). These men subsequently formed the cadre of the Lithuanian government party.

The Lithuanian colony in Petrograd set up a Lithuanian National Council at an early stage – 26 March – and this Council then elected a Provisional Administrative Council consisting of twelve members. A delegation led by the Duma delegate Yčas, which was sent to Prince Lvov by the Petrograd Council, was told that the Russian Government would give due consideration to its desire for Lithuanian autonomy. This assurance was quickly followed by demands for the unification of all the territories inhabited by Lithuanian communities and the incorporation into Lithuania of the eastern part of East Prussia. On 27 May a Provincial Diet (*Seimas*), convened in Petrograd and attended by 336 delegates, called for an independent Lithuanian state. This led to the withdrawal from the Diet of the ultra-leftists, but later, when the Russian Government – under Kerensky – was seen to be dragging its heels over the question of concessions, including those relating to Lithuanian autonomy, there was a *rapprochement* between the two wings of the Lithuanian political movement. Meanwhile, the Lithuanian expatriates had also been active. We have already seen that the Lithuanians in the U.S.A. put forward a number of important ideas at this time. In Geneva a Lithuanian information centre was set up in 1915, which established contact with the western allies, while in Stockholm a Lithuanian conference held in October 1917 recognised the *Taryba* as the competent instrument for the reconstruction of the Lithuanian state. This was a particularly significant development, for it showed that a certain concensus of opinion had been achieved among Lithuanians of all persuasions (save those on the extreme left).

In its endeavours to obtain a declaration of Lithuanian independence from the German Government the *Taryba* was greatly hampered by the fact that the German Chancellery, the Reichstag and the Army Command were themselves at loggerheads as to what should be done with their territory.

The *Taryba*'s principal ally in Germany was Matthias Erzberger, a Reichstag delegate and a member of the *Zentrumspartei*, who ardently promoted the Lithuanian cause from 1917 onwards.

The turning-point in this campaign came on 13 November 1917, when Smetona gave a lecture in Berlin, in which he called for an independent Lithuanian state based on the ethnological and not the historical boundaries of the Lithuanian community, and gave an assurance that all future Lithuanian governments would maintain close ties with Germany. Two weeks later Count Hertling, the German Chancellor, informed the Reichstag that his government proposed to recognise Lithuanian sovereignty, and on 11 December 1917 the *Taryba* was able to proclaim 'the restoration of the independent state of Lithuania with its capital city of Vilnius'. But the Lithuanians were still anxious to obtain a definitive assurance from the Germans, especially after the initiation of the peace talks in Brest-Litovsk, which they regarded as a serious threat, and on 16 February 1918 it tried to bring pressure to bear on Berlin by issuing a second proclamation, specifically stating that the new Lithuanian state must be totally independent of both Russia and Poland.

The Germans still bided their time, and it was only after the *Taryba* had given explicit assurances of close collaboration in the political, military, commercial and financial spheres that Kaiser Wilhelm II signed the document authorising the establishment of an independent Lithuanian state. This document was dated 23 March 1918.

As a result of this development the Lithuanians were caught up in the rivalries which marked the relationships between different states within the German Empire. One German political group, which enjoyed the support of the Army Command, was agitating for a union between Lithuania on the one hand and either Saxony or Prussia on the other, a project which Erberger and his associates in the Reichstag were determined to frustrate. In order to achieve this end Erzberger espoused the cause of Duke Wilhelm von Urach, a descendant of a collateral Catholic line of the Württemberg dynasty, who was aspiring to the position of head of state of the new Lithuanian nation, and on 9 July 1918 the Duke's

Lith

candidacy was endorsed by the *Taryba*, which appointed him *Monarchy* King of Lithuania with the name Mindove II. But although Germany had authorised the establishment of a Lithuanian state, she had yet to give her approval to the *Taryba*; and meanwhile Yčas and Voldemaras, the Duma delegates, who had returned from Russia to join the *Taryba*, were beginning to express misgivings. Eventually, however, the new German Chancellor Prince Max von Baden, who had appointed Erzberger as one of his secretaries of state with a seat in the cabinet, broke the deadlock, and on 2 November the *Taryba* was duly authorised to proclaim itself the legislative organ of the new monarchy. It immediately convened a constituent session and drew up a provisional constitution. This constitution was entirely democratic, which is a point of some consequence in view of the fact that the *Taryba* itself had not been democratically constituted. Three days later the *Taryba* appointed Augustinas Voldemaras President of Lithuania.

Voldemaras (1883–1944) was one of the most contradictory and controversial figures of the early period of Baltic independence. He was the gifted son of a small farmer from the Vilnius district, and he studied classical philology and history in St. Petersburg, graduating with honours. He became a university lecturer in 1911, and after making several journeys abroad was appointed assistant professor at the University of Perm in the eastern part of European Russia. When the February Revolution broke out in 1917 he returned to Petrograd and threw himself into Lithuanian politics.

But by 11 November when Voldemaras' cabinet was sworn in, the German Empire had collapsed, and Lithuania was faced with an entirely new situation.

In Lithuania the German military administrators dealt with the Lithuanians. But in Courland, and later in Livonia and Estonia, they dealt with the Baltic Germans and not with the Latvians or Estonians. They had good reasons for adopting this approach, for the major part of the Latvian population had fled the country, and the members of the Baltic German upper class were deeply committed to their Baltic homeland. Nonetheless, this was a fateful decision, and one calculated to create considerable problems.

The German military administration under Major von

Gossler formed an integral and subordinate part of the *Ober-Ost-Verwaltung*, the general administration responsible for all aspects of German policy in the conquered Baltic territories. Under the terms of this policy Courland was specified as a future colonisation area for demobilised German soldiers. This was first announced in a decree promulgated by the Commander-in-Chief Eastern Front on 20 April 1917, and was endorsed in a formal resolution of the Courland nobility dated 22 September 1917, which stipulated that one-third of all arable land in Courland was to be allocated to German settlers. The Baltic barons in the other territories did not follow this particular example. In general, however, the political objectives pursued by the German administration were the same in all the Baltic territories. The implementation of particular projects may have varied in respect of detail, but it soon became abundantly clear that the policy decisions taken by the administration were designed to pave the way for eventual annexation.

After the fall of Riga and the occupation of the Baltic Islands in September–October 1917, the German Army was poised for the conquest of the whole Baltic area. From then onwards – due to the Bolshevik take-over in Russia and the ascendancy of the pro-Bolshevik councils in Estonia and Latvia – the German troops appeared in the role of crusaders who had come to liberate the Baltic peoples from the proletarian yoke. In both Estonia and Latvia there were many members of the indigenous population who were prepared to overlook past grievances and who placed their hopes for the future in a German victory. As for the members of the Baltic German upper class, there could be no doubt about their attitude. Various representatives of the nobility in both Livonia and Estonia had long been urging the authorities in Berlin, and more especially the German Army Command, to renew the offensive on the Baltic front. Other Baltic Germans had tried to involve the Latvian and Estonian rural communities; they had risked their lives collecting signatures for petitions, which they then smuggled through the front line or across the frozen winter sea to Saaremaa.

The determination of the Baltic provinces to break away from the Russian Empire also found expression in a diplomatic initiative undertaken early in 1918, when a plenipotentiary was sent to Stockholm to present a declaration of independence to the Soviet Commercial Attaché Vorovsky on behalf of the Baltic barons of Livonia and Estonia. In this declaration, which was handed to Vorovsky on 28 January, the barons referred to the constitutional privileges granted to the Baltic territories by Peter the Great in 1721 under the terms of the Treaty of Nystad, and then went on to remind the Soviets of Lenin's undertaking that the non-Russian peoples within the Russian Empire would be allowed to determine their own future.

Both the Stockholm declaration and the call for a renewed German offensive were bitterly resented by the Communist authorities in Tallinn, who took severe reprisals. Many of the leading Baltic German politicians were arrested; some 567 people, including a number of Estonians, were deported to Central Russia; and the whole of the Baltic nobility was outlawed. The deportees were not able to return until the Peace of Brest-Litovsk had been signed.

The sophisticated historical arguments adduced by the Baltic German nobility in support of the declaration of independence naturally carried little weight with the Latvian and Estonian bourgeoisie. Ever since the October Revolution, the members of the latter class had been virtually at one in their determination to break away from Russia, but since they had no desire to exchange one taskmaster for another, they were equally opposed to German hegemony. On 19 February 1918 the Council of Elders of the Estonian *Maapäev* vested supreme power in a committee of three, the so-called Liberation Committee, which consisted of K. Päts, J. Vilms and K. Konik. This Liberation Committee proved highly resourceful, for in the night of 24–25 February (during the brief interval between the Bolshevik withdrawal from Tallinn and the German take-over) it published an official manifesto, in which it proclaimed the independent Republic of Estonia, and vested supreme power in a Provisional Government headed by Päts. From then onwards the annual celebrations to mark the founding of the Republic were held on February 24. At first, this proclamation of independence had little effect. Baron von Seckendorff, the general commanding the occupation troops, refused to recognise the Estonian Government, which was forced to go underground; and on 16 June Päts was arrested and sent to an internment camp.

The German–Soviet peace negotiations opened in Brest-Litovsk in December 1917, but it soon became apparent that the Soviets were not prepared to accede to Germany's demands, whereupon the German Army Command ordered an immediate offensive. German troops from Riga then advanced northwards to Tartu, which fell on 24 February, while a second force pressed forwards from Saaremaa to take Tallinn on 25 February, and Narva on 4 March.

This offensive had the desired effect, for on 3 March the Soviets put their signature to the Peace of Brest-Litovsk. Under the terms of this settlement Russia surrendered Courland, Riga and Saaremaa, whose future status was to be determined by the German authorities in accordance with the wishes of the local population. As for Estonia and Livonia, they were to remain under German occupation until law and order were restored. Later, under the terms of the supplementary agreements appended to the Treaty on 27 August 1918, the Soviet Government was forced to renounce its claims to Estonia and Livonia.

And so the German Army liberated the whole of the Baltic area from Bolshevik rule. In certain districts it even crossed the frontier into Russia proper, advancing as far as Pskov. Local reaction to the German occupation varied from district to district. Among the Estonian and Latvian communities, however, the Germans were able to find only very few pro-German elements who were prepared to collaborate; and these did not include any of the really important politicians, who were quite adamant in their opposition. Later, when the Germans revealed their colonisation plans, attitudes hardened still further among the Estonian and Latvian leaders, and when the Baltic economy was bled by the army to further the war effort, their hostility came to be shared by the general populace.

A number of leading Baltic German politicians did their utmost to protect the rights of their Baltic confederates during the German occupation. One such was Baron Eduard von Dellingshausen. After returning from deportation, he made a determined attempt to persuade the German Military Administration in Estonia to confiscate only estate land for colonisation purposes, and to leave the peasants' land untouched. Alexander Eggers, a government inspector of schools in the city of Tallinn, also tried to help the indigenous community by urging the authorities not to prohibit the use of the vernacular tongue in Estonian schools. But the Germans showed themselves insensitive to the educational requirements of the Baltic peoples. Thus, on 15 August 1918, when they reopened the University of Tartu, the occupation authorities based the new statutes on the university's early German tradition and completely disregarded the needs of the Estonian and Latvian communities. Professor Theodor Schiemann, from Berlin, the newly-appointed provost, was roundly criticised at the time for his part in this affair by his nephew Paul Schiemann, the future politician (see pp. 204–6).

Germany's Baltic policy was highly ambivalent. Initially, Germany was clearly intent on annexing the territory and using it as a means of furthering its own agrarian and economic interests; but later it became conscious of the need to avoid giving undue offence to a future bourgeois Russian government by making excessive territorial demands. However, neither in the Baltic territories nor in Germany itself did it occur to the politicians to act on the principle of self-determination by acceding to the democratic demands of their Estonian and Latvian counterparts. It would have been surprising had they done so, for such a response would have been entirely out of their keeping with contemporary attitudes. Thus, partly because of preoccupation with their own victorious offensive, and partly because of their fear of Bolshevism, the Germans failed to recognise the intensity and vitality of Estonian and Latvian nationalism.

The political leaders of the Baltic German community sought the support of the occupation authorities, and of a small group of Estonian and Latvian conservatives, in order to press their plan for the incorporation of the Baltic territories into the German Empire. In April 1918 provincial assemblies were convened, at the instigation of the Baltic German nobility, in Livonia and Estonia and on the island of Saaremaa, which were essentially the same as the assembly that had already been held in Courland, the members of which were elected by the various estates voting in separate ballots. These provincial assemblies then elected the delegates to a General Provincial Assembly, with a membership consisting of thirty-five Germans, thirteen Estonians and ten Latvians. This General Assembly met on 12 April in Riga, where it passed a resolution calling upon the German Emperor to recognise the Baltic provinces as a monarchy, and to make this monarchy a German protectorate. It was hoped initially that the new territory would be linked with Prussia by an act of union, but later an alternative proposal was advanced for a United Baltic Duchy under Duke Adolf Friedrich of Mecklenburg (1873–1969).

Once the Baltic territories had been occupied by the German Army, the Estonian and Latvian politicians were no longer able to influence the course of events. The Latvians had two political instruments at their disposal (the Democratic Bloc, formed in September 1917, and the National Council, which came into being two months later), neither of which was able to function at that time. The situation was exactly the same in Petrograd, where the new wave of Bolshevik terror that had begun in January 1918 prevented the members of the Latvian National Council from playing their part in political life. At the end of June these members met in the apartment of the former Duma delegate Goldmanis, and decided to press the western Allies to support them in their quest for independence. Subsequently, they opened offices in Switzerland, Sweden and France to propagate their cause.

Meanwhile, ever since February 1918, the Estonians had been stepping up their pressure on the western Allies. On 25 April 1918 Julius Seljamaa (the former Duma delegate who subsequently became the Estonian envoy in Riga and Moscow and, from 1933 onwards, Foreign Minister) handed Brändström, the Swedish envoy in Petrograd, a memorandum in which the Estonians protested against the resolution passed by the General Provincial Council on 12 April. Copies of this memorandum were also handed to the representatives of the western Allies, and in the months that followed, the Estonian and Latvian politicians continued to protest, both at home and abroad, against the measures taken by the German Military Administration. This policy soon paid dividends, for on 3 May 1918 the Estonians persuaded the English, French and Italian governments to give *de facto* recognition to the *Maapäev*.

In the summer of 1918 the western powers were far too preoccupied with the prosecution of the war to think of helping the Baltic territories. Of course, Germany's plans for the Baltic region were also hampered by the heavy fighting in the west, and it was not until the autumn of 1918 that it was possible to proceed with the implementation of what was hoped would be the definitive political structure of the *Land Ober-Ost*. On 7 November 1918 the General Provincial Council elected four Germans, three Latvians and three Estonians to serve on a Regency Council, which was to act as a provisional government. The President of this Council was Baron A. Pilar von Pilchau, who had previously been Provincial Marshal of Livonia.

But by this time the bell had already begun to toll for the German Empire. Since August 1918 it had been clear to all concerned, including the German Army Command, that there was no point in prolonging the war. On 4 October the Germans asked the Allies for an armistice, and on 9 November, the day on which the new Baltic Regency Council convened for its constituent session, revolution broke out in Germany.

5. *The War of Liberation*

From mid-November 1918 onwards, the situation in the Baltic territories was alarming. Although the German withdrawal had cleared the way for the development of independent political institutions, the Bolshevik offensive barred it again. The German collapse left the Baltic peoples virtually defenceless, for their own sparse forces were scarcely equal to the task which faced them.

On 13 November the Soviet Government repudiated the Peace of Brest-Litovsk in order, as we are told in a Soviet-Estonian account, 'to embark on the political and military struggle for the liberation of Estonia and Latvia from the yoke of German Imperialism'. And in this connection, the author continues, 'the working masses of the occupied territories' were promised 'the support of the Russian workers and peasants'. On 11 November the Commander-in-Chief of the

Red Army, the Latvian Vācietis, ordered the 6th Soviet Russian Division under General I. Ivanov to take up position near Jamburg, just east of the Estonian border. Including reserves, Ivanov's force numbered some 3,000 men.

On 22 November the main body of this force marched on Narva. The initial attacks were repelled by remnants of the German Army and a few small Estonian units composed largely of volunteers, many of them schoolboys. But a few days later a detachment of Soviet marines landed near Narva-Jõesuu at the mouth of the Narova, and on 29 November Narva fell into Communist hands. Before the day was out the victors had proclaimed a Soviet Republic of Estonia, under the name of the 'Estonian Work Commune'. The new Republic, which was headed by the Communist leader Jaan Anvelt, was recognised by Moscow on 7 December. Meanwhile, the Communist elements among the indigenous population began to play an active part in the development of the territory.

From Narva the Bolshevik troops advanced westwards, and on 24 December they took the important railway junction of Tapa, where the line branches off to Tartu and Riga, before pressing on to within some 30 km. of Tallinn. Meanwhile, a second Bolshevik force had been advancing from Pskov whose German garrison had pulled out on 25 November) towards the west and the north-west. Tartu fell on 21 December. Soon afterwards Viljandi and Pärnu were being threatened, and to the south of Pärnu the Bolsheviks fought their way through to the coast.

The invasion of Livonia was carried out by the Latvian light infantry regiments supported by units of the Red Army. A three-pronged attack was mounted: against Riga via Pskov, Valga, Valmiera and Cēsis; against Liepaja via Zilupe; and against Liepaja via Polotsk and Dvinsk. Valga was taken by the 1st and 6th Light Infantry Regiments on 18 December, and was nominated as the seat of the Latvian Soviet Government. By the end of the year almost the whole of Livonia was in Communist hands. Valmiera fell on 25 December; Riga was evacuated on 2 January and was taken over by the Bolsheviks the following day. A week later Jelgava also fell into their hands. It was not until the end of January that the front was stabilised along the line of the Ventspils.

Advancing from Courland into Northern Lithuania, the Bolsheviks pressed forwards towards Kaunas, taking Šiauliai, Panevežys, Ukmergè and Telšiai *en route*. On this front their advance was halted near Kedainiai. Meanwhile, the so-called White Russian and Lithuanian Army, which consisted of the 2nd Soviet Russian Pskov Division and a few smaller units, advanced from the east and entered Vilnius on 5/6 January, whereupon the Lithuanian Government withdrew to Kaunas, and Smetona and Voldemaras went abroad in search of foreign aid. Shortly after Vilnius had been occupied, Lida fell into Communist hands; and in the west the Red Army reached the Memel. By this time more than half of Lithuania had been conquered. But unlike Estonia and Livonia, Lithuania had not produced an embryonic Communist organisation in the winter of 1917-18. Consequently the Bolsheviks had to create not only a Lithuanian Communist Government but a whole network of councils as well. The Government was headed by Mickevičius-Kapsukas and Z. Angarietis, who were assisted by A. A. Yoffe, the Soviet adviser. In order to ensure that Lithuania was firmly integrated into the Soviet community it was proposed that a federal union should be established between the Lithuanian and the White Russian Soviet Republics.

By the beginning of 1919 the nationalist cause in the Baltic territories seemed doomed. In Lithuania the situation was extremely threatening, in Estonia it was grim, and in Latvia apparently hopeless.

The conquest of the Baltic area constituted one specific stage of the world revolution planned by the Bolshevik leadership in Moscow. As early as 16 November 1918 the Soviet War Commissar Leon Trotsky had announced that the Red Army would advance into Western Europe. Apparently, contact was to have been established with the Austrian Revolutionaries via Kiev, and with the German Revolutionaries via Pskov and Vilnius. Similar ideas were expressed in a Latvian Communist Manifesto published on 17 December, in which it was stated that Germany and the other countries of Western Europe would soon be in the grip of the Communist Revolution, and that in due course all those countries would have to be amalgamated into a 'Union of Soviet

Republics'. Eight days after the publication of this manifesto, on 25 December, the Party Secretary in Petrograd, G. Zinoviev, pointed out that Lithuania, Latvia and Estonia formed a barrier which cut off Soviet Russia from revolutionary Germany, and said that this barrier must be removed so that the Bolsheviks could agitate for a socialist revolution in the Scandinavian countries, and the Baltic could be transformed into 'an ocean of socialist revolution'. On 29 December Zinoviev returned to this theme, insisting that the 'White Bands' must be driven from the Baltic territories, and all land 'snatched' from Soviet Russia must be restored.

The initial Soviet offensive in Estonia was a failure, largely because even before the German occupation the Estonian politicians had started to construct an administrative infrastructure, which stood them in good stead during this crucial period. Piip has pointed out in this connection that, despite contemporary scepticism about the methods and tendencies developed under the German occupation, it was significant that in February 1918 the Estonians were able to drive out the Russian invaders and rid themselves of the local Bolsheviks at one fell swoop, thus facilitating the subsequent development of their territory after the German withdrawal.

The Estonian Provisional Government first entered the scene on 11 November, the day the German forces finally laid down their arms. The officer commanding the German army in Estonia then lifted the ban on the *Maapäev*, and on 19 November the German plenipotentiary August Winnig gave *de facto* recognition to the Estonian Government, thus enabling Premier Päts and his colleagues to proceed with the construction of the Estonian state. The first priority was to build and train a national army, and to this end the government mobilised all Estonian officers on 16 November and appealed for volunteer recruits. But after the fall of Narva it was obvious that a volunteer army could never defeat the Bolsheviks and that conscription would have to be introduced. In December 1918 Lieutenant-Colonel Johan Laidoner (1884–19?), who had returned home via Finland from Russia, was appointed Commander-in-Chief of the Estonian Army. Under this capable officer, who also had a sound political instinct, the expansion and organisation of the army made excellent progress. Laidoner was the son of a farm labourer from the Viljandi district. He passed out from the Military Academy in St. Petersburg in 1912, and during the First World War served with the Russian Army, becoming a Divisional Chief of Staff. After the collapse of the tsarist regime Laidoner assumed command of the Estonian Division. In the Estonian Army his Chief of Staff was Lieutenant-Colonel Jaan Soots.

In a number of Estonian towns the Baltic German communities started to form volunteer units to help with the defence of the country. At first, the Estonian Government was rather dubious about the advisability of this move, but on 27 November Päts authorised the recruitment of Baltic German volunteers of military age. Subsequently a number of these units were combined, and the Baltic Battalion which was subsequently brought up to regimental strength– was formed in Rakvere. This battalion, commanded by Colonel C. von Weiss, was immediately deployed on the Narva front. On 6 December the government also came to terms with a Russian anti-Bolshevik force of some 3,500 men, which had been formed in Pskov on 10 October with the approval of the German Army Command. In addition, the Estonians were able to draw some comfort from the presence of a British naval squadron, which had entered the Baltic and, after passing Liepaja, anchored off Tallinn. In an engagement with ships of the Soviet fleet the English squadron had captured two destroyers, and handed them over to the Estonian Government. But in terms of foreign aid the crucial factor was the intervention of Finnish volunteers, who reached Tallinn on 31 December, at the precise moment when the Bolsheviks were threatening to break through.

The arrival of the Finnish contingent turned the tide in favour of the Estonians, who began to advance at the beginning of January 1919, and drove the Bolsheviks back across the Narova before the end of the month. Apart from the Finnish and German contingents and the 2,500 men of the Estonian Regular Army, there was also a force of partisans fighting on this front under the command of Lieutenant Julius Kuperjanow, who was killed in the battle for Valga. Kuperjanow's force played a major part in the campaign and was largely responsible for the liberation of Tartu on

14 January. There was subsequently fierce fighting along the railway line linking Tartu with Valga, where the Estonians fought, and finally routed, units of the Latvian light infantry regiments. Early in February Valga and Võru were taken, and by 24 February 1919 – the first anniversary of the founding of the Estonian state – the whole country had been liberated.

The Soviet invasion of Lithuania also hit its peak in January 1919. After an abortive attempt to flank Kaunas and press on to the Memel to the south and west of the town, the Red Army fell into disarray, and Bolshevik units began to retreat eastwards. In February the *Taryba* was able to meet in Kaunas. The Lithuanian Army – which had been created on 23 November 1918 but was still a ragged force – was then able to organise and equip itself with arms and war materials left by the retreating German Army. By the late summer of 1919 the Bolshevik invaders had been driven from every corner of the territory. Of course, the Lithuanians were then faced with other problems, which we shall be dealing with later.

The situation in Latvia was much more difficult than in either Lithuania or Estonia, for the Latvians first had to create a political base for their liberation movement. When the National Council, which had been established in Petrograd, failed to reach an agreement with the Democratic Bloc, which had been founded in Riga, a new representative body had to be set up. This was done on 17 November 1918, when the Latvian People's Council was created under the chairmanship of J. Čakste (1859–1927). On 18 November this Council met in Riga to proclaim Latvian independence, and adopt a new political platform, which dealt with a whole series of crucial questions, including the question of Latvian nationalism. The Premier of the first government of the independent Republic of Latvia was Karlis Ulmanis, one of the leaders of the Peasants' League.

Ulmanis was a highly intelligent and ambitious politician who eventually came to dominate Latvian politics. He was born into a peasant family in 1877 in the district of Jelgava in Courland. After studying agriculture in Germany and Switzerland, he was obliged to emigrate following the 1905 Revolution, and continued his studies in the U.S.A., where he gained experience and a knowledge of foreign languages. He returned home just before the outbreak of the First World War and devoted himself to politics.

The perseverance of the Latvian representatives sent to woo the western Allies was finally rewarded on 11 November 1918, when Great Britain gave *de facto* recognition to the new Latvian state, thus placing it on a par with Estonia, which had received its *de facto* recognition from Britain on 3 May 1918. Z. Meirovics played a leading part in this initiative. We have already seen that A. Winnig, the German plenipotentiary in Riga, gave *de facto* recognition to Latvia on behalf of Germany on 26 November. This was followed, on 7 December, by an agreement drawn up by Winnig and the Latvian Minister of Defence Zālitis, providing for the transfer of arms and equipment from German army stores to a Baltic militia called the 'Baltische Landeswehr', a volunteer force already being formed at that time by a group of Baltic Germans. Initially, this force also embraced a Latvian unit commanded by Colonel O. Kalpaks.

Paradoxically, the western Allies – and especially Britain – wanted the German troops who had stayed on in Latvia after the capitulation to undertake the initial defence of the country against the Bolshevik invaders in accordance with Article 12 of the Armistice signed in Compiègne. German volunteers were enrolled in the Iron Division and, in order to encourage recruitment, the Latvian Government agreed to Winnig's suggestion that all Germans who fought for Latvia should be given the opportunity of acquiring Latvian citizenship when hostilities ended. But this concession was bitterly resented by many Latvians, who regarded it as an underhand attempt to revive the German colonisation scheme. The Social Democrats walked out of the People's Council in protest, and one of the three Latvian army companies mutinied on 30 December. It seemed as if the sympathies of the majority of the Latvian people lay with the Latvian light infantry regiments, which formed the nucleus of the invading Bolshevik Army.

But what precisely was this Bolshevik Army? What was the nationality of the men who fought in it?

Let us first consider the situation in Estonia. The 6th Soviet Russian Division, which fought on the Narva front, contained two Estonian light infantry regiments, one of which had been formed in Viljandi, the other in Tartu. By the end of 1918 these regiments had suffered heavy losses, and it seems probable that a large proportion of the replacements would have been Russian. According to a report drafted by the Estonian High Command in February 1919 there had been thirty-five Communist regiments fighting in Estonia, only four of which had been Estonian. And according to Martna, the proportion of Estonian soldiers in those regiments varied from 25 to 75 per cent. Certainly the vast majority of the Estonian population regarded the Bolshevik troops as foreign invaders. Laaman tells us that even Stučka, the Latvian Communist leader, expected that the Bolshevik troops would have to conquer Estonia by force of arms. Unlike Latvia – where Stučka anticipated a relatively easy military campaign – Estonia had thrown up very few Bolshevik sympathisers, and those few were all concentrated in the industrial areas of Reval and Narva. Stučka's prognosis was borne out by the course of events. When the Estonian troops went over to the offensive, it took them just twelve days to liberate their country. The Soviet Government of Estonia had held office for only six weeks, during which time it achieved nothing of any consequence; and when a Communist revolt was launched on the island of Saaremaa on 16 February 1919 it was suppressed within a week.

In Latvia the situation was rather different. Although the Latvian light infantry regiments had been stiffened by the incorporation of Russian units, they remained predominantly Latvian. Above all, the major part of their officers were Latvian. Moreover, ever since the Bolshevik take-over in Russia in October 1917 the Latvian light infantry regiments had proved extremely reliable. On 1 November 1917 Lenin had seconded several Latvian units to Petrograd, to guard the members of his government, and in July 1918 the Latvian regiments had suppressed the revolts staged by the Social Revolutionaries in and around Moscow with exemplary despatch. Subsequently they were deployed on the Volga front, which was threatened by the advance of the Czechoslovak Legion from Siberia, and in 1919 some 5,000 Latvian soldiers fought against Denikin's White Armies on the southern front. In September 1918 the Latvian Jakums Vācietis (1873–1938), who had already risen from Commander of the Latvian 5th

Light Infantry Regiment to Commander of the Russian 12th Army, was appointed Commander-in-Chief of the Red Army of the Russian S.F.S.R. Other Latvian officers achieved high rank in the Red Army (such as J. Alksnis, R. Bērzins, R. Eidemanis and J. Fabricius) and a number of Latvian functionaries were promoted to senior positions within the Communist Party (such as J. Rudzutaks, R. Eiche, I. Smilga, V. Mezlauk, J. Bērziņš and J. Pēters).

In view of all this, it would have been surprising if the invading Soviet troops had not been welcomed more warmly by the indigenous population in Latvia than their colleagues on the Estonian front.

The first measures taken at the behest of Moscow to pave the way for a Communist take-over in Latvia date from November 1918. Šilf-Jaunzemš, a member of the Central Committee of the Latvian Communist Party, was instructed to prepare for a General Congress of the Latvian Councils; Pētēris Stučka (1865–1932), who had been one of the leading lights of the Latvian Social Democratic movement ever since the turn of the century, was chosen as the future head of a Latvian Soviet Government, in which Jūlijs Daniševskis (1884–1937), President of the Soldiers' Council of the Latvian light infantry regiments, was to serve as his deputy. On 14 December the independent Soviet Republic of Latvia was officially proclaimed in Moscow, and on 22 December it was recognised by the Soviet Government in a decree signed by Lenin.

The Latvian Soviet Government lasted much longer and was much more active than its Estonian counterpart. Of course, it enjoyed certain advantages. For example, it was able to build on the resolutions passed at the end of 1917; and it also had in Stučka a head of government who belonged to the top flight of the Bolshevik leadership in Moscow. In 1917–18 Stučka held the post of People's Commissar for Justice in Soviet Russia, and in this capacity played an important part in the preparation of the first Soviet Russian constitution, drafted in 1918. In February 1918 he was a member of the Soviet peace delegation at Brest-Litovsk.

We get some idea of the importance which the Soviet Russians attached to their Latvian satellite from the attendance at the General Congress of the Latvian Councils, which met in

c*

January 1919 to pass the constitution law, of two top party representatives from Moscow: Sverdlov, who, as Chairman of the All-Russian Central Executive Committee, was Head of State of the Russian Soviet Republic, and Kamenev, a member of the Central Committee of the Russian Communist Party.

The constitution of the Latvian Soviet Republic was based on that of the R.S.F.S.R., from which it departed in only a few respects. Significantly, the Latvian constitution did not call for a People's Commissar for Foreign Affairs, and Stučka pointed out in this connection that, in view of the close affinity which existed between Latvia and the R.S.F.S.R., there was no need for formal treaties between them such as those concluded by the R.S.F.S.R. with the Soviet Ukraine or Soviet White Russia. The General Congress also stated that it would maintain the 'closest possible links with the R.S.F.S.R. and join in the common struggle against the foreign Imperialists'. Basically, the Latvian Bolsheviks thought of their Republic as an integral part of the R.S.F.S.R., but one enjoying autonomy in respect of its internal affairs. Consequently, because their economy was more highly developed than that of many of the Central Provinces of Russia, they claimed the right to evolve their own policies in certain important fields such as agrarian reform and the structure of the unions.

The friendly welcome which the Latvian Communist troops received from large sections of the local population was soon withdrawn, due to the steady growth in the use of terror tactics, the drop in living standards, the disappointment felt over the continuation of the war, and the failure of the world revolution. The internal policies pursued in Latvia – and, for that matter, in Estonia – were greatly influenced by the government's anti-bourgeois class struggle, which led to the expropriation of private property by the state, the arrest of private individuals on political charges, and the use of physical intimidation.

In Estonia, the first wave of terror, which lasted from October 1917 to February 1918, was followed by a second shorter wave, from November 1918 to January 1919. In Latvia the first wave, which was confined to the Latvian part of Livonia, also lasted from October 1917 to February 1918. But the second, which affected the whole of Latvia, went on for a full six months, from November 1918 to May 1919. During the winter of 1917–18 the Bolshevik terrorists concentrated almost exclusively on the members of the Baltic German community, but in the following winter they harassed all property owners, irrespective of nationality, and all persons who had received a bourgeois education.

Bolshevik behaviour in Tartu and Riga was particularly brutal. Just before Christmas 1918 a considerable number of people – many of them priests of different denominations – were arrested in Tartu; on 9 January 1919 a number of German estate owners were shot on the icebound river; and on 14 January, just before the town was liberated, the Communists staged a bloodbath in the basement of one of the town banks, in which both the university preacher and professor, Pastor Traugott Hahn, and the Estonian Orthodox Bishop Platon (Paul Kulbusch) lost their lives. All in all, forty pastors of the Protestant Church were shot in Estonia and Latvia by the Bolsheviks. In Riga the great killer in the winter of 1918–19 was hunger: it has been estimated that 8,000 people starved to death in that city alone. In May 1919 several hundred people were held as hostages in Riga's central prison, and when the anti-Bolshevik forces were approaching the city, thirty-two of them, including several clerics and a number of women, were shot, others being forced to march off to the east with the retreating army. These acts of terror were the death throes of a regime. It had first begun to disintegrate in the spring of 1919, when the mounting discontent of the Latvian peasant population was augmented by the disenchantment of the industrial workers, especially in Riga.

After the fall of Riga the Latvian Provisional Government, headed by Ulmanis, fled to Liepaja, where it was able to exert only a marginal influence on the course of events. Once again the focal point of Latvian political activity moved to Western Europe. As for the military initiative in the Republic, that had clearly passed to the German army units.

Towards the end of 1918 the German Government became extremely anxious about the situation in the Baltic territories. In view of the revolutionary activities taking place within Germany itself, it was felt that the Bolshevik advance, which had almost reached the borders of East Prussia, created an acute threat that could not be ignored. So Germany decided to act. The First *Garde-Reserve* Division was moved from East Prussia to Courland; the 'Baltische Landeswehr' was placed under the command of Major Fletcher, and the Iron Division under the command of Major Bischoff, both of whom were capable and forceful officers; finally, the German High Command appointed Major-General Count Rüdiger von der Goltz, who had commanded the German auxiliaries in Finland in 1918, Commander-in-Chief of all German Forces in the Baltic area.

The German counter-offensive was launched at the end of February, and made rapid progress. Ventspils was taken on 24 February, and Jelgava on 18 March; and within a very short space of time the major part of Courland had been liberated. A Latvian brigade also took part in this campaign; it was commanded by Colonel Jānis Balodis, who later became Latvian Minister of War. One of Balodis' senior officers, Colonel O. Kalpaks, was killed on 6 March, when a German and a Latvian unit fired on one another by mistake.

Although the Latvians obviously benefited from the Germans' military successes, they grew more and more suspicious of their political motives. General von der Goltz was a self-willed officer with political ambitions which went far beyond anything envisaged by the German Government. All that Germany wanted at that time was to reconquer Courland. But von der Goltz had dreamed up a quixotic scheme for the overthrow of the Russian Bolshevik Government as a first step towards the conclusion of an alliance between Germany and some future Russian bourgeois government, which would create a united front capable of combating the western powers. However, it was not von der Goltz's romantic notions which perturbed the Latvians. What worried them was that, with the support of the German Government and its eastern army, the Baltic Germans might come to reassert their former predominance.

The Latvian Government then tried to strengthen its own army by introducing conscription. But von der Goltz objected to this move – which was, of course, designed to reduce the imbalance between German and Latvian armed strength – whereupon the Latvians appealed to the western Allies. At this point a detachment of shock troops attached to the 'Baltische Landeswehr' decided to take matters into their own hands.

Led by their youthful commander, Baron Hans von Manteuffel, who acted without von der Goltz's authority, these troops overthrew the Latvian Government on 16 April in the Liepaja *putsch*. Premier Ulmanis and most of his ministers managed to avoid arrest and sought sanctuary on board a British warship. Subsequently Ulmanis called on the British envoy in Copenhagen, who gave an assurance that his government would honour its obligations under the defence agreement between Britain and Latvia, which had been signed on 11 February.

After the Libau *putsch* Manteuffel tried, but failed, to obtain Colonel Balodis' support for a plan to set up a military junta, whereupon the leading members of the Baltic German community began to look around for a Latvian politician able and willing to form a more co-operative government. The man they settled on was Andrievs Niedra (1871–1942), a pastor and author, and long-standing adversary of Ulmanis. At first Niedra tried to come to terms with the members of Ulmanis' government, and it was only when they refused to collaborate that he formed his own cabinet, which consisted of six Latvian and three German ministers. But Niedra had no popular support worth mentioning; he was indeed little more than a puppet of the German armed forces.

The Allied Armistice Commission in Paris had been watching the growth of Germany's military power in Courland with mounting suspicion, and when the counter-offensive was launched in February 1919, the Commission turned down Germany's request for merchant ships to transport men and materials to the new war zone. It is hardly surprising, therefore, that when the Commission met on 22 April to consider the implications of the Liepaja *putsch*, it should have demanded the restoration of the old *status quo*. The British representative was particularly adamant.

Thus the conflict between the Latvian and German leaders became an international issue. After the *putsch*, the Armistice Commission insisted that the German Government should recall Count von der Goltz and place all German military units in Latvia under Latvian command. But when the Germans refused to comply with this instruction and threatened to pull out of Latvia altogether, the Commission was obliged to yield, for allied policy in Latvia depended on the continuing presence there of a German military force. In fact, everybody wanted the offensive against the Bolsheviks to be maintained. Meanwhile, the 'Baltische Landeswehr' had been urging acceptance of its project for the relief of Riga, where the Bolshevik reign of terror had reached its peak. With the backing of Admiral Sinclair, the officer commanding the British Fleet in the Baltic, von der Goltz – who needed a military victory in order to win support for the new Latvian Government – authorised an attack, which was carried out by a combined force consisting of German troops, the Latvian Balodis Brigade and a Russian detachment commanded by Colonel Prince A. Lieven. After the shock troops of the 'Baltische Landeswehr' had stormed the bridges over the Daugava, Riga was taken on 22 May.

The conquest of Riga was to assume a significance which extended far beyond the borders of Latvia and the Baltic territories. The vision of a European Revolution, conjured up by the Russian Bolshevik leaders, was to remain a vision. And it should be remembered in this connection that the 'Miracle on the Vistula', which thwarted Moscow's plans for the bolshevisation of Poland, was preceded by the 'Miracle on the Daugava' of 22 May, 1919.

The policies pursued by the western powers in respect of the Baltic territories were strangely divergent. The British were genuinely interested, but the French were concerned only in so far as developments in the Baltic region affected the establishment of the new Polish state, while the Americans soon withdrew from their initial involvement. The American withdrawal was particularly regrettable since Lieutenant-Colonel W. Greene, who was in Latvia in April and May 1919 as head of an American military mission, showed a keen appreciation of the complexity of the country's multi-ethnic society. His delared objective at the time was to unite all the different communities, including the Baltic German community, in defence of Latvian autonomy.

In the minds of all Allied politicians, the Baltic question was indissolubly linked with the Russian question, and for a while the Allies' Baltic policy was dictated by the requirements of their Russian policy, which called for intervention in the civil war. However, the attitude of the British Government under Lloyd George was decidedly ambivalent, for a large section of British public and political opinion was opposed to intervention, a fact which the government had to take into account. But almost all shades of British opinion were behind the border territories in their quest for independence. In this connection it is interesting to note that in December 1918, when the situation in the Baltic territories had reached its most critical stage, one of the members of an Estonian delegation to Western Europe tried to persuade Lord Robert Cecil that it would be to Britain's advantage to establish a naval base on the island of Oesel. But although this idea re-emerged from time to time in the years that followed, and was advocated by Jaan Tõnisson on several occasions, it was never worked out in detail. Basically, British politicians wanted to prevent both Germany and Russia from reasserting themselves in the Baltic region, and it was for this reason that they took such a keen interest in the Baltic independence movement. The French and the Americans, on the other hand, had serious doubts about this movement. Although they had little sympathy for Russian Communism, they both had good reasons – although not always the same reasons – for wanting to see a strong and united Russia, an aim that was not easily reconciled with the nationalist aspirations of the Baltic territories.

But the western powers were in a grave dilemma. After the bitter and protracted fighting of the First World War, none of them was either willing or able to put an army into the field in the Baltic territories. A group of British politicians tried to persuade the Scandinavian countries to send a full-scale expeditionary force, but without avail. The solution finally adopted, *faute de mieux*, of retaining, and subsequently reinforcing, part of the German army of occupation, not only went against the principles underlying the Armistice conditions, but also appeared to be undermining the Baltic liberation movement. In the event, this solution received its pragmatic justification through the fall of Riga. But as the fighting continued, it became apparent that the different groups in the Baltic territories had strongly conflicting interests. And so, on 23 May, the Council of Foreign Ministers at the Paris Peace Conference drew the moral from the Liepaja *putsch* by deciding to ask the Germans to withdraw their troops from both Latvia and Lithuania as soon as the indigenous peoples were able to provide adequate replacements. The Council also recommended that a military mission be sent to advise on the formation of local army units.

Until then General von der Goltz had successfully prevented the introduction of general mobilisation in Latvia. But a Latvian army unit had been formed on Estonian territory under Captain Jorgis Zēmitāns (1873–1928) from 2 February onwards, and this unit was expanded in the course of May 1919. Zēmitāns advocated the policies pursued by Ulmanis, as did the Estonian Government, which from May 1919 onwards was headed by Otto Strandman. The reason why the Estonians sided with Ulmanis was that, like him, they feared the growth of German influence and the possibility of collaboration between the German army units and the Russian detachment commanded by Prince Lieven. And so, at the end of May, the mobilisation ordered by Ulmanis immediately prior to the Liepaja *putsch* was put into effect in the northern districts of Latvia, which had been liberated with the help of Estonian troops.

After the collapse of Bolshevik rule in Riga, the Estonians had also gone over to the offensive. Advancing towards Eastern Latvia from the north, the Estonian forces had liberated Aluksne, and then pressed on to Jekabpils on the Daugava. On 3 June they joined up with the troops of the 'Baltische Landeswehr' who had also advanced ino Central Livonia after 22 May.

At that point the rational course of action for the Estonian and German troops would have been to join forces and proceed together against their common enemy. But the acrimony and mutual suspicion which were part and parcel of Latvian political life did not make for rational behaviour; and so instead of combining, both armies adopted a mutually hostile posture. The Estonian commanders insisted on the German troops pulling back behind the Livonian Aa, while the Germans and the members of the Niedra Government wanted the Estonians to withdraw into their own territory. There were men of peace on both sides, but they were unable to assert themselves.

Immediately after this military confrontation on 3 June, the American observer Lieutenant-Colonel Greene proposed a compromise solution which would have enabled the Estonian and German forces to combine against the Bolsheviks. Negotiations were conducted to this end in Cesis, but were adjourned on 9 June at the request of the Estonians. Meanwhile, a new Allied military mission arrived. It was headed by the British General, Sir Hubert Gough, who made no secret of his antipathy towards the Germans. Gough took the Estonians' side and demanded the repatriation of 50 per cent of all German troops stationed in the Baltic territories. When this demand was rejected by von der Goltz, the stage was set for the Battle of Cēsis, which took place on 22 June.

I have already referred to the suspicion with which the two sides regarded one another. But was this suspicion justified? To suggest that the Germans intended to invade Estonian territory and overthrow the government would be ludicrous. On the other hand, they had undoubtedly failed to treat the Estonian Government with due respect. It was as if they had not realised that it was a legally constituted body and, as such, responsible for the political administration of all Estonian territory. Moreover, although General von der Goltz did not take an active part in the battle, he made no attempt to stop the Volunteer Corps from joining the 'Baltische Landeswehr' in support of the Niedra Government, whose War Minister, Vankins, assumed command of the German forces. The Latvians under Balodis and Prince Lieven's Russian detachment were not involved in the battle, which was joined at the precise moment when the German Government agreed to sign the Peace of Versailles. This can hardly have been a coincidence; and it must be assumed that von der Goltz calculated that, in the circumstances, the Allies would refuse to accept Germany's signature, a step which would have had unforseeable consequences for the situation in the east. But great gambler though he was, von der Goltz was realistic enough to ask the Allies to intercede when the 'Baltische Landeswehr' was defeated.

Major-General Ernst Põdder commanded the Estonian troops, who fought with immense courage and *élan*. They were, of course, inspired both by feelings of social antagonism and by a sense of patriotism. This brief but extremely violent engagement was later to be described as an initiation ceremony, in which the Estonian people finally asserted themselves as an independent nation. The turning point in the battle came with the deployment of the Estonian tanks and the Kuperjanov partisans. By 23 June victory was assured. The Germans were forced to withdraw to Riga, pursued by the Estonians, who began to prepare for an attack on the city.

The armistice, concluded on 3 July 1919 at Strazdumuiža near Riga, called for the withdrawal of all German troops from Latvia at the earliest possible moment. Meanwhile, the Germans were ordered to evacuate Riga, and the Estonians had to pull back to Inčukalns. On 4 July the Latvian units commanded by Balodis and Zēmitāns entered the capital, thus sealing the fate of the Niedra Government, which stood down on 8 July to make way for Ulmanis. In Ulmanis' new government Z. Meierovics returned to the Foreign Ministry, and M. Valters to the Ministry for Internal Affairs. However, at the request of the Allies, two German politicians were also given ministerial posts. Nor was the government the only Latvian institution to be reorganised under the terms of the armistice. The 'Baltische Landeswehr' was reformed as well; German nationals serving with the Landeswehr – i.e. Germans born within the borders of Germany – were discharged, and its control passed to General Sīmonson, the Latvian Commander-in-Chief, who was accountable to the Latvian Government. The new commander appointed by Sīmonson was the British Colonel Alexander (later Field-Marshal Lord Alexander of Tunis). Alexander testified to the fighting spirit of his Baltic German troops, who were very different from the licientious soldiery of the German Volunteer Corps.

Following the resolution of the conflict between the Baltic Germans on the one hand and the Estonians and Latvians on the other, the Russian anti-Bolshevik forces began to play a more prominent part in the military campaign. When the Soviet troops on the Northern Sector withdrew from Estonia, the Estonian Army was able to advance beyond the Narova and Lake Peipsi, thus creating a salient, which protected the forces in the south from a flank attack and so enabled them to prepare for a new offensive without being harassed by the Bolsheviks. The offensive was launched in May 1919, when the Northern Corps advanced from the Narva district towards Petrograd. This White Russian contingent, which had been brought up to a strength of nearly 5,000 men by volunteers and deserters, was supported during the initial phase of its advance by Estonian units. On 25 May these Estonian troops captured Pskov, only to hand it over a few days later to a White Russian detachment, which successfully held the town until August, but tarnished its reputation in the process by taking brutal reprisals on the population.

As the weeks passed, the Estonians came to realise that collaboration with the Russians was both militarily and politically problematical, especially since the officers commanding the anti-Communist Russian forces had given no indication that they were prepared to recognise Estonian independence. Of course, once their own territory had been liberated and their Latvian neighbours were no longer in any immediate danger, the Estonians had no particular interest in continuing the war against the Bolsheviks. In view of this, and also in view of the difficulties posed by their alliance with the White Russians, it is not surprising that General Laidoner should have decided to relinquish his command of the Northern Corps, which then passed to General Judenič. Under Judenič the corps received reinforcements – in the form of Lieven's Russian detachment – and was renamed the North-Western Army to distinguish it from the Russian Northern Army, which was operating in the Archangel region. But, of course, this North-Western Army continued to depend on the Estonians for its supplies.

It was at this stage that the British military representative, General Marsh, intervened. On 10 August in Tallinn he made the White Russians set up a government for the north-western region under Lianozov, and then forced this government to recognise Lithuanian independence. But Marsh's solution did not meet with general support among the western Allies, who were divided on this issue; and when the Council of Foreign Ministers met to discuss the problem on 20 August at the Paris Peace Conference, all that they could suggest was that the Baltic States and the White Russians should try to come to terms. This suggestion was seized upon by the Allied officials on the spot, who persuaded the military representatives of the Baltic States, Poland, the Russian North-Western Army and the Russian Western Army to commit themselves to a combined offensive against the Bolsheviks in mid-September. The real driving force behind this agreement, which was reached in Riga on 26 August, was of course General Marsh.

When the Russian Western Army was formed, attention was focused yet again on the German troops still stationed in the Baltic region. General Gough, it will be remembered, had stipulated that these troops should all be evacuated by 19 July. But General von der Goltz had sought to extend this deadline in the hope that he might yet succeed in obtaining agricultural land on which his soldiers could settle. The fact that the Latvian Government was by then insisting that the agreements concluded on 29 December 1918 had been invalidated by the Treaty of Versailles did not deter him. Accordingly, von der Goltz supported the project for the formation of Russian army units composed of former prisoners of war because if German contingents could be incorporated into this force, then those of his soldiers who wished to stay on in the Baltic territories would be able to do so. The project was duly put into effect, and when Prince Lieven's detachment was transferred to the northern sector, it was replaced by this new force, which came to be known as the Russian Western Army and was commanded by an adventurer from the Caucasus, Colonel P. M. Bermondt-Avalov. At one point Bermondt's army numbered some 40,000 men.

Against the background of the Russian civil war, this new German initiative appeared positively alarming to the western Allies, who even considered sending a Polish force under Allied command to drive the Germans out. But it was Bermondt who made the first move. He asked the Latvian Government to grant him transit rights for his army through Latvian territory so that he could launch an offensive against the Bolsheviks; and when he failed to receive a satisfactory response, his troops attacked the Latvian positions on the Daugava on 8 October, and subsequently fought their way into the suburbs of Riga. Bermondt then offered the Latvian Government an armistice.

At this point the Latvians' northern neighbours and brothers-in-arms came to the rescue. Two columns of Estonian tanks intervened and enabled the Latvian Army Command to stabilise its front. Meanwhile, the British fleet had appeared off Riga. With this Bermondt's position became untenable, and on 9 October his armistice offer was rejected. By then the Latvians were in a position to launch a counter-attack, and on 11 November they drove Bermondt's troops out of Riga. Bermondt then placed his army under the command of Lieutenant-General von Eberhard – von der Goltz's successor – in order to safeguard his political position, whereupon the Latvians did not hesitate to break off diplomatic relations with Berlin. This action was taken on 23 November. A few days later, the last of Bermondt's troops were driven from Latvian soil.

In September and October other units of the Russian Western Army had occupied parts of Lithuania, mostly in the Šiauliai district, where they caused a great deal of damage to property. On 21–22 November they were engaged in violent clashes with the Lithuanian Army near Radviliškis. But the Allied military mission sent out to Lithuania under the French General Niessel intervened, and ordered the invading force to leave the country. This order was complied with, and by 15 December 1919 Bermondt's troops had re-crossed the frontier.

While Bermondt was mounting his infamous assault on Riga, Judenič was preparing to attack Petrograd. Not surprisingly, the combined offensive planned on 26 August failed to materialise. The Estonians sent some of their troops from the Narva front to help the Latvians against Bermondt, while the British ordered part of their fleet, which was steaming off Petrograd, to Riga for the same purpose. And the two Russian armies, which were fighting on the northern and southern sectors, failed to establish effective liaison.

At the beginning of this offensive, Yudenič commanded a force of some 17,000 men, and for a while he made rapid progress. On 20 October his troops occupied Tsarskoe Selo and Gatchina, which lay just outside the gates of St. Petersburg. But due partly to the lack of discipline in his own army command, and partly to the fanatical resistance offered by the inhabitants of Petrograd under Trotsky, his assault quickly lost its initial impetus. Within two days the tide had turned. The Red Army went over to the offensive, routing the regiments of the North-Western Army and driving them back in disarray to the Estonian border. By 20 November the last of the White Russian units had crossed over into Estonia, where they were disarmed and interned. Trotsky wanted to pursue the enemy into Estonia, but Lenin rejected this proposal and the Red Army halted on the bank of the Narova.

6. *The Peace Treaties*

The desire for freedom evinced by the Baltic peoples had proved stronger than the political machinations of the Germans and the White Russians. The indigenous communities had prevailed. Now they had to persuade Soviet Russia to desist from further aggression and agree to a peace settlement. This seemed a perfectly viable undertaking, for at that time the Soviet Government was interested primarily in putting an end to the civil war in Central Russia, and so was likely to prove amenable to proposals which would enable it to concentrate on its internal problems. It had, in fact, been trying to conclude a peace treaty with Estonia since the spring of 1919. In deciding to seek a settlement, the Russians were undoubtedly influenced by the Estonians' military success; but they must also have been conscious of the need to deny the Russian North-Western Army the right to marshal its forces on Estonian territory.

In response to feelers put out by the Estonian Communist leader Kingissepp, Bela Kun's Hungarian Communist Party, which had just assumed power, offered its services as mediator. But it was not until the Soviet Russians broached the question of peace talks in a broadcast transmitted on 27 and 28 April that positive steps were taken. Meanwhile, from early February 1919 onwards, leading Estonian politicians such as Jaan Tõnisson, had also been considering the possibility of peace talks, but they ran into difficulties with the western Allies, who were still pursuing an interventionist policy and were pressing for a combined offensive against the Bolsheviks. Then, on 21 July, the Soviet Russians returned to the question of a Soviet–Estonian peace treaty in a further broadcast, whereupon an English journalist began to sound out the Commissar for Foreign Affairs, Chicherin, on the subject. As a result the Soviet Government made a formal offer, on 31 August 1919, to enter into peace negotiations. The Estonian Government accepted this offer on 4 September and it was agreed that the negotiations should be opened in Pskov on 10 September.

But within a week Estonia decided to break off the talks. There were two compelling reasons for this decision. First, Estonia realised that she was being isolated from the other border territories; and she wanted to avoid this at all costs. (It is perfectly true that Moscow had also offered to conclude peace treaties with Latvia, Lithuania and Finland on 11 September, but until such time as Latgale had been liberated from Bolshevik rule it would have been naïve to expect the Latvians to respond to such an offer.) And secondly, the Estonians found themselves in a difficult situation *vis-à-vis* the Russian North-Western Army, which had just begun to prepare for a second offensive against Petrograd. Meanwhile, the Allies – and especially France – had also adopted a much tougher attitude to the question of a unilateral peace between Estonia and Soviet Russia. Eventually, it was decided at a conference held in Tartu from 29 September to 1 October 1919, attended by the Premiers and Foreign Ministers of Finland and the Baltic States, to postpone the negotiations with Moscow so that the Estonian Government could await the outcome of Judenič's second offensive. The new date suggested to Chicherin was 25 October.

When Judenič's army was defeated yet again by the Petrograd garrison, it seemed at first that the other Baltic States would also agree to enter into peace talks. On 17 November representatives of Estonia, Latvia and Lithuania met a Russian delegation headed by Maxim Litvinov in Tartu to arrange for an exchange of prisoners, and two days later an agreement regulating the exchange was duly signed by all four parties. But although Litvinov gave an undertaking that the R.S.F.S.R. would recognise all three Baltic territories as independent states, and indicated that the Soviet troops in Latgale might be withdrawn, the Latvians and Lithuanians remained sceptical.

Since they were unable to reach agreement with their neighbours, and since the defeat of Judenič's army had created an extremely threatening situation on the Narva front, the Estonians finally decided to go it alone. Accordingly, the peace negotiations between Estonia and Soviet Russia were officially opened in Tartu on 4 December. The Soviet delegation was led by L. Krasin and M. Yoffe, the Estonian by J. Poska. At first the Soviets tried to exploit the new military situation by insisting that Estonia should cede the Petseri district and the eastern part of Virumaa, i.e. the area between Kunda and Narva, which contained valuable deposits of oil shale. These demands were backed up by a renewed Soviet offensive on the Narva front, which again saw bitter fighting. But under the command of General A. Tõnisson, the Estonians held their line. The Soviet delegation then proved much more flexible, and on 31 December an armistice agreement was duly signed.

Meanwhile, the general political situation had undergone a radical change. At a meeting of the Allied Supreme Council in London on 13 December 1919, it was decided to withdraw support from the White Russian armies, and on 16 January 1920 the blockade of the Soviet Russian ports was lifted. This did not stop the Polish representative at the Helsinki Conference, which was held in mid-January 1920 and was attended by representatives of Finland and the Baltic States, from pressing for the establishment of a united anti-Bolshevik front. There was, of course, considerable tension at Helsinki – Poland and Lithuania disagreed on many issues, as did Estonia and Latvia – and it is hardly surprising that the conference should have failed to produce any really positive results. The Estonians stuck to their decision to negotiate with the Soviet Russians, and on 2 February 1920 a peace treaty was concluded in Tartu.

Estonia derived considerable benefits from the Tartu Treaty. Under its terms the R.S.F.S.R. renounced all claim to Estonian territory, and recognised the independence of the new republic. Moreover, Estonia not only retained the eastern part of Virumaa, but was also allocated the Petseri district and a strip of land on the eastern bank of the Narova. Both states gave an undertaking that they would not allow foreign armies to establish bases, or foreign political organisations to operate, within their territories. Thus the Soviet Russians were spared the prospect of repeated anti-Bolshevik incursions across the Estonian border, while the Estonians could safely dismiss the possibility of a new Estonian Soviet Government being formed on Russian soil. As for reparations, the R.S.F.S.R. absolved Estonia of all responsibility for the debts still outstanding from tsarist times, and undertook to pay 15 million gold roubles towards the construction of the new Estonian state. Further provisions covered the exchange of prisoners and internees, the restoration of works of art removed during the war, and the right of the Estonian population to decide for themselves whether they wished to adopt Russian or Estonian citizenship. Provision was also made for a trade agreement with preferential tariffs. Finally, Estonia undertook to allow the R.S.F.S.R. to build a free port in Tallinn, or some other Estonian harbour, and to erect a power station on the Narova. In exchange, the Estonians were given concessions to exploit one million hectares of Russian forest land, and to build a railway line from the Estonian border to Moscow.

And so, as Hehn has rightly pointed out, the treaty signed at Tartu in February 1920 brought the Estonians a measure of success which, before 1917, not even the most ardent nationalist would have thought possible. However, the Soviet Russians also regarded this treaty as a highly satisfactory solution, for it deprived the anti-Bolshevik forces of their invasion base in the north-west, and broke up the anti-Soviet united front of Baltic territories. Lenin himself expressed his satisfaction with the peace when he described it as 'a window on Western Europe opened by the Russian workers', and as 'an incomparable victory over Western imperialism'. This statement was, of course, also a very neat exercise in the art of propaganda, for it diverted attention from the failure of the Bolshevik campaign to incorporate the Baltic territories into the new Soviet Russian state.

Once Bermondt had been forced to abandon his invasion of their territory, the Latvians began to prepare for an offensive against the Bolsheviks with the object of liberating Latgale. An important feature of this offensive was the offer of military aid given by the Poles, who were intent on maintaining good relations with Latvia in order to offset their bad relations with Lithuania. On 29 December 1919, the Latvian and Polish high commands agreed on the terms of a combined operation, which was duly mounted on 3 January 1920 and in which three Polish divisions and the 'Baltische Landeswehr' took part. The extremely welcome support afforded by Poland was readily understandable in the light of the general hostility which existed between the Poles and the Soviet Russians. But there was also a more immediate reason for Polish intervention, namely that Warsaw wanted to ensure that Daugavpils passed to Latvia and not to Lithuania. In this connection, it would seem that Pilsudksi may well have toyed with the idea of incorporating Latvia into his plans for a great East and Central European federation. Within a few weeks Latgale was liberated, thus removing the only impediment to an armistice between Latvia and Soviet Russia; and on 1 February such an armistice agreement was duly signed.

Moscow's principal object in concluding this agreement was to put an end to the Latvian–Polish alliance, while the Latvian Government, for its part, simply wanted a speedy peace settlement. The Latvian people were war-weary, having been involved in almost continuous fighting for five years. It was felt that if a lasting peace could be procured, the people would be unlikely to revolt against the existing social order, but that until such time as it was procured they would obviously be vulnerable to Communist agitation. This was, no doubt, the reason why, after signing the armistice agreement, Moscow began to drag its heels over the opening of peace negotiations. It was only when Poland invited Estonia, Latvia and Finland to send delegates to a conference in Warsaw in mid-March 1920 to discuss the establishment of an East European bloc that the Soviet Government was prepared to act. To counter this Polish initiative, Moscow suggested to both the Latvians and the Lithuanians that they should nominate representatives to negotiate peace terms.

The Latvian–Soviet negotiations were opened in Moscow on 16 April. On 12 June a preliminary agreement was signed covering the repatriation of Latvian refugees from Russia, and on 1 August 1920, just fourteen days before Pilsudski's counter-offensive turned the tide in the Polish–Soviet war, a full peace treaty was signed in Riga. This treaty was essentially the same as that concluded in Tartu between Soviet Russia and Estonia. Under its terms Latvia's eastern frontier was drawn along ethnological lines, with the result that it acquired the districts of Daugavpils, Rezekne and Ludza, which had previously formed part of the government of Vitebsk, together with an area in the district of Dissa and a strip of land running along the border of the government of Pskov, which contained Pytalova, an important town on the railway line from Livonia to Latgale. And so as a result of this treaty, Latgale, which had been separated from Livonia ever since 1629, was reunited with the rest of Latvia.

Meanwhile, the state of war which had existed between Latvia and Germany had been brought to an end on 5 July 1920. Germany was obliged to make reparations, and gave *de jure* recognition to the new Latvian Republic.

After defeating the Bolshevik troops in the late summer and autumn of 1919, the Lithuanian Army disposed of Bermondt's force before the year was out. Peace negotiations were then opened in Moscow on 9 May 1920, and these led to the conclusion of a peace treaty on 12 July, which also corresponded in the main to the Treaty of Tartu. Under its terms the R.S.F.S.R. expressly recognised the Vilnius district as part of Lithuania.

After defeating the White Russian Army commanded by General Wrangell in southern Russia and making peace with Finland (on 14 October 1920) and Poland (on 12 March 1921), the Soviet Government was able to devote itself exclusively to the task of national reconstruction. The period of civil war and foreign intervention was over. Meanwhile, the three Baltic States embarked on their period of independence. Although they had received substantial help from foreign powers, they owed this new-found independence above all to their own military prowess and political courage.

CHAPTER II

THE EARLY STAGES OF INDEPENDENCE

1. *Constitutions and National Emblems*

Like most of the new European states which came into being after the First World War, the Baltic States were set up as democratic republics. During the German occupation the Baltic German nationalists had thought in terms of a constitutional monarchy, but after November 1918 this was no longer a viable proposition. By then it was taken for granted by the Lithuanians, the Latvians and the Estonians that their future constitution would be republican and that under its terms the government would be fully accountable to a democratically elected parliament. And indeed it soon became apparent in all three Baltic States that the legislature was to become the most powerful body. All three states moreover, adopted a single-chamber system of parliamentary rule, which was felt to be perfectly adequate for their needs and which was extremely democratic. Finally, all three introduced a universal and equal franchise based on proportional representation and direct and secret ballots.

The elections held in Estonia to set up a Constituent Assembly took place in April 1919, i.e. after the country had been liberated but before the Bolshevik military threat had been fully averted. The delegates – 120 in all – met in Tallinn on 22 April under the chairmanship of the Socialist August Rei (1886–1963). This Constituent Assembly was more radical than any of the parliamentary assemblies of later years. Of the members 40 per cent were Socialists and 25 per cent were Radical Democrats, which means that between them the left wing and left of centre delegates had a sizeable majority. The Conservative opposition consisted of the Liberal Democrats, who held 25 per cent of the seats, and the Agrarians, who held 6·5 per cent. The Socialists and Radical Democrats tackled the problem of agrarian reform with great verve, and were able

76

to force a very radical bill through the chamber by 10 October, 1919.

Meanwhile, progress was also made on the bill to establish a new constitution. This was passed by the full assembly on 15 June, 1920 and became the law of the land on 21 December. The Estonian constitution was remarkable for its extreme parliamentary bias. The powers of parliament (*Riigikogu*) were so great that in effect the government was little more than a parliamentary commission. The Premier was referred to as the 'Senior Statesman' (*Riigivanem*), and acted as head of state on all ceremonial occasions, for – like the Swiss Confederation – Estonia had no President of the Republic. The Senior Statesman was not appointed Commander-in-Chief of the Army, nor was he authorized to proclaim new laws, this being the prerogative of parliament, whose president acquired considerable prestige on this account. But there was also a certain measure of popular participation in Estonian politics. Thus the electorate was able to contribute to the work of parliament through the referendum and initiative; and the only way in which the Estonian parliament could be dissolved before the expiry of its terms was through a referendum.

The first Provisional Government of Estonia, which was formed in 1918, was headed by Konstantin Päts, the leader of the Farmers' Union. Päts held power until the spring of 1919, when Otto Strandman, a member of the radical democratic Workers' Party, succeeded him as Premier. A few months later Strandman handed over to Jaan Tõnisson, the Leader of the People's Party, who remained in office until 1920. In the following year the first constitutional parliamentary elections were held, and produced a sharp swing to the right with a victory for the Farmers' Union. The Estonian Government had its seat in Tallinn, where the ministers and senior officials established themselves in the historic buildings on the Domberg. The new blue, black and white flag of the Estonian Republic fluttered at the top of 'Long Hermann's Tower', which formed part of the ancient residence of the Teutonic Order, and was one of the focal points of the town. The three stalking leopards, blue on a golden ground, which had first appeared in Estonian heraldry during the period of Danish rule and had featured on the coat-of-arms of the Knighthood of Estonia from 1284 onwards, were taken over by the young republic and became the dominant emblem on the new Estonian coat-of-arms.

In Latvia the Constituent Assembly was not able to convene until 1 May, 1920. The final draft of the new constitution was approved by the Assembly on 15 February, 1922 and passed into law on 7 November of the same year. In many respects the Latvian constitution followed the republican constitutions established by the French, the Swiss and the (Weimar) Germans. Ultimate power was vested in the Latvian parliament (*Saeima*), which was responsible for electing the President of the Republic and for appointing the members of the judiciary. Despite opposition from the Social Democrats, who wanted an Estonian-type constitution, the President of the Republic was appointed Commander-in-Chief of the Army; and under Paragraph 81 he was also authorized to enact emergency legislation during parliamentary recesses, although all decrees promulgated in this way had to be confirmed by parliament when it reconvened.

The Provisional Government set up in Latvia was headed by Kārlis Ulmanis, the Leader of the Peasant's League from 1918 to 1920, and by Z. Meierovics from 1921 to 1923. The first President of the Republic, who was elected for a five-year term in 1922, was Janis Čakste (1859–1927). After working as a lawyer in Jelgava, Čakste, who came from peasant stock in Courland, went to St. Petersburg as one of the Latvian delegates to the Russian Imperial Duma, and in 1919 was asked to head the Latvian Peace Delegation in Paris. Like the Estonians, the Latvians chose an historic building as their seat of government: Riga Castle, which was built by the Knights of the Sword on the banks of the Daugava and had subsequently housed both the Swedish and the Russian governors, was designated as the President's official residence. On the strength of a passage in the writings of the thirteenth-century chronicler, Heinrich von Lettland, the Latvians chose as their national emblem a dark red flag divided down the centre by a narrow white stripe. Their coat-of-arms combined the traditional emblems of the two Latvian provinces – the Livonian Griffin and the Lion of Courland – which appeared beneath a rising sun. Thus – like the Estonians and Lithuanians – the Latvians were intent on reviving historical emblems. As far as the Lithuanians were concerned, this was a logical step, since they were able to look back on a period of national independence in the Middle Ages. But in the case of the Latvians and Estonians this step seems at first sight somewhat surprising, for their historical emblems had been symbols of foreign rule. Clearly, the need to strengthen their young states by establishing links with the past and so creating a sense of historical continuity was felt to be of overriding importance.

In Lithuania, where the German withdrawal was followed by a Bolshevik invasion and, subsequently, the arrival of Bermondt's force, the political situation remained undecided for a much longer period than in either Estonia or Latvia, with the result that the elections to the Lithuanian Constituent Assembly could not be held until April 1920. This Assembly, which was composed of 112 delegates, passed a bill establishing a provisional constitution on 10 June, 1920, which was superseded by a permanent constitution on 1 August, 1922. Under its terms the *Taryba*, or National Council, was replaced by a parliament (*Seimas*), which became the supreme authority of the land, the President of the Republic being no more than a figurehead. Smetona, who had been President of the *Taryba* and, from April 1919, provisional President of the Republic, stood down in 1922 in favour of Aleksandras Stulginskis, the first President elected for a full five-year term under the new constitution. In both the Constituent Assembly and the first Parliament the Conservative Christian Democrats were the majority party; next in line came the People's Socialists, followed by the Social Democrats. Prior to the proclamation of the constitution, three Lithuanian cabinets were formed under A. Voldemaras (1918), N. Sleževičius (1918–19) and E. Galvanauskas (1919–20) respectively; the first cabinet following the proclamation (1920–3) was formed by K. Grinius. When the Poles seized Vilnius in October 1922, the Lithuanians were obliged to nominate the town of Kaunas as their temporary capital. The Lithuanian coat-of-arms featured a thirteenth-century emblem that had once been a focal point of Lithuanian life but had long since been submerged in the ethnic subconscious: a white knight bearing a sword and a shield decorated with a cross. The Lithuanian tricolour was yellow, green and red.

When they first emerged as independent republics the three Baltic States had several common features. All owed their independence to the collapse of the tsarist regime; all had multiracial populations: and all had agrarian-based economies (agriculture provided employment for 79 per cent of the Lithuanian, 66·2 per cent of the Latvian, and 58·58 per cent of the Estonian population). We see from these statistics that the dependence of the Baltic peoples on agriculture at this time was strongest in the south, and diminished progressively towards the north. This pattern was also reflected in the population densities of the three territories, which revealed the same overall trend: Lithuania had 42·5 people per sq. km., Latvia 26·6, and Estonia 23·4 (while Finland, an even more northerly territory, had only 9·2). Needless to say, the decrease in population density and agricultural dependence was matched by an increase in the spread of industrialisation. There was also a definite progression in respect of the national composition of the three Baltic States, only here the movement did not follow a geographical pattern. Latvia had the largest number of minorities (26·6 per cent of the population), followed by Lithuania (19·8 per cent) and Estonia (12·4 per cent).

After their experiences at the hands of the Bolsheviks the peoples of the Baltic States were at one in their opposition to the Soviet Union, and unequivocally embraced the political and cultural traditions of the West. The vast majority of the leading Baltic politicians of the period came from peasant stock, and most of them were the first members of their families to be educated. And so, in the late 1910s and early 1920s, completely untapped forces were suddenly brought into play in these newly-emerging nations, whose leaders were determined to make their own individual contribution to world politics and so prove their worth on the great stage of history.

But once the peace treaties had been signed and the Baltic States secured against external enemies, they had to concentrate – at least during the early period of independence – on their internal affairs. In order to develop their national economies they had to implement agrarian reforms and train technologists. They also had to extend and develop their educational systems so as to keep pace with the civilized nations of the West. All this had to be achieved without prejudice to the cultural interests of the minorities.

The foreign policy of the Baltic States was based on two fundamental propositions: close co-operation with one another and, where possible, with the other nations bordering the Baltic; and friendly relations with the western powers, who had given positive proof of their good intentions during the struggle for independence. The Allied Supreme Council gave *de jure* recognition to Estonia and Latvia on 21 January, 1921; and the U.S.A. followed suit on 22 July, 1922. Later the same year, on 20 December, the Allies also recognised Lithuania. Meanwhile, on 22 September, the Baltic States had been admitted to the League of Nations.

2. *Demographic Developments and the Nationalities*

Before trying to assess the demographic developments in the Baltic territories during the period of tsarist rule and the period of independence, I must first deal briefly with the administrative organisation of the Russian Empire. Under the Tsar the Estonians lived both in Estonia and the northern part of Livonia and on a number of Baltic islands, such as Saaremaa, Hiiumaa and Muhu, while the Latvians occupied Courland, the southern part of Livonia, and part of the government of Vitebsk. According to the last major census of tsarist Russia, taken in 1897, the population of the territory which later became the Republic of Estonia was 960,000. The corresponding figure for the Republic of Latvia was 1,930,000.

During the First World War the population of the former Russian Baltic provinces was reduced by nearly 1,000,000, due partly to military wastage and revolutionary and counter-revolutionary losses, partly to the deportation of indigenous inhabitants, and partly to the emigration of Russian and Baltic German nationals. This drop in the population was off-set to a certain extent by the repatriation from Russia of some 100,000 people, who had opted for Baltic citizenship under the terms of the peace treaties concluded with the Soviet Russians. Most of these were Latvians, but they also included Estonians, Germans and Jews. On the other hand, there was a

D

further – albeit much smaller – group of Baltic nationals who emigrated overseas at that time.

But if we compare the returns on the 1897 census with the returns made for Estonia in 1934 (1,126,413) and for Latvia in 1935 (1,950,000), we find that, after allowing for the territorial expansion of these two states along their eastern frontiers, there is little difference between the two sets of figures. Incidentally, the number of Estonians and Latvians living abroad was estimated at 200,000 and 300,000 respectively.

In 1922 there were 970,000 Estonian nationals (87·6 per cent of the total population) living in Estonia; and by 1934 this figure had risen to 992,000 (88·1 per cent). In ethnic terms, Estonia was the purest of the Baltic States. Its largest single minority was a group of Russian nationals (91,109 or 8·2 per cent of the total population in 1922, and 92,656 or 8·2 per cent in 1934). Most of these Russians lived in the same part of the Republic, i.e. beyond the eastern border of the lands once ruled by the Teutonic Order, where they had joined with the russified and largely Greek Orthodox members of small Finno-Ugrian or Estonian ethnic groups – such as the Ingrians on the eastern bank of the Narova and the Setu in the Petseri district and on the western shore of Peipsi Lake – to form a more or less homogeneous settlement. Russian urban elements had also appeared in Narva, Tallinn and Tartu.

There were 1·35 million Latvians living in Latvia in 1920 and 1·47 million (75·5 per cent of the total population) in 1935. Ethnically, the Latvian community was less pure than the Estonian, and contained various minorities, the largest of which – as in Estonia – was the Russian. The Russian minority in Latvia numbered 124,746 (7·8 per cent of the total population) in 1920 and 206,499 (10·6 per cent) in 1935. Then there was the Slav minority – 75,630 (4·7 per cent) in 1920 and 26,867 (1·4 per cent) in 1935 – and the White Russian and Polish minority – 54,567 (3·4 per cent) in 1920 and 48,949 (2·5 per cent) in 1935. These last two minority groups had also settled in the eastern border areas, primarily in Latgale, which is why the figures for 1935 are lower than those for 1920. During this fifteen-year period many of the inhabitants of Latgale had been assimilated into the Latvian community

Latgale posed a very special problem for the new Republic

of Latvia. Although the Set in the south-east of Estonia were probably quite as numerous, the occupants of Latgale – 567,164 in 1935 – were a far more significant group, for they had embraced the Roman Catholic religion during the period of Polish rule (1561–1795), and had been administered quite independently of the Baltic provinces under the tsarist regime (1795–1917). But there was also a small Lithuanian community in Latvia. In the south and east of Courland – primarily in the Illukst district – and in the town of Riga there were 26,083 Lithuanian industrial workers (1·6 per cent of the total population) in 1920 and 22,913 (1·2 per cent) in 1935.

Where the Latvians had their Slav minorities, the Estonians had a long-established Swedish minority, which had settled on the north-west coast and on the smaller offshore islands. In 1922 there were 7,850 Swedes in these localities (0·7 per cent of the total population) and in 1934 7,641 (also 0·7 per cent). Most of these people were inshore fishermen or peasants, and some of their forbears had come to Estonia in the fourteenth century.

The second largest minority in Estonia was the German community. According to the census returns this embraced 18,319 people in 1922 (1·7 per cent of the total population) and 16,346 in 1934 (1·5 per cent). The German community in Latvia – which was only the fourth largest minority in the country, the Jews being the third largest – none the less embraced 70,964 people in 1925 (3·6 per cent of the total population) and 62,144 in 1935 (3·2 per cent). Thus, during the first fifteen years of independence the total figure for both countries fluctuated between 78,000 and 89,000. Back in 1881 there had been 180,000 Baltic Germans in Latvia and Estonia. By 1914 this figure had been reduced to 162,000, after which – due partly to the Bolshevik terror campaign and partly to the new agrarian laws – many Baltic Germans emigrated, mostly to Germany, although in the course of the 1920s about 10,000 of these emigrants returned. But of the 20,000 German farmers who had settled in Courland and Livonia between 1905 and 1914 under the twentieth-century German colonisation scheme, only half continued to farm after 1919. Between 1919 and 1939 there was a marked drift away from the land within the Baltic German community, which suffered from a surplus of women and a low birth rate. According to the census taken in 1934–5 the largest concentrations of Baltic Germans at that time were in Riga (38,523 or 61·19 per cent of the Latvian Baltic German community), Liepaja (4,620 or 7·4 per cent), Jelgava (2,319 or 3·7 per cent), Tallinn (6,575 or 40 percent of the Estonian Baltic German community) and Tartu (2,706 or 16·5 per cent). But these official figures may well have been on the low side, for in the 1930s there was considerable anti-minority feeling in both Latvia and Estonia, and it seems highly probable that a number of Baltic Germans will have concealed their nationality to protect either their families or their professional positions. By the same token, the census returns for the other minority groups are also suspect.

For the Jewish minority the liberation of the Baltic territories from Russian rule was of great significance. Before the Russian Revolution the Jews had been subject to residential, educational and professional restrictions, and on various occasions had been systematically persecuted by the Russian authorities. Moreover, with the partial relaxation of these restrictions in 1905, the tsarist regime had made a determined attempt to assimilate the Jewish minority into the Russian nation. This entirely negative state of affairs was swept away by the Baltic War of Liberation, which left the Baltic Jews free to develop a new sense of national and religious identity based on the Zionist precepts of Theodor Herzl.

In Estonia there were 4,566 Jews (0·4 per cent of the total population) in 1922 and 4,434 (also 0·4 per cent) in 1934; in Latvia there were 79,644 (5 per cent of the total population) in 1920, 95,675 (5·2 per cent) in 1925, and 93,479 (4·8 per cent) in 1935. The Latvian Jewish community, which was so much bigger than its Estonian counterpart, was concentrated primarily in Courland and Latgale, and in the city of Riga. The marked increase in the number of Latvian Jews in the early 1920s was due to the repatriation of Jewish families from Russia under the terms of the Latvian–Soviet peace treaty. However, the biggest of all the Baltic Jewish communities, in both absolute and proportional terms, was that in Lithuania, which embraced 153,743 people and accounted for 7·6 per cent of the total population. The Lithuanian Jews, most of them urban dwellers, included manufacturers, craftsman and – to a much larger extent than in either Latvia or Estonia – academics and students. The Lithuanian Government acknowledged the importance of the Jewish minority by setting up a Ministry for Jewish Affairs, which remained in existence until 1924. Meanwhile, the Jews were intent on developing their own institutions, with the result that by 1935 there were 105 Jewish primary schools, attended by approximately 8,000 pupils, and fourteen Jewish secondary schools, attended by approximately 13,000 pupils. There was no inherent anti-Semitism in the Baltic States, but with the growth of nationalist feeling in the 1930s anti-Semitic tendencies began to appear, especially in Latvia.

After the Jews, the Poles were the largest minority group in Lithuania, numbering 65,599 and accounting for 3·2 per cent of the total population in 1923. It should be remembered, however, that many of these Lithuanian Poles, especially among the gentry, had originally come from Lithuanian stock. The size of the Russian minority, which included a group of estate owners who had acquired their lands as a result of the expropriation of Polish landlords following the 1863 insurrection, had been greatly reduced due to the effects of the war, and by 1923 the Russians numbered no more than 50,460 (2·5 per cent of the total population). There were also 29,231 Germans (1·4 per cent) in Lithuania in 1923, 3,269 of them in Kaunas and the remainder distributed amongst the western districts, especially along the Courland border; and, finally, there were a few White Russians and Latvians in the northern and eastern border districts.

Under the Tsar the Lithuanians had been concentrated in the government of Kaunas, where they formed the majority group, and the governments of Vilnius and Suwalki, where they were in the minority. At that time, the total number of Lithuanians living in these Russian provinces was estimated at between 2 and 2·5 millions. In 1923 the population of the Lithuanian Republic – excluding the Klaipeda and Vilnius territories – numbered 2,035,121, and by 1937 this figure had risen to 2,397,008 (the population density in 1937 being 45·8 persons to 1 sq. km.). Of this latter figure, 1,701,863 (i.e. 84·2 per cent) were Lithuanian, while the remainder belonged to the various minorities. In 1923 the average age of the Lithuanian population was lower than that of either the Estonian or the Latvian population. According to the census returns for that year 28 per cent of Lithuanians were under fifteen years of age compared with 27 per cent of Estonians and 23 per cent of Latvians. The Lithuanian community living abroad was also much larger than either the Latvian or the Estonian. In the U.S.A. alone there were between 700,000 and 800,000 Lithuanians (nearly one-third of the total emigrant community) in neighbouring Latvia there were 50,000; while in Poland (including the Vilnius territory) there were a further 80,000; finally, the Lithuanians living in East Prussia prior to 1919 were estimated at 200,000 (although German statistics gave a lower figure).

A survey carried out in 1922 revealed that 78·3 per cent of the Estonian population were Protestant and that, due primarily to the conversion campaign mounted by the Russian Church in the mid-nineteenth century, rather less than 19 per cent were Greek Orthodox. Thus, Estonia was a predominantly Protestant country. In Latvia there were fewer Greek Orthodox believers (13 per cent) but considerably more Roman Catholics, especially in Latgale and parts of Courland (22·6 per cent in 1925 and 24·5 per cent in 1935). In order to facilitate the integration of Latgale, which posed very special problems, the Latvian Government signed a concordat with the Holy See. But despite this concession to the Catholic Church, the majority of the Latvian population remained Protestant (57·2 per cent in 1925 and 55·1 per cent in 1935). In Lithuania 85·7 per cent of the population were Catholic.

It is significant that the highest birth rates in Estonia and Latvia were recorded in the eastern districts, which were not Protestant and which, in some cases, were occupied by non-Estonian and non-Latvian minority groups. The Estonian birth rate fell from 16·2 per thousand in 1925 to 15·2 per thousand in 1934. In Latvia the downward trend was even more marked: from 20·8 per thousand in 1925 to 16·4 per thousand in 1934. In both Latvia and Estonia there was a surplus of women and a disproportionately large number of old people. Lithuania also had these problems, but not to the same extent.

3. *Agrarian Reforms*

There were several motivitations for the agrarian reforms introduced in the Baltic States. The first and most important was of a social order. It was, quite simply, the desire to redistribute the land on a more equitable basis, thus providing the previously landless peasants with small properties of their own, and removing the gross discrepancy between this class and the former estate owners. In 1918, 58 per cent of all agricultural land in Estonia had been in the hands of the large estate owners while two-thirds of the rural population — some half a million people – had owned no land at all. The situation had been almost as bad in Latvia, where prior to the agrarian reform 48 per cent of agricultural land (3·16 million hectares) had belonged to the estate owners, 39 per cent to the small farmers and 10 per cent to the state.

The second motivation was political. It was argued that the only effective way of combating the social and economic policies advocated by the Soviet Russians was to expropriate all agricultural land and redistribute it in the form of smallholdings to the indigenous peasants. When the agrarian reforms were first debated, the Baltic War of Liberation was still being fought, and in those circumstances it is hardly surprising that the Baltic nationalists should have sought to immunise the rural proletariat against the propaganda put out from Moscow by appeasing their hunger for land.

The third motivation was also political, but in a nationalist sense. A major problem facing the Baltic nationalist politicians was the need to undermine the political influence exerted by the members of the foreign upper class within their territories, and one of the most effective ways of doing this was to undermine their economic position. In fact, there were those who maintained that if the existing system of land and property ownership were allowed to continue, it might well threaten the whole independence movement. As far as Estonia was concerned, this particular motivation was reinforced by the armed clash between units of the Estonian Army and the 'Baltische Landeswehr' at Cēsis, which coincided with the debate of the agrarian reform bill in the Estonian parliament. During the very first reading of the bill Otto Strandman (the leader of the radical democratic Workers' Party, who became Premier later the same year) stated categorically that one of the principal objects of the bill was to undermine the economic and political power of the Baltic German upper class.

The Baltic German delegates to the Constituent Assembly had a hard time of it, especially in June and July 1919. Their proposal that one-third of the agricultural land on the Baltic German estates should be taken over by the nation, against suitable compensation, and redistributed among the peasants was not even discussed; a further proposal put forward by the more moderate Estonian parties with the approval of such well-known politicians as Päts, Uluots and Teemant, which envisaged the gradual appropriation of a certain percentage of the agricultural land on the large estates, was rejected out of hand; and even Tõnisson's proposal, which was also based on a compromise, was turned down by the Assembly. The final outcome of all the parliamentary debates was the expropriation law of 10 October 1919. This was passed by sixty-three votes to nine with one abstention after the delegates of the Peoples' Party and the Christian Peoples' Party had walked out in protest before the division. This law, which was on the statute book before the constitution law, represented an intervention on the part of the state in the established system of land ownership that was positively revolutionary.

Under the terms of the new law, 1,065 estates (96·6 per cent of all the estates in the country) were expropriated, together with their farms and summer villas. Although the vast majority of these properties belonged to Baltic Germans, fifty-seven Estonian estate owners were also affected by this measure. The expropriation was carried out over a two-year period, the question of compensation being left over for settlement at a later date. It was obvious from the outset that if the state had attempted to compensate the owners to the full value of their property, the country would have been bankrupted, which would have defeated the whole purpose of the agrarian reform. After long deliberations a law was passed on 1 March 1926 fixing the level of compensation at 3 Estonian crowns per hectare, which was about 3 per cent of the real value of the estates. This was bad enough in itself, and the vast majority of the estate owners were reduced to near penury by the low

level of compensation. But worse was to come, for no compensation at all was given in respect of forest land, and instead of
compensating the owners of confiscated agricultural land in
cash, the state in most cases issued debenture bonds. These
estate owners were later authorised to apply for the restitution
of up to 50 hectares of land. A few, who had run 'model
estates', were more fortunate. For economic reasons they were
exempted from the provisions of the expropriation law.

Prior to the agrarian reform there had been some 51,000
farms in Estonia, and as a result of the expropriation law a
further 56,000 smallholdings were created, which were then
distributed to landless peasants. But these smallholdings were
too small to be profitable, and the peasants who worked them
were scarcely able to earn a living wage, let alone set money
aside for investment purposes. Consequently, the state was
obliged to lend them money in the form of low interest,
long-term credits so that they could build houses for their
families and buy agricultural equipment. In the course of the
1920s it became apparent that there were many organisational
problems attendant on the kind of major agricultural reforms
that had been carried out in Estonia. Of course, the profitability
of the smallholdings also depended on the fertility of the soil,
which was high in the Viljandi and Tartu areas, but low in the
west. By and large, however, agricultural units of less than 20
hectares were found to be uneconomic, which meant that
the only really viable units in Estonia were the farms that had
already been in existence prior to 1919. The average size of
such farms was 34 hectares. In order to improve the output
of the smallholdings the Estonians established co-operative
societies, which soon began to play an important part in
agricultural production by providing modern machinery for
the use of smallholders and farmers, and by taking over the
marketing of livestock. In 1937, 72 per cent of Estonia's
agricultural produce went to the home market. Between 1914
and 1934 the number of hectares used for cereal production
was increased by 20 per cent.

In Latvia the Minister for Agriculture H. Celmiņš submitted
an agrarian bill to the Constituent Assembly, which was passed
on 16 September 1920 after various compromise solutions
proposed by the Latvian estate owners had been rejected.

D*

Under the terms of this bill, 1,300 estate owners were to be
dispossessed and 3·7 million hectares were to change hands.
Unlike the Estonians, the Latvians decided from the outset
that those estate owners whose properties were taken over
should be allowed to retain up to 50 hectares, together with an
appropriate amount of stock and equipment, for their private
use. Although no less than 1,887 persons benefited from this
concession, the amount of land involved was only 1·7 per cent
of the total confiscated. In 1924 the Latvian parliament decided by 50 votes to 35 that no compensation would be paid
to the former estate owners, a decision which doubtless
contributed to the revulsion felt in Western Europe, where the
Latvian agrarian reform was considered to be almost as
radical as the Soviet Russian.

In both Estonia and Latvia army veterans were given
priority in the queue for smallholdings. The Estonians imposed
no restrictions in respect of ethnic origin, although for various
reasons many German veterans preferred not to apply. But
the Latvians passed special legislation in 1929 to deprive
former members of the 'Baltische Landeswehr' of this privi-
leged status (whereupon the Minister of Justice, Magnus
– a Baltic German – tendered his resignation). A petition
submitted to the League of Nations by the Latvian estate
owners in 1926 proved ineffective.

After the agrarian reforms in Latvia, 35 per cent of all
land – chiefly forest land – belonged to the state, 39·3 per
cent remained in the hands of the small farmers, and 22·2 per
cent was allocated to the new smallholders. Gradually Latvian
agricultural production improved under the new dispensation.
For example, the national beef herd rose from 912,000 head
in 1913 to 1,278,000 head in 1939, and the annual butter
yield increased from 108 kg. per cow in 1913 to 130 kg. in
1939.

In Lithuania only very few estates were in German hands.
The largest group of landowners were the Poles, followed by
the Russians, who had acquired their properties following
the Polish revolts of 1830 and 1863, when the tsarist regime
confiscated a considerable number of Polish estates. Initially,
the Lithuanians proposed to drive out the Russian settlers by
nationalising their lands, and to reduce the economic pre-

dominance of the other – chiefly Polish – estate owners by fixing 80 hectares as the maximum permitted size for any private holding. Such a reform would have been quite as radical as the reforms implemented in Latvia and Estonia. In the event, however, the Lithuanians introduced a far more lenient measure, due largely to the moderating influence of the Christian Democrats. Not that the Russians benefited from this change of heart – their lands and forests were still taken over by the state. But the non-Russian estate owners gained a great deal, for the agrarian law of 29 March 1922 laid down that the maximum size for private agricultural holdings was to be fixed at 150, and not 80, hectares. In addition, a small measure of compensation was paid out.

The Lithuanian agrarian reform also had a considerable effect on the character of country life. Under the terms of the new law the traditional village communities were broken up in much the same way as in Russia under the Stolypin reforms. This produced a radical change in the life of the rural population, which began to follow the Estonian and Latvian pattern. Opinions differ as to the advisability of this particular measure. Its advocates point to the increased prosperity which it brought to the Lithuanian farmers while its detractors insist that this was outweighed by the harmful social effects of enforced isolation. Incidentally, the smallholders who were allocated plots of land on the expropriated estates did not share in this prosperity. For them life was hard, and many gave up the unequal struggle and went to seek work in the towns, while many more emigrated to America, which had been a promised land for Lithuanians ever since the nineteenth century.

4. *The Political Parties*

Estonia and Latvia had much the same kind of party-political structure. In both countries a more or less conservative agrarian party – the Farmers' Union in Estonia and the Peasants' League in Latvia – was opposed by a Social Democratic Party, while the middle ground was occupied by one or more National Liberal parties, which represented the views of the indigenous intellectuals. Much the same kind of set-up was to be found in Finland, but not in Lithuania, where different forces were at work.

However, although the Latvian and Estonian political parties both operated within the same kind of tripartite system, they none the less differed from one another in certain important respects. The Estonian Farmers' Union (*Eesti Maarahva Liit* and later *Põllumeestekogud*) sent only eight representatives to the Constituent Assembly, but by 1920 it had twenty-one delegates in the Estonian parliament, and by 1929 twenty-four. In 1932 it formed a coalition with the Settlers' Party (*Asunike Koondis*), which favoured rather more radical policies than the Union, and this coalition then became the strongest group in the Estonian parliament with a total of forty-two delegates. But the coalition lasted little more than a year, and by 1934 the Farmers' Union had been reduced to twenty delegates, only one more than the Settlers' Party. Up to 1932 the Farmers' Union had represented the interests of the 'old peasants', i.e. the members of the old peasant class who had owned their own farms and had adopted a more moderate attitude to the question of agrarian reform than either the Social Democrats or the Radical Democratic Workers' Party. It had also supplied ten of the twenty heads of government to form cabinets between 1919 and 1934. (Of the remaining eleven, four had come from the Workers' Party, four from the People's Party, two from the Christian People's Party and one from the Social Democratic Party.) The most important representatives of the Farmers' Union were Konstantin Päts (Premier 1923–4, 1931–2, 1932, 1933 and 1938 and State president 1938–40); Jaan Teemant (Premier 1925–7); the Professor of Constitutional Law, Jüri Uluots (Premier 1939–40); Kaarel Einbund or Eenpalu – Premier 1932 and 1938–40); Jaan Hünerson (Minister of Education); Jaan Soots; and Johan Laidoner (Commander-in-Chief of the Estonian forces in the War of Liberation).

Whereas the Estonian Farmers' Union became more and more popular in the course of the 1920s and early 1930s, the popularity of the Latvian Peasants' League declined. After winning 17·8 per cent of the popular vote in 1920 it received 16·8 per cent in 1922, 15 per cent in 1925, 14·9 per cent in 1928 and 12·2 per cent in 1931. Unlike their Estonian counter-

parts, the members of the Latvian Peasants' League failed
to come to terms with the smallholders, who formed a Latvian
Settlers' Party (*Jaunsaimnieku*) under A. Blodnieks in 1925. In
fact, far from attracting fresh support, they even failed to
maintain the unity of their own party, for in 1931 a splinter
group broke away to form the New Peasants' League (*Jaunā
zemnieku apvienība*). And yet the Peasants' League continued to
exert considerable political influence throughout the whole
of this period. It was represented in practically every Latvian
government, and provided no less than twelve of the eighteen
Premiers appointed prior to 1934. Its most important members
were: Kārlis Ulmanis (Premier 1918–21, 1925–6, 1931, 1934,
1934–40; President of the Republic 1936–40); General J.
Balodis (Minister of War 1939–40); V. Gulbis (Minister of
Agriculture 1928, 1930, 1931–4); A. Kviesis (President of the
Republic 1930–6); H. Celmiņš (President of the Republic
1924–5); and A. Bērziņš (Minister for Public Affairs 1937–40).
But there was one political organisation in Latvia which had
no counterpart in Estonia. This was the National Association
(*Nacionālā apvienībā*), which was set up between 1919 and 1921
under the leadership of the publicist and lawyer Arveds Bergs.
This group, which stood to the right of the Peasants' League,
has some power in the early 1920s, but towards the end of
the decade, when the right-wing radicals began to form extra-
parliamentary organisations, their influence was progressively
undermined.

The middle ground in Estonia was occupied by the Peoples'
Party (*Rahvaerakond*), which was founded and led by Jaan
Tõnisson (Premier 1919–20, 1927–8 and 1933) and in which
Jüri Jaakson (Premier 1924–25) played an important part.
As a National Liberal organisation, the People's Party was
centred on Tartu, where it enjoyed the support of *Postimees*,
a newspaper with a long tradition dating back to the early
days of Estonian political journalism. The People's Party had
its great moment in the Constituent Assembly, where it was
represented by twenty-five delegates. Although these twenty-
five were reduced to nine in the subsequent parliamentary
assemblies, the People's Party nonetheless participated in
seventeen of the twenty coalition governments formed between
1919 and 1933. The smaller Christian People's Party, which

was founded by the Tallinn eye specialist Dr. Friedrich Akel (Premier 1924) and had five parliamentary delegates in 1919, merged with the People's Party in 1931. Its members included a number of leading Evangelical clerics.

Whereas the Christian People's Party was more conservative then the People's Party, the Radical Democratic Workers' Party (*Eesti tööerakond*), which also merged with the People's Party (in 1932), was rather more radical. Indeed, its original programme had been more or less in line with that pursued by the Russian *Trudoviki* in the Imperial Duma. But it was not long before the Workers' Party dropped its revolutionary socialist demands and moved towards the bourgeois parties of the political Centre, after which it began to gain support in Tallinn and the smaller provincial towns, especially among the middle-grade officials. Like the People's Party, it reached its peak in the Constituent Assembly, where it was represented by thirty delegates. In the parliamentary assemblies of the 1920s its influence was also greatly reduced, and by 1929 it had only ten parliamentary delegates. The leaders of the Workers' Party included Otto Strandman (Premier 1919 and 1929–31), the Professor of International Law, Ants Piip (Premier 1920–2), and Juhan Kukk (Premier 1922–3). After the mergers between the People's Party and the Christian People's Party in 1931, and the Workers' Party in 1932, a National Centre Party (*Rahvuslik Keskerakond*) came into being. But this Centre Party started out with only twenty-three parliamentary delegates, for ever since 1919 the Centre had been losing ground in Estonian politics.

In Latvia the three main Centre parties – the Democratic Party, the Radical Democratic Party and the People's Party – joined forces back in 1922 to form the Democratic Centre (*Demokratiskais centrs*). This new coalition, which had its grassroots among the urban liberals, dedicated itself to the eradication of class conflicts within Latvian society. But later, in the course of the 1930s, the Democratic Centre adopted a narrow nationalist platform based on anti-minority feeling. With the help of the *Jaunākās Ziņas*, the biggest of the Latvian daily newspapers (the circulation of which rose at one point to 190,000), it exerted a dominant influence on Latvian public opinion. In parliament, however, the Democratic Centre and the smaller Centre parties, such as the Progressive Association (*Progresīvā apvienība*), never had more than nineteen delegates, and at one stage were reduced to nine. But, of course, the Centre held the balance in parliament at all times, for the right- and left-wing parties were too evenly divided for either of them to form a completely independent government. Consequently, the Latvian Centre was much more powerful than the Estonian Centre.

In both Latvia and Estonia the Social Democratic Party was the only major party with a set ideology. But despite its Marxist base, it remained completely democratic and, true to its Menshevik origins, was always on the right of the Socialist camp. In the Estonian Constituent Assembly the Social Democrats were represented by forty-one delegates and were the strongest single group. But they lost ground in successive parliamentary elections, and by 1923 had only fifteen delegates. Their party membership also declined from about 10,000 in 1920 to 2,273 in 1924. Subsequently, they attracted many new members in the urban areas, due no doubt to the international economic crisis, and by 1932 their membership had risen to 12,525. Although the importance attached by the party to Social Democratic theory diminished from one election to the next, this did not mean that the Social Democrats had given up their nationalisation plans, but merely that they had deferred them. This was made quite apparent by an enquiry conducted in 1930.

There was a second Socialist Party in Estonia. The Independent Socialists started out with seven delegates in 1919, and subsequently succeeded in increasing their representation. But this success was short-lived, and in 1925 they merged with the Social Democrats to form the Socialist Workers' Party, which had twenty-five seats in the 1929 parliament. The foremost Estonian Social Democrats were August Rei (Premier 1928–29) and Mihkel Martna.

The Latvian Social Democratic Party (*Latvijas Sociāldemokratiskā Strādnieku Partija*), whose leaders included Dr. Paul Kalniņš (President of the *Saema* 1925–34), Fricis Menders, Félikss Cielēns and Bruno Kalniņš, also won the largest number of seats in the Constituent Assembly. But like its Estonian counterpart, it then entered into a progressive decline. Thus, after gaining 38·7 per cent of the popular vote at the 1920 parliamentary election, its share of the poll was reduced to 24·8 per cent in 1928 and 19·2 per cent in 1931. In fact, this decline first set in at the Constituent Assembly, when seventeen of the party's delegates broke away under the leadership of M. Skujenieks (President of the Republic 1926–8 and 1933) and R. Dukurs. Later the members of this splinter group founded the Latvian Progressive Association, which started out as an internationalist, Marxist party but subsequently gravitated towards the Centre. Dukurs, however, found his way back to the Social Democratic fold in 1928.

In the countryside the Social Democrats lost ground as a result of the agrarian reforms, for the landless peasants who were allocated smallholdings under the terms of these acts soon abandoned their radical ideas once they had become settlers. And in the course of time the old class-war slogans also lost their appeal for the industrial workers of the towns, who gradually transferred their allegiance to the new nationalist movements. By 1933–4 the Estonian and Latvian Social Democrats were quite unable to advance a Socialist alternative to the presidential form of democratic government which had been established in both their countries. Instead, they concentrated on their opposition role, and tended to fight shy of governmental responsibility. Only once did the Lithuanian Socialists agree to take part in a coalition government, and only once did the Estonian Socialists produce a head of government.

There were no Communist delegates at the Constituent Assembly in either Estonia or Latvia. At the first Estonian parliamentary elections the Communists won 5·3 per cent of the popular vote, which gave them five seats in the chamber; and between 1921 and 1923 they increased their support amongst the electorate, with the result that ten Communist delegates were returned in 1923, who received 43,711 votes between them (9·5 per cent). But after the Communist *putsch* of 1 December 1924, it was apparent to all concerned that the Communist Party had no intention of respecting the constitution, and it was duly proscribed by the government of the day. The Communists then stood for parliament under an assumed name, and won six seats in 1926 and 1929, and five in 1932.

But these delegates were of no real consequence. As for the Lithuanian Communist Party, that had been proscribed during the War of Liberation. Subsequently, the Lithuanian Communists also stood for parliament under an assumed name, and in 1928 and 1931 a few managed to gain election as members of the Workers' and Peasants' Association (*Strādnieku un nabadzīgie zemnieku*). But they were even less significant than their Estonian comrades.

Apart from the national minorities there were no regional groups in Estonia. This was not the case in Latvia, where Latgale threw up a number of regional groups. The largest of these was the Party of Christian Peasants and Catholics (*Kristīgie zemnieki un katoli*), which was headed by the Catholic Bishop J. Rancāns. In 1920 this party received 15·9 per cent of the popular vote, and in 1931 27·2 per cent. The next largest regional group was the Progressive Peasants Association of Latgale (*Latg. progresīvo zemnieku apvienība*), which was closely aligned to the Latvian Centre parties. These regional parties were important in so far as they introduced a clerical element into Latvian political life which had been quite unknown in the old Baltic provinces.

The three-party system (Nationalist Liberals, Agrarian Conservatives and Social Democrats), found in Estonia, Latvia and – to a lesser extent – Finland, was also established in Lithuania. But in Lithuania there was a greater imbalance between the component groups. There the devout Catholicism of the indigenous population, and the essentially agrarian structure of the economy, led to the predominance of the Christian Democratic Party, an agrarian association in which the Church played an important part. This party represented the interests of the Lithuanian Peasants' League (*Ūkininku Sajunga*) and the so-called Workers' Federation (*Darbininku Federacija*), i.e. the non-Marxist section of the industrial proletariat. The leaders of the Christian Democratic Party were S. Šilingas (1885–1962) and L. Bistras (1890–1959).

The principal left-wing party in Lithuania was the Social Democratic Party; but although this was the oldest political organisation in the country, it never acquired much influence. The principal Centre – or, to be more precise, left of Centre – party was the Party of the People's Socialists (*Valstiečiai*

Liaudininkai: literally, Party of Rural People), a leftist Liberal association, which had adopted some of the Marxist ideas advanced by the Russian *Narodniki* and Constitutional Democrats. The People's Socialists were led by M. Sleževičius, who was the Premier in various Lithuanian governments, Dr. K. Grinius and the former Duma delegate P. Leonas (1854–1938). The Lithuanian Communist Party had established close contact with Lenin prior to 1917, but was proscribed by the Lithuanian Government in 1919, as we have already seen. Its leader, Mickevičius-Kapsukas (1880–1935), went to live in Moscow in 1921. When the party reappeared in Lithuania in 1922 in the guise of a Workers' Association, it failed to acquire any great influence.

The National Party (*Tautininkai*), which subsequently played such an important part in Lithuanian politics, was hardly in evidence during the early years of the new republic. This party, it will be remembered, was founded by a group of Lithuanian intellectuals, which had formed around Antanas Smetona and his newspaper *Viltis* (Hope) in Vilnius. Apart from Smetona, nearly all the leading figures in the Lithuanian quest for independence – men like Basanavičius, Voldemaras and M. Yčas, who established personal contact with General Žukauskas and General Plechavičius of the Lithuanian Army – belonged to the National Party. On the face of it, it seems remarkable that these politicians – especially Smetona and Voldemaras – who had, as it were, lifted the infant republic out of its cradle, and who were eventually to become the dominant figures in the Lithuanian nationalist movement, should have faded into the background once the foundations of the new state had been laid. In fact it was the Christian Democrats who asserted their supremacy, both in the Constituent Assembly (of 1920) and in the first three parliaments (of 1922, 1923 and 1926). In 1920 they won fifty-nine out of a total of 112 seats, in 1922 thirty-eight out of a total of seventy-eight, in 1923 forty out of a total of seventy-eight, and in 1926 thirty out of a total of eighty-five. At the same four elections the People's Socialists won twenty-nine, nineteen, sixteen and twenty-two seats, while the Social Democrats won fourteen, eleven, nine and fifteen. The *Tautininkai* had their first success at the polls in 1926, when they won three seats.

The Lithuanian constitution, which passed into law in 1922, gave ample opportunity for party manoeuvring, and the Lithuanian politicians were not slow to exploit the situation. As a result, the men who had done most to achieve independence soon found that they had been eliminated from the leadership race by new party leaders with little political experience. During these early years Lithuania's financial and social policies were not soundly based, and its taxation and welfare systems had yet to be evolved. No state sickness benefits were paid until the 1930s.

5. *The Vilnius and Klaipeda (Memel) Questions*

There were various frontier disputes between Estonia and Latvia, but these were not serious and were quickly settled.

The principal points at issue were Hainaši on the Gulf of Riga, the island of Ruhnu, and the border town of Valga. According to the census of 1897 there were 4,453 Latvians living in Valga compared with 3,594 Estonians, and in the municipal elections of 1917 the Latvians won a majority of the local government offices. But two years later, when the question of this border town came up for settlement, the Estonians insisted that the Latvians' electoral success had been due to the presence in Valga of a large Latvian refugee community. The Latvians countered this argument by reminding the Estonians that Valga was the principal town of a Latvian district, and pointed out that of the five railway lines which passed through the town, three came from Latvia. A Latvian–Estonian commission was then set up to decide the issue, and on 22 March 1920 a compromise solution was reached. It was agreed that Hainaši was to go to Latvia and the island of Ruhnu to Estonia, while Valga was to be shared equally by both states. This settlement was entirely successful, for it was never questioned by either party.

Latvia and Lithuania had fallen out during the War of Liberation over the town of Daugavpils, which they both claimed. The Latvians had the better case, for their claim was backed by powerful ethnic and historical arguments. Moreover, the Lithuanians were inhibited from pressing their case by the Poles, to whom they were indebted for their help in the Latgale campaign, and who did not want Daugavpils to pass to Lithuania. However, the Latvians were prepared to accommodate the Lithuanians in the matter of access to the Baltic. Consequently, the commission headed by the Englishman Sir James Simpson was able to negotiate a settlement in March 1921, whereby Lithuania was given a narrow strip of coastal territory in Courland containing the small fishing port of Polangen together with the district of Heoligenaa, while the Latvians were compensated by border adjustments, both in the vicinity of Oknist and to the south of Autz, between the Memel and the Muhs.

But Lithuania's real border problems were in the east and west. Between them, the Vilnius and Klaipeda (Memel) disputes imposed an intolerable burden on this young state, which threatened to cloud its relations with its more powerful neighbours. Having had to bow to foreign aggression on its eastern border, the Lithuanian Government sought compensation for its loss by indulging in aggression on its own account on its south-western border. In doing so it evidently failed to consider that, if Poland and Germany were to come to terms, there was every likelihood that Lithuania would find it extremely difficult to hold on to the Klaipeda territory and virtually impossible to win back the Vilnius district.

On 2 January 1919 the Lithuanian authorities were forced to withdraw from their historic capital when it was threatened by Bolshevik troops. Three days later the Bolsheviks marched into Vilnius, and the Lithuanian Government moved to Kaunas. Then, in the spring of 1919, the Lithuanian Army began to move eastwards again while Polish troops of General Haller's army advanced north-eastwards in pursuit of the retreating Russians. Both the Lithuanians and the Poles were heading for Vilnius. The Poles arrived first, and occupied the city on 19 April, thus depriving the Lithuanians of what they had hoped would be their crowning achievement. Pilsudski offered to set up a Polish–Lithuanian federation, but his offer was rejected. Diplomatic contacts were established but brought no positive result.

It was only when the tide of war turned against the Poles in the summer of 1920 that the Lithuanians were given a further chance of regaining Vilnius. On 12 July they had signed a peace treaty with Soviet Russia, and on 15 July the Russians offered to restore Vilnius to them provided the Lithuanian Army joined forces with the advancing Red Army, or alternatively allowed Russian troops to pass through their territory. The Lithuanian Government accepted this offer and opted for the second alternative, thus exposing itself to the machinations of the Lithuanian Communist Leader Kapsukas, who had entered Vilnius with the Red Army. The situation was not without its dangers. In fact, but for the 'Miracle on the Vistula' of 20 August, Lithuania might well have become Communist, despite its peace treaty. As it was, this Polish victory set the seal on Lithuanian sovereignty, and forced Kapsukas to go underground. Towards the end of August the Red Army handed Vilnius over to the Lithuanians, who proclaimed it as their capital city on 26 August. The Military Control Commission sent out by the League of Nations under the French Colonel Chardigny then brought pressure to bear on the Poles, who agreed to sign a treaty with the Lithuanians. This was duly concluded in Suwalki on 7 October 1920, and under its terms the Lithuanians gained control over Vilnius and the surrounding district, an area of 14,500 sq. km. with a population of nearly half a million.

Two days later, on 9 October the Polish General L. Zeligowski launched a surprise attack and occupied the city. The Polish Government disclaimed all knowledge of this coup, maintaining that the General had acted on his own initiative, although it was quite evident that Warsaw had in fact given its blessing to the venture. In attempting to realise his dream of a new Jagiellonic Empire, Pilsudski had tried but failed to advance into the Ukraine. It was then that Zeligowski, following the line of least resistance, had invaded the Vilnius district. At that time the Poles frequently referred to the great love they bore the Lithuanians, and maintained that it was purely on this account that they wanted to set up a Polish–Lithuanian federation. Unfortunately for Warsaw, the Lithuanians failed to respond to these ardent overtures, as they doubted whether Poland was capable of entering into a confederate relationship without seeking to assert her predominance. For eighteen months Vilnius was a Polish dependency, and as such served as a buffer state, which was known in

Warsaw as Central Lithuania. The Polish language was used for all administrative purposes, and the territory was governed by a commission set up by Zeligowski and composed entirely of Poles.

Finding themselves opposed by a superior force, the Lithuanian troops had been obliged to withdraw from the Vilnius territory. Of course, ever since 1919 there had been repeated clashes between Polish and Lithuanian troops, and by the time Zeligowski had occupied Vilnius the relationship between the two countries bordered on a state of war. Numerous attempts were made to persuade the Polish and Lithuanian governments to enter into direct negotiations. But these were no more successful than the initiative undertaken by the League of Nations, which set up an arbitration commission under the former Belgian Foreign Minister Hymans, who recommended the establishment of a new Polish–Lithuanian union with common economic, military and foreign policies, within which Vilnius, Kaunas and the Klaipeda territory – which had been allocated to Lithuania – would function as autonomous cantons, each with its own provincial diet. Hymans' plan was, of course, rejected by both parties, for the Poles had no intention of withdrawing from the Vilnius territory, while the Lithuanians regarded the whole project as an attempt to deprive them of their independence. Hymans then produced modified proposals, but although these were approved by the League of Nations they still proved unacceptable.

The 'Central Lithuanian' administration introduced by the Poles turned out to be a temporary expedient. On 8 January 1922 elections were held to establish a *Sejm* for the Vilnius territory, which was enlarged for this purpose by the incorporation of two large areas extending to the banks of the Deugava in the north and embracing the town and district of Lida in the south. Within these new borders the Poles outnumbered the Lithuanians by nearly ten to one (68·3 to 7·2 per cent of the total population). Not surprisingly, the elections were boycotted, not only by the vast majority of Lithuanians but also by the Jews, who sympathised with them. Of the 387,397 persons entitled to vote, only 249,325 (64·4 per cent) went to the polls. In the city of Vilnius the turnout was even longer (54·8 per cent). In the circumstances the outcome of the election was a foregone conclusion: a large majority for union with Poland. The resolution to this effect passed by the Provincial Diet on 20 February 1922 was ratified by the Polish parliament in Vilnius on 20 April.

Subsequently, Lithuania called on Poland to return to the conditions agreed upon in the Treaty of Suwalki, and when this demand was rejected, she brought the issue before the International Court of Justice in The Hague. But this also failed to produce a firm decision and the border question was not resolved. As a result, Lithuania continued to look upon her border with Poland as a temporary demarcation line, and refused to establish diplomatic relations. Vilnius remained the nominal capital, and Kaunas was still regarded as a purely temporary seat of government.

The dispute between Poland and Lithuania also affected the recognition of Lithuanian independence by the great powers. Although Lithuania, like Estonia and Latvia, had become a member of the League of Nations on 22 September 1921, the entente powers refused to recognise the government until it settled its relations with Poland. The principal stumbling block for Lithuania was, of course, the attitude of the French, who were backing Poland to the hilt. A note sent to the Lithuanian Government by the Conference of Ambassadors on 13 July 1922 enumerated the conditions under which Lithuania might receive recognition. The principal point at issue concerned Articles 343 and 345 of the Treaty of Versailles, which stated that the River Memel/Nemunas was to be designated as an international waterway. At first the Lithuanian Government tried to barter by offering to abide by this directive in exchange for international approval of Lithuania's claim to the Klaipeda territory. Later it dropped this condition, and on 20 December 1922 the English and French governments undertook to give *de jure* recognition. The U.S.A. had already done so in July 1922.

All this time the Vilnius question had proved intractable, and for this reason the Conference of Ambassadors met on 15 March 1923 to consider the Lithuanian problem. Meanwhile, various allied commissions and tribunals had tried, but failed, to negotiate the reopening of the River Memel/Nemunas to international shipping, a project of great importance to the

Poles as well as the Lithuanians. The other party to the Klaipeda dispute was, of course, Germany, and by the time the Vilna question came up for discussion in March 1923 Lithuanian's international position had been further complicated by her dispute with Germany over the Klaipeda affair.

It will be remembered that on 24 March 1919 a Lithuanian delegation had called on the Allied Supreme Council to transfer parts of the eastern region of East Prussia to Lithuania. But although the Treaty of Versailles stipulated that Germany was to cede the whole of the Klaipeda territory, instead of passing to Lithuania, this was administered in the first instance by a French general as an Allied condominium. The decision as to whether it would be transferred to Lithuania at some future date was deferred.

Faced with this indeterminate situation, the Lithuanian Government eventually decided to take matters into its own hands, and on 10 January 1923, the day the French Army marched into the Ruhr, units of the Lithuanian Army, posing as a volunteer force, invaded the Klaipeda territory. The French garrison, which had been occupying the territory since February 1920, offered no resistance and agreed to withdraw. The Conference of Ambassadors protested to the Lithuanian Government. But this protest was a mere formality, for on 16 February 1923 the conference approved the transfer of the Klaipeda territory to Lithuania.

On 8 May 1924 a Klaipeda Convention was signed, and this document listed the conditions under which Lithuania was to assume rights of sovereignty. In the preamble to the new statutes the Lithuanian Government undertook to respect the internal autonomy of its new province, while in the statutes proper it was decreed that the province was to be governed by a Provincial government, whose members were to be elected by the Provincial Diet, but whose President was to be appointed by the Lithuanian Governor. In the 1925 census 71,156 of the inhabitants of the Klaipeda province claimed German nationality, and 67,259 Lithuanian. But in the elections to the Provincial Diet, which were held in October 1925, the German United Front won twenty-seven of the twenty-nine seats.

It was quite obvious that Lithuania's annexation of the Klaipeda territory would cloud her relations with Germany.

The western powers, for their part, had hoped that if the Lithuanian Government was allowed to keep this strip of land, it would more readily resign itself to the loss of Vilnius. But this proved a false assumption, for subsequently the Lithuanians treated the Vilnius affair as a major threat to their national prestige, and in December 1927 this question became a burning issue when Pilsudski and Voldemaras met face to face in Geneva. Both of these men were extremely forceful politicians, and both had been elected as the leaders of authoritarian regimes in the previous year.

But even before this meeting took place there was a marked deterioration in Polish–Lithuanian relations, and for a while it looked as if war might break out at any moment. Pilsudski, who had close personal connections with the Vilnius territory, took part in various anti-Lithuanian demonstrations in the city of Vilnius, including celebrations to mark the seventh anniversary of Zeligowski's coup. Meanwhile, both the German and the Soviet governments – who had maintained much closer contact since the Berlin Treaty of 1926 – advised Lithuania to enter into direct negotiations with Poland. On 24 November 1927 the Soviet envoy to Warsaw warned Pilsudski not to attack Lithuania. The French envoy also urged moderation.

It was against this background that Pilsudski and Voldemaras met at the League of Nations in Geneva on 9 December 1927. Voldemaras, never a very exciting speaker, had embarked on a long-winded presentation of the Lithuanian case when Pilsudski suddenly interrupted him. Pounding the table with his fist, the Polish leader shouted across the hall: 'I didn't come all the way from Warsaw to Geneva just to listen to your long speeches. There's only one thing I want to know: do you want war or peace?' When Voldemaras told him that he wanted peace, Pilsudski seemed satisfied.

A resolution was then passed by the League of Nations which called upon the Poles and Lithuanians to enter into negotiations on neutral soil. Accordingly, a conference was convened in Königsberg in 1928, but brought no positive result. The demarcation line which served as a common frontier remained closed, there were no rail communications between the two countries, and no shipping passed along the Memel (Nemunas).

Even letters from Lithuania to Poland went via Latvia or Germany. This state of affairs was to continue for a further ten years.

One interesting by-product of this development was the establishment of a better understanding between Lithuania and Germany. German–Polish relations had also been strained, and so, despite the antagonism caused by the Klaipeda dispute, the Germans came to look upon the Lithuanians as natural allies. After lengthy negotiations a German–Lithuanian frontier agreement was signed in 1928, and was followed by a trade agreement in 1929. Significantly, it was only after Voldemaras had been overthrown that this *rapprochement* was weakened.

CHAPTER III

BALTIC POLITICS IN THE 1920s

1. Federation Projects after 1920: the Latvian–Estonian Alliance

The concept of a Baltic federation emerged at a quite early stage and was given serious consideration by a number of politicians and political commentators. The first people to think along these lines were a group of Lithuanian publicists, who debated the possibility of a union with Latvia before 1917. Later, when he was living as an exile in Switzerland, the Latvian poet Rainis also became interested in this idea. Meanwhile, the Estonian delegates to Western Europe – men such as A. Piip and K. R. Pusta – had been advocating the establishment of some form of federal association between the Baltic territories, and J. Tõnisson had sounded out the Scandinavians in Stockholm to see if this proposal could be extended so as to create a great northern bloc. When the Finnish volunteers arrived in Tallinn in late December 1918 and turned the tide of battle against the Bolsheviks, the idea of a Finno-Estonian union elicited a warm response from many Estonians. At the same time, the Baltic German politician Paul Schiemann was urging the creation of a Latvian–Estonian association.

During the War of Liberation Estonian, Latvian, Lithuanian and Finnish representatives met on various occasions to discuss the feasibility of a federal union, and the first Estonian Foreign Minister subsequently submitted proposals along these lines to the Supreme Allied Council in Paris. However, it soon became apparent that the time was not yet ripe for the establishment of a Baltic bloc, and that further detailed discussions would have to be held before this idea could be put into practice.

The attempts to establish closer co-operation between the

107

various Baltic States took place in three phases: 1920–5, 1925–34 and 1934–40.

The first phase was initiated in January 1920 when an international conference was held in Helsinki to discuss the feasibility of a defensive alliance between Finland, Estonia, Latvia, Lithuania and Poland. In August the same year the delegates to this conference met again, this time in Bulduri near Riga. Although each of these states had negotiated a separate peace with the Soviet Russians, it nonetheless seemed as if a pan-Baltic bloc was beginning to emerge. But then came the Vilnius dispute. After the occupation of the Lithuanian capital by Polish troops in October 1920, the establishment of a federal union embracing both Lithuania and Poland was clearly impossible. Consequently, when a second conference was convened in Helsinki in July 1921, it was attended by only four foreign ministers: those of Estonia, Latvia, Poland and Finland.

Instead of collaborating with Poland, the Baltic States could, of course, have tried to forge closer links with the Scandinavian countries. On the face of it, this would have seemed an entirely reasonable alternative, and there were some who openly advocated such a policy. Back in January 1920 the Lithuanian representatives in Helsinki had tried to drum up support for Jaan Tõnisson's ideas, and in February 1922 the Lithuanian Premier Galvanauskas said that he would welcome an alliance between the Scandinavian and Baltic states. But it was to be demonstrated time and again in the inter-war years that this project was based on a fallacy. The truth of the matter was that the Scandinavian countries were extremely loth to become embroiled in international politics. Subsequently, even the Finns had second thoughts about the advisability of forming really close links with their southern neighbours.

At the second Helsinki Conference, which was held in July 1921, the Finnish Foreign Minister R. Holsti urged the conclusion of a quadripartite alliance between Finland, Estonia, Latvia and Poland. Holsti's proposal received the immediate support of the Poles, who then became the principal driving force in this attempt to create a new power bloc. The French, whose whole eastern policy prior to 1932 was based on their desire to set up a *cordon sanitaire* against Soviet Russia, also backed this initiative, although they regarded it as a purely defensive arrangement. The discussions conducted in Helsinki were continued in Warsaw in the early spring of 1922, and on 17 March a non-aggression pact was signed, which provided for consultation in the event of an unprovoked attack on any of the four signatories, who undertook not to conclude agreements prejudicial to their allies.

Although the Russians insisted that the Warsaw Pact was an anti-Soviet measure pure and simple, this was not in fact so. As far as the Poles were concerned, it was also designed to inhibit any attempt by the Germans to redraw their eastern borders. On the face of it, this concern must have seemed excessive to both the Germans and the Russians, who clearly felt that Poland had emerged from the First World War as a great European power. Certainly, Poland laid claim to such status; and although in reality she lacked the resources to make good this claim, the sheer size of the Polish state made it hardly surprising that Soviet Russia should have feared Polish influence in the Baltic region and considered Polish policies more dangerous than they really were. As for the Baltic States and Finland, it was readily apparent that they constituted no threat whatsoever to the security of the Soviet Union. They simply wanted to consolidate their new-found independence and establish a communal framework for the Baltic region by means of inter-state agreements. But because Poland was determined to increase her influence, the Baltic States ran the risk of being caught up, much against their will, in a Soviet–Polish dispute that could only be prejudicial to their interests.

Since Moscow regarded the Warsaw pact as an anti-Soviet device, it naturally sought to undermine it. Accordingly, the delegation sent to represent Soviet Russia at the Genoa Conference broke its journey in Riga, where it engaged in a discussion with representatives of the Latvian, Estonian and Polish governments, which led to the conclusion of a number of relatively unimportant trade agreements, and the convening of a disarmament conference in Moscow, to be attended by all four parties to the discussion. Commenting on this project, a Soviet observer openly conceded that the Soviet Union was seeking 'to weaken the united front established by the Baltic States, and blunt the anti-Soviet edge of the resolutions passed in Warsaw'.

Subsequently, Finland and Lithuania were also invited to take part in the Moscow Conference. However, the latter proved completely abortive because the Soviet Union refused to countenance the proposal put forward by the Baltic States, who insisted that disarmament must be preceded by the conclusion of non-aggression pacts. However, in the late autumn of 1923, when a further Communist rising seemed imminent in Germany, the Soviet Russians, fearing Polish intervention, made renewed overtures to the Baltic States. In November the same year the Soviet envoy V. Kopp offered to guarantee Latvian independence in exchange for an assurance of Latvian neutrality. It is even possible that the Soviet Union was hoping to persuade the Latvian Government to allow Soviet troops to pass through Latvian territory in order to help the German insurgents. Subsequently, a similar offer was made to Estonia. But neither Latvia nor Estonia was prepared to enter into bilateral negotiations, and neither was very happy about a Soviet guarantee. Instead they suggested than an arbitration agreement be concluded. This, of course, was unacceptable to Moscow, and when events in Germany went against the Communists, the Soviet Russians allowed the negotiations to lapse.

The resolutions framed by the signatories to the Warsaw Pact were not ratified by their respective governments and so did not pass into law. Clearly, this constituted a considerable success for Soviet diplomacy. It was at this point that the Finns began to adopt a more cautious attitude towards the Baltic States. After accusing their Foreign Minister Holsti – who had been the principal advocate of the proposed bloc – of having exceeded his brief, they gradually weakened their links with their southern neighbours and aligned themselves with the Scandinavian States. By 1925 the regular discussions conducted by the foreign ministers of Finland, Estonia, Latvia and Poland had been broken off.

With the dissolution of the quadripartite bloc, Estonia and Latvia were thrown back on their own resources, and they consequently set about the task of putting their own houses in order. Following a Conference of Baltic States, which was convened in Tallinn in mid-October 1923 and was concerned primarily with economic questions, a discussion was held between Latvian and Estonian representatives which led to the conclusion of a bilateral agreement on 1 November. This agreement was later enlarged, but even in its original form it went part of the way towards the establishment of a Latvian–Estonian alliance. Among other things, it set out the terms of a definitive border agreement, which resolved the thorny problem of Valga by dividing the town into an Estonian and a Latvian sector, and of a mutual defence pact, which was to run for a period of ten years.

The principal object of the Latvian–Estonian entente was to keep the Baltic territories out of the clutches of the great powers. Its guiding spirit was Z. A. Meierovics (1887–1925), Prime Minister of the Latvian Republic (1921–3) and Latvian Foreign Minister, and one of the most remarkable Baltic politicians of the early 1920s. The son of a Jewish doctor from the district of Liepaja, Meierovics had studied commerce and subsequently worked in a bank in Riga. Like his Estonian colleagues, he first sought to create economic and industrial links between Latvia and Estonia, which were meant to pave the way for the establishment of joint administrative bodies.

The Latvian–Estonian alliance was to become the model for all later alliances in the Baltic region. Admittedly, it was more a marriage of convenience than one of love, and it had its fair share of misunderstandings. But by and large the agreement of 1923 proved viable, not least because it was made by two neighbouring territories with strong historical associations.

2. *The Communist Putsch in Tallinn*

Although the parliamentary system of democratic government adopted in Estonia and Latvia was essentially liberal, the Estonian and Latvian Communist parties were both pro- CP's scribed. The only way in which they could take part in illegal elections was by standing under an assumed party name. The Estonian Communists won five seats at the first national election (1920) by this means, and at the second (1923) they won ten. The decision to ban the Estonian and Latvian Communist parties was made because they were suspected – and justifiably so – of taking their orders from the Communist International. Nor was proscription the final sanction. On 3 May 1922 Viktor Kingissepp, one of the leading Estonian Communists, was arrested, accused of anti-Estonian activities, and condemned to death. Yet, in the municipal elections held in Tallinn in the autumn of 1923, at a time when there was rising unemployment, the Communists won thirty-six out of a total of 100 seats, and later the same year they gained nearly 25 per cent of the popular vote at the Tartu elections.

At the beginning of 1924 the Communist organisations became much more active. But so too did the Ministry of Internal Affairs, which was headed by K. Einbund (Eenpalu). On 22 January the police raided all known Communist cells in the country, arresting some 200 ringleaders and forcing others to seek refuge in the Soviet Union.

However, this police action failed to curb the Communist agitators, who continued to concentrate on two particular groups: the workers in the major towns – especially the Tallinn dockers – and the Russian-speaking inhabitants of the border areas, from Narva to Petseri. In Tallinn Communist-inspired workers' demonstrations were staged in June and August 1924. In Tartu the police uncovered a projected *putsch* in September, and the thirty people arrested in this connection included the Communist parliamentary delegate Heidemann and a number of soldiers. In November an attempt was made to free Communist prisoners from the remand prison in Tallinn. A few days later, on 10 November, 149 Communists were arraigned before a military court in Tallinn, charged with espionage and plotting to overthrow the government. Judgement was given on 27 November: seven of the accused were acquitted, thirty-nine were sentenced to penal servitude for life, while thirty were given fifteen years, and the rest three to ten years' imprisonment. The trade union leader and parliamentary delegate Jaan Tomp, who openly denounced the trial, was promptly arrested and sentenced to death by a drumhead court. He was executed by firing squad on 15 November.

Predictably, the Soviet Russians took exception to these harsh measures. The Soviet envoy Kobetsky, who had been accredited to Tallinn in July 1924, protested to Foreign Minister Pusta on 18 November against Tomp's execvtion, and then left immediately for the Soviet Union. Demonstrations were staged in front of the Estonian Consulate in Leningrad; and when the Soviet newspapers, especially those in Leningrad, reported the trial, they spoke of 'bloody reprisals' taken against the Estonian proletariat.

The Tallinn trial was the prelude to a Communist insurrection which was mounted on 1 December 1924. Shortly after 5 a.m. small groups of between five and twenty armed men moved through the streets of Tallinn to the most important strategic points in the town: the Baltic railway station, the officers' school, the barracks of the Armoured Division, the telephone and telegraph office, and the airfield. The entire Communist force consisted of no more than 400 or 500 men. The main attack was launched on the government buildings on the Toompea (citadel), where Premier Akel narrowly escaped assassination. The Minister of Communications Karl Kark was less fortunate. He had set out to catch the early train to Tartu, where the police had uncovered a Communist plot to blow up one of the bridges over the Emajõgi, and met his death at the Baltic railway station.

The government reacted quickly and decisively. A state of emergency was declared, and General Johan Laidoner, who had been Commander-in-Chief of the Estonian Liberation Army, was given special powers to deal with the situation. These measures were taken within an hour or two, and by mid-day order had been restored. A few of the ringleaders managed to escape in two aircraft, which flew off to the East; and Jaan Anvelt, who had headed the Estonian Soviet Government in November 1918 and was the leader of the insurrection, found temporary refuge in the Soviet Embassy. All in all, twenty-one people were killed and forty-one wounded. The army had remained loyal to the regime; so too had the vast majority of the workers.

During the brief battle twelve of the rebels were killed, and by the evening a further 140 had been arrested. Thirty of these were sentenced to death by special military courts and executed on the spot. A few further death sentences were carried out in the next few days. It was been suggested that the number of insurgents executed by the government was much larger, but this seems unlikely. Subsequently, the Estonian parliament gave the government far-reaching powers to maintain the security of the state: General Laidoner, whose decisive leadership was one of the principal factors in securing the speedy defeat of the Communist insurgents, was re-appointed Commander-in-Chief of the Army; a volunteer militia (*Kaitseliit*), similar to the Finnish militia, was formed to help the army maintain national security; Premier Akel's cabinet, which had assumed office in March 1924, was replaced by a coalition government under the leadership of Jüri Jaakson; and the Estonian Communist Party was proscribed.

The Communist *putsch* in Tallinn was regarded with great alarm, not only in the other Baltic territories, but in every country of Europe. It revived memories of the Soviet coup in Georgia in 1922, and of the abortive revolutions in Germany and Bulgaria in October 1923. Was the *putsch* planned and directed from Moscow? Certainly, it could hardly have come at a worse time for the Soviet Commissariat for Foreign Affairs. After the failure of the German revolution towards the end of 1923, Chicherin had been trying to establish normal political relations with the European nations. *De jure* recognition of the Soviet Union had been given by Great Britain, the Scandinavian States, Italy, and finally – on 24 October 1923 – France. But no sooner had France recognised the Soviet Government than there were difficulties with Britain over the Zinoviev letter. Although this letter was doubtless a forgery, the British were inclined to accept it at its face value, and they deferred the signing of an Anglo-Soviet trade agreement on this account. Trotsky suggested at the time that for the Soviet Government to have supported the Communist insurrection in Tallinn would have been a desperate measure, and in the light of these events his comment appears eminently reasonable.

On the other hand there appears to have been some substance in the rumours, which were circulating in Tallinn during the early days of December, of Soviet troop concentrations on the Estonian border. We know for a fact that the Red Army recalled four groups of reservists from the Petrograd and Pskov districts for a three-week period of exercises on 29 November;

and although there is no firm evidence to support the contention that Soviet naval units left Kronstadt and steamed off Tallinn, it was subsequently learnt that of the 400 or 500 men who took part in the insurrection, about sixty were smuggled into the country by sea, which might perhaps be taken as an indication of Soviet naval activity.

On the available evidence, it seems that Zinoviev, who was both Party Secretary in Petrograd and Chairman of the Comintern, was the guiding spirit behind the Tallinn *putsch*. This was strongly implied by a number of Soviet functionaries – such as Viktor Serge – who defected to the West. Zinoviev was able to call on the services of local units of the Petrograd G.P.U.; he knew that the Executive Committee of the Communist International would back him in such a venture, and he may well have counted on the support of army units from the Petrograd and Pskov military districts. He would, of course, have collaborated with Anvelt, the Estonian Communist leader, who was living in Petrograd at that time. But although Anvelt euphemistically described the Tallinn action as a continuation of the class struggle, rather than a *putsch*, in an article published in *Pravda* on 24 March 1925, it does not necessarily follow that he was in favour of this venture. It seems, in fact, that considerable pressure was brought to bear on the Estonian members of the Comintern. Rumour had it that they were offered a straight choice by their Russian comrades: to approve the project or be transported to Siberia.

Assuming that Zinoviev was responsible for the insurrection, we have to ask ourselves why he should have chosen to pursue such a course. The answer appears fairly obvious. Zinoviev was an extremely ambitious man, whose personal prestige had been severely undermined, even within the Comintern, towards the end of 1923. Subsequently, with the death of Lenin, a fierce struggle for power set in, and Zinoviev was no doubt looking for ways of strengthening his own position. A successful *putsch* in Estonia, leading to the establishment of an Estonian Soviet Republic and the acquisition for Soviet Russia of a more or less ice-free port in Tallinn, would undoubtedly have helped to restore his shattered fortunes. As it was, the Estonians remained loyal to their parliamentary government, and the whole episode proved a costly failure.

In all, seventy-seven Communist ringleaders were arrested and brought to trial. Judgement was passed on 22 July 1925: five were acquitted, one – Heidemann – was condemned to death, and the remaining seventy-one were sentenced to penal servitude for life. Anvelt, who managed to escape to the Soviet Union, perished in the Stalinist purges of the 1930s.

In the aftermath of the Tallinn *putsch*, the Estonians decided that the time had come to strengthen their ties with Latvia. The Latvians, for their part, were well aware that if the Communists had succeeded in Estonia, they would undoubtedly have tried to take over the other Baltic States as well, and so when the Estonian President Jaakson visited Riga shortly after the insurrection he was received with every possible mark of honour. Subsequently, negotiations were conducted with a view to forging closer economic links between the two states, that would eventually lead to the creation of a customs union. On 5 February 1927 an interim agreement was signed regulating inter-state trade until a full economic union could be established.

The Tallinn *putsch* also provided Poland with an opportunity of reviving her 1922 plan for an East European bloc. Her new overtures met with some success, especially in Estonia, where the Foreign Minister Kaarel R. Pusta, who was a great francophile, ardently advocated closer collaboration with Poland. Estonian army circles also reacted favourably to Polish proposals for a closer military liaison. Meanwhile, the Latvian Foreign Minister Meierovics was urging acceptance of the Lithuanian scheme for a smaller Baltic bloc consisting only of Lithuania, Latvia and Estonia. For Lithuania this was a matter of great importance, for if the Polish plan had gone through, she would have been faced with a choice between two evils: progressive isolation or – if she accepted the state of affairs in the Vilnius territory and joined the larger bloc – total dependence on Poland. It happened that at that time relations between Latvia and Poland were particularly strained, due to the tactless propaganda put out by the Poles in Latgale, which had once been a Polish province. Of course, from the Latvian and Estonian point of view, Lithuania was not exactly an ideal ally, for she was doubly encumbered with the Vilnius and Memel problems.

In January 1925 Estonian, Latvian, Polish and Finnish representatives met yet again at a four-power conference in Helsinki, where they signed an arbitration agreement on 17 January. A further conference was convened in Riga in March 1925, which was also attended by a Rumanian representative, whose government had entered into a military alliance with Poland. At this conference a joint policy was evolved that was designed to enable these five countries to adopt a common attitude to the questions of arms sales and communications at the forthcoming disarmament negotiations in Geneva. Before leaving Riga the representatives arranged to reconvene in August the same year to continue their discussions. Meanwhile, however, Meierovics was tragically killed in a road accident, and instead of holding a second conference in Riga the five governments concerned decided that any outstanding matters could be dealt with just as effectively by their League of Nations delegates when they met in Geneva for the September session. These delegates duly consulted with one another, but apart from reaffirming their intention of adopting a common policy at the negotiations, they achieved nothing of any consequence. For all practical purposes, the decision to cancel the second Riga conference put an end to the plan for a quadripartite Eastern bloc and – much to the satisfaction of the Soviet Union – destroyed Poland's hopes of dominating the Baltic area. However, this brought little comfort to the Lithuanians, for their own plan for a tripartite bloc also seemed doomed to failure at that time.

3. *Moscow's Policy on Lithuania*

After the Locarno Pact had been signed in October 1925, the Soviet Government decided to approach the Baltic States one by one and try to conclude bilateral agreements with each in turn. It was felt that this was the best way of countering the repeated attempts to form an anti-Soviet bloc and of increasing Soviet influence in those states. And since Lithuania had received such a firm rebuff from Poland, Moscow assumed that she would prove the most co-operative.

The late spring of 1926 saw a complete transformation of the political scene in Lithuania. After a long period of Christian

Democratic rule, the new elections, which were held in May, produced a coalition government comprising People's Socialists and Social Democrats, headed by M. Sleževičius. Even the presidency passed to a People's Socialist delegate, Dr. K. Grinius, who held office from June to December 1926.

The first problem with which the incoming government was confronted concerned Lithuania's relations with the Vatican, which had deteriorated under the Christian Democrats, despite their Catholic learnings. This has led to a conflict between State and Church in Lithuania, which could not be ignored, since 85·7 per cent of the Lithuanian population was Roman Catholic. The trouble had started in 1925 when the Pope made a concordat with Poland, in which he appeared to give his blessing to the Polish occupation of the Vilnius territory, and which consequently gave offence to both the nationalists and the leftists in Lithuania. An official protest was made to the Vatican, and the papal nuncio Zecchini was not allowed to return to his post in Kaunas.

Not surprisingly, the coalition government had difficulties with the army. But its most controversial act was the decision to pardon a number of leading Communists. This caused great resentment among the Christian Democrats, which was subsequently reinforced by the government's foreign policy initiatives. It soon became apparent that Sleževičius was trying to come to terms with Poland, and to this end he invited representatives of the Polish minority to join his government. Unfortunately for him, however, Pilsudski – whom the Lithuanian Christian Democrats regarded as the arch-villain of the Vilnius affair – seized power in Poland in May 1926 with the result that Sleževičius' attempted *rapprochement* began to look perilously like a sell-out.

It was against this background that Moscow launched its new initiative. Of course, ever since 1920 the Soviet Russians had had much friendlier relations with the Lithuanians than with the Latvians or Estonians. This was due partly to the tensions which had developed between Lithuania and Poland, and partly to the mediation of J. Baltrušaitis, a bilingual Symbolist poet of the school of Alexander Blok, who was the Lithuanian envoy to Moscow in the early 1920s.

In the circumstances, the Soviet Commissar for External

Affairs Chicherin, who had already put out feelers in Kaunas in December 1925, could be reasonably certain that his government's proposals would meet with a favourable reception. This in fact proved to be the case. Sleževičius's cabinet agreed to enter into direct negotiations, and on 28 September 1926 a non-agression pact was signed by Lithuania and the U.S.S.R. At the signing ceremony in Moscow the Soviet Government stated yet again that it recognised Lithuania's claim to Vilnius.

Meanwhile, Moscow had also approached the other Baltic States. On 21 May both Tallinn and Riga were offered non-aggression pacts, which would have guaranteed their borders, regulated their trade with the Soviet Union, and established an arbitration procedure to settle any differences that might have arisen. These proposals triggered a series of discussions between the Latvian and Estonian governments. The Latvian Premier and Foreign Minister K. Ulmanis went to Kaunas; and it was no accident that L. K. Relander, who was President of Finland from 1925 to 1931, visited the Baltic States at that time. A major factor in these discussions was the agreement signed in Berlin on 24 April 1926 between Germany and the Soviet Union. In general, this agreement had helped to stabilise the political situation in Central and Eastern Europe, and the Russians had been able to hold it up as a desirable precedent in their negotiations with the Lithuanians. But although the Lithuanians had been favourably impressed by the Soviet–German agreement, their neighbours had not. On the contrary, they were extremely perturbed by this development. And so, partly for this reason and partly because the Russians refused to set up the kind of arbitration tribunal which they wanted, the Estonians and Latvians were decidedly sceptical about the whole affair, and were loth to commit themselves. Consequently, this Soviet initiative tended to hang fire. Meanwhile, of course, the Poles were disturbed by the *rapprochement* between Lithuania and Russia. They were afraid that Lithuania might become a Soviet satellite and that Moscow would then actively support the Lithuanian claim to Vilnius. Notes were exchanged by the Polish and Soviet governments, and the British Government also warned Moscow on this account.

But Polish fears were soon to be allayed, for the right-wing parties in Lithuania had been opposed to the negotiations with the Soviet Union from the outset, and when the non-aggression pact was finally concluded on 28 September, the nationalist party, the *Tautininkai*, and the rightist elements in the army decided to take matters into their own hands. On the night of 16–17 December 1926 a group of officers led by General K. Ladyga forced their way into the parliament building and broke up the assembly. Sleževičius's cabinet was dismissed, together with the President of the Republic, and General P. Plechavičius was appointed head of state with dictatorial powers. A state of emergency was then declared and a minority government was subsequently formed by the *Tautininkai* and the Christian Democrats, who at that time held thirty-five of the eighty-five seats in the national assembly, the *Seimas*. The new Premier was Voldemaras, and the new President of the Republic Antanas Smetona. Smetona remained in office until 1940.

In the period leading up to the military coup, Voldemaras had been engaged in academic work, and had played an active part in the founding of the University of Kaunas, where he was appointed Dean of the Faculty of Social Sciences in 1922. But when approached by General Ladyga and his associates, he readily accepted the premiership, which he combined with the office of Foreign Minister. It soon became apparent that the deposed People's Socialists and Social Democrats were able to command little popular support, and that the army was the only power factor of any consequence. The officers responsible for the *coup* had obviously been inspired by the Polish colonels, who had seized power and set up an authoritarian regime under Pilsudski in May 1926. The coalition government appointed by the Lithuanian army rebels following their successful take-over was extremely short-lived. The Christian Democrats fell out with the *Tautininkai* in the early months of 1927 and withdrew from the government. The parliamentary delegates then withheld their support from the *Tautininkai*, whereupon Smetona dissolved parliament in April 1927. This unconstitutional act was the prelude to a period of authoritarian rule: on 15 May 1928 Smetona proclaimed a new constitution, which gave greatly increased powers to the President of the

Dictatorship

Republic; from then onwards parliament faded into the background and the country was ruled largely by decree.

In his foreign policy Voldemaras proceeded with great caution. Although he had been perturbed by the *rapprochement* between the Lithuanian Socialists and the Soviet Russians, it was the fact that it had been established by a left-wing government, and not the *rapprochement* itself, to which he objected. He felt that a left-wing Lithuanian Government would have been far too vulnerable to Soviet pressures, but was quite confident in his own ability to resist them. Consequently, far from repudiating the non-aggression pact of September 1926, he enlarged it by concluding a series of trade and cultural agreements with the U.S.S.R. At the same time, Voldemaras tried to improve Lithuania's relations with Germany, an initiative resented by many of his compatriots, who came to regard him as a Germanophile of the worst kind. But Voldemaras was not a man to be deterred by considerations of personal popularity. He stuck to his guns, for he was convinced that the only effective way of preserving Lithuanian independence was by pursuing a policy of friendly co-existence with both Russia and Germany, a policy which, incidentally, provided these two great powers with a neutral meeting place.

We have already seen that Moscow's attempts to conclude a non-aggression pact with the Estonians and Latvians had proved abortive. One of the major stumbling-blocks in this connection was that Riga and Tallinn wanted to conclude a joint pact while Moscow insisted on separate pacts. The Russians feared – quite justifiably – that a joint pact would leave so many loopholes that Warsaw would still be able to dominate the Baltic area, while the Estonians and Latvians feared that if they signed bilateral agreements they would inevitably be dominated by their more powerful partner. But towards the end of 1926 a left-wing government assumed power in Latvia under M. Skujenieks, who agreed to enter into further talks with the Russians. As a result, the Latvian Foreign Minister Cielēns and the Soviet envoy Avalov were able to initial a Latvian–Soviet non-aggression pact on 9 March 1927. This was the first occasion on which the Soviet Union agreed to the nomination of a neutral chairman for the arbitration commission that was to deal with possible disputes between

E*

Latvia and the U.S.S.R. (although the choice of a specific chairman was left open). The Latvian negotiator Cielēns was interested primarily in the question of Latvian–Soviet trade. He continued to press the Russians in this connection, and on 2 June 1927 a trade agreement was duly signed, which was ratified on 26 October. Under the terms of this agreement – to which Moscow attached particular importance in so far as it established a welcome link with the western world following the breaking off of Anglo-Soviet diplomatic relations in May 1927 – the Soviet trade delegation in Riga was granted extraterritorial status and a Soviet free port area was authorised in Liepaja.

Meanwhile, the Lithuanians soon discovered that co-existence with Soviet Russia was not without its dangers. The government uncovered pro-Soviet intrigues in the early months of 1927, and on 19 May 1927 the former Chief of the Lithuanian General Staff K. Klešinsky was sentenced to death as a Soviet spy. On the day of the execution the Soviet envoy Alexandrovsky left the country. At the same time, Pilsudski also adopted a hostile attitude towards the Lithuanian Government, so much so that by 27 November 1927 the Soviet Union found itself obliged to draw the attention of the German and French governments to the need for immediate steps to ensure the preservation of Lithuania's independence. The fact that this was threatened quite as much by the U.S.S.R. as by Poland was further demonstrated in January 1928 when a Communist conspiracy was exposed in Kaunas.

A big spy trial held in Rezekne in October 1927, showed that Soviet spy rings had also been active in Latvia, where the G.P.U. had recruited agents among the frontier guards and railway workers. As a result of this exposure, Latvia refused to sign the non-aggression pact initialled on 9 March. Moreover, the trade agreement concluded in June 1927, which was to run for a five-year period in the first instance, was not renewed. Cielēns, who had negotiated both the pact and the agreements for the Latvian Government, was accused of gullibility and weakness in his dealings with Moscow, especially in agrarian circles. At the end of 1927 there was a political crisis in Latvia which brought down the government. Jurašesvkis then formed a caretaker cabinet, which was replaced in December 1928 by an agrarian cabinet composed of members of the Peasants' League and headed by H. Celmiņš. Under Celmiņš Latvia enjoyed stable government until 1931.

As for the Estonians, they stuck to their original decision and refused absolutely to enter into bilateral agreements with the Soviet Union. They were alienated first by the Tallinn *putsch*, and subsequently by the G.P.U. attempt, which appears to have met with some success, to subvert the Estonian envoy in Moscow, Ado Birk. Birk, who had formerly held office as Foreign Minister, was arrested on his return in March 1927. With this, Soviet–Estonian relations entered upon a new and much cooler phase.

4. *Development of the Economy and Foreign Trade*

Even under tsarist rule there were certain differences in the economic structure of the three Baltic territories. Thus, while Lithuania retained its predominantly agrarian character until well into the twentieth century, Estonia and Latvia began to build up native industries from the late 1890s onwards, which soon acquired a certain significance in terms of the general economy of these two provinces, for they included the Narva textile factories and the Riga metal works and harbour installations. We have already seen that during the First World War many of the industrial installations in the Baltic area were dismantled and transported to Central Russia. Riga, whose population had reached half a million by 1914, was the principal victim of this evacuation policy. Between 1915 and 1917, when the German front line lay just to the south of Riga, severe inroads were made on the industrial potential of this major city, and part of its population either fled or was ordered to leave by the Russians. After the armistice agreement had been concluded with Soviet Russia, it became immediately apparent that the Baltic territories had lost their economic hinterland. Fundamental changes were called for, and the whole economy was eventually remodelled to meet the needs of the West European market. The Russian carrying trade had been reduced to 30 per cent of its pre-war volume.

In Estonia the number of workers employed in large industrial concerns (those with more than twenty workers) fell from

44,600 in 1913 to 32,000 in 1930, then rose to 39,100 in 1935. The initial decline – between 1913 and 1930 – was particularly marked in the textile and metal industries. But despite this decline, 17·4 per cent of the Estonian population was still employed in industry in 1930 compared with 13·5 per cent in Latvia and 6 per cent in Lithuania.

In 1920 the Soviet Russians paid 15 million gold roubles to Estonia by way of war reparations, which the young republic was able to use for capital investment. A large part of this money was spent on opening up the deposits of oil shale in Virumaa between the Gulf of Finland and Lake Peipsi, which yielded some 5,000 million tons. Previously, only very modest amounts of oil shale had been employed as industrial fuel, but from the early 1920s onwards its use was greatly increased, and this enabled the Estonians to reduce their imports of anthracite. Even more important for the Estonian economy was the production of oil, petrol and asphalt, which was undertaken in Kiviöli, Kohtla-Järve and other places. Exports of these products – mostly to Germany, with whom Estonia signed a special agreement in 1935 – were doubled between 1933 and 1935. By 1939 Estonian oil production was one-third as big as Poland's, and one-fifth as big as Germany's.

Of the traditional Estonian industries the one that adapted best to the new economic conditions of the 1920s and 1930s was the textile industry, centred on Narva. By 1926 the Kreenholm Works had 3,833 power looms and jennies with nearly 500,000 spindles; and by 1936 no less than thirty-eight large textile works had been opened in Estonia. The paper and woodworking industries also expanded. The Northern Cellulose and Paper Factory was opened in Tallinn, and the Sulphate-Cellulose Factory in Kehra; and Tallinn also possessed a number of plywood and furniture factories. The adaptation of the metal goods and cement industries was less successful, because they had been geared almost exclusively to the Russian market. Nonetheless, a number of small factories in Tallinn, which produced machinery and metal goods, made a useful contribution to the economy. So too did the Railway Wagon Works in Tallinn and Valga, and the Telephone Factory in Tartu. When the Becker Dockyard was dismantled and transported to Russia during the war, two other large

dockyards – the Russian Baltic and the Peter Dockyards – had
to be closed down, as had the Dvigatel Wagon Works in
Tallinn. One of the two major cement works – that in Asseri –
was also closed down, production being transferred to Kunda.
However, the artificial fertiliser industry made considerable
progress following the introduction of phosphates. All in all,
the Estonians responded well to the demands of twentieth-
century industrial life. They introduced new processes wherever
possible, and rationalised their factories to good effect. Their
woodworking and food-producing industries underwent a
further expansion in the 1930s, which seemed to hold out great
promise for the future.

In Estonia the largest employer of urban labour was the
textile industry. In Latvia it was the metal goods industry,
which employed 18,500 workers. Next came the woodworking
industry with 18,400 workers, followed by the food-producing
industry with 17,600, and the textile industry with 17,000.
In 1920 Latvia had 1,430 industrial concerns and 61,000
industrial workers: in 1937 she had 5,700 concerns and 205,000
workers. A number of large industrial complexes were built
during this period, including a sugar refinery in Jelgava and a
power station in Keggum, which supplied 40 per cent of the
country's electricity. In addition, several small dockyards
were built in the harbours of Riga, Liepaja and Ventspils.

But, of course, agricultural products – butter, eggs, pigs,
bacon, skins, furs and flax – were the basis of the export trade,
not only in Estonia and Latvia, but in Lithuania as well.
Thanks to the change-over, initiated in the 1920s, to high-
quality meat products, there were more or less guaranteed
markets for Baltic produce in England, Germany and – to
a smaller extent – the U.S.A.

Between 1922 and 1935 the revenue from Estonian exports
rose from 52·8 to 80·1 million kroons, while her expenditure
on imports dropped from 61·4 to 68·8 million kroons. In 1922
Germany was Estonia's biggest customer, buying 54·7 per
cent of Estonian exports while Britain bought only 22·2 per
cent. By 1935, however, the situation had changed. In that
year Germany bought 26·3 per cent and Britain 37 per cent.

In Latvia both imports and exports rose steadily up to 1929.
Then came the slump. But in 1931 the upward trend re-

appeared, and continued throughout the rest of the decade. Timber and wooden articles formed an important part of Latvia's export trade. Britain was the principal market for Latvian goods; in 1938 she bought 41·9 per cent of all Latvian exports, while Latvia bought only 20·8 per cent of her imports from Britain. In the same year Latvia bought 38·9 per cent of her imports from Germany, to whom she sold 29·5 per cent of her exports.

Trade with the Soviet Union declined in both Estonia and Latvia. In 1922, 25 per cent of Estonia's trade had been with the Soviet Union, but by 1935 this had fallen to 3 per cent. In 1938 Latvian imports from the Soviet Union stood at 3·5 per cent of total imports. Between 1927 and 1929, following the conclusion of the Latvian–Soviet trade agreement, Latvian exports to the Soviet Union rose from 2 to 15 per cent of the country's total exports, only to drop back to 1 per cent by 1933. Later there was a further slight increase, and by 1938 about 3 per cent of Latvian exports went to the Soviet Union.

We get some idea of the progress made by the three Baltic states if we consider their trading position in 1938, when they exported $65.8 million worth of goods, which was about half the amount exported by the Soviet Union in that year.

After a difficult initial period the economic situation in Estonia and Latvia improved, and then remained relatively good until 1925/6. In the following year Estonia made a determined attempt to stabilise her currency, going over from the mark to the kroon in the process. But subsequently the situation deteriorated, due to the impact of the worldwide economic crisis, and prices for agricultural products slumped, especially in the period 1930–2. In Estonia the revenue from agricultural production dropped from 247 million kroons in 1927 to 133 million in 1933. The government then introduced a series of stringent measures – it devalued the kroon, rationed foreign currency, set up a state monopoly for certain goods, and stopped importing wheat – which enabled it to redress its adverse balance of payments and so resolve the crisis. As a result, the revenue from agricultural production in Estonia rose to 216 million kroons by 1937/8, which was only a little below the 1927 level. The industrial workforce in Estonia, which had been cut back to 25,000 in 1933, also expanded during this period, and numbered some 45,000 by 1939. Unemployment, which had first appeared in Estonia and, to a lesser extent, in Latvia in 1923/4, and which looked as if it might pose a major problem in both countries from 1930 onwards, was completely eradicated by 1936. Moreover, the Estonian and Latvian workers were protected by up-to-date industrial legislation. Among other things, they had a guaranteed eight-hour working day, and were entitled to elect their own works representatives. The unions, which were independent of the government, were extremely active, for apart from socio-political initiatives, they also launched a number of ambitious educational programmes.

In Lithuania agriculture and forestry retained their traditional predominance for much longer than in Estonia or Latvia. Particular importance was attached to animal husbandry and poultry breeding; pigs, sheep and geese were reared on a large scale. Moreover, the major part of Lithuanian industry, which developed very slowly, was concerned with the processing of agricultural products, foodstuffs and leather. There were also a number of factories – most of them in Klaipeda – which produced wooden articles, cellulose and paper, and a few which produced textiles. Later, in Kaunas, metal goods were manufactured, the raw materials being imported from Sweden. The Swedes were very much interested in Lithuania at this time; a considerable amount of Swedish capital was invested in the new republic, and there was active trading between the two countries. By 1931 Lithuania had 1,132 industrial concerns, employing 21,692 workers.

But even in the 1930s Lithuania's foreign trade was still based on her agricultural products. From 1932 onwards Britain replaced Germany as Lithuania's principal export market, while most of Lithuania's imports – petrol, mineral oils, salt, sugar, cotton goods, locomotives and wagons – came from the U.S.S.R. Ever since the early 1920s the Soviet Russians had been trying to build up their trade with Lithuania, and in 1926 the left-wing Lithuanian Government sent a delegation to Moscow in order to negotiate a trading agreement. But, as we have already seen, this initiative was frustrated by the *coup d'état* of December 1926. In 1924/5 Lithuanian exports to the Soviet Union – which consisted primarily of leather goods and cellulose – were worth between 4·5 and 6·4 million litai. Between 1925 and 1930 their value rose to between 8·7 and 19 million litai. After the conclusion of a trade protocol in August 1931 it rose yet again to 25·5 million, and after a second protocol had been signed in February 1935, it reached 26·6 million litai. Even so, this constituted only a fraction of Lithuania's total exports, which brought in no less than 280 million litai in that year.

Towards the end of the 1920s Lithuania became an important export market for the Soviet Union. Large consignments of timber were shipped to Memel and, after being processed in Lithuanian sawmills, were sent on to East Prussia via inland waterways. This Soviet transit trade increased sharply from c. 20,000 tons in 1924 to c. 283,000 tons in 1926. However, despite this extremely promising development, the Smetona regime was reluctant to increase its trade with the Soviet Union for fear of the political consequences.

5. Education and Culture

Although it was quite evident that the nationalist movement, which first emerged in the Baltic territories in the second half of the nineteenth century, was an extremely vital development, its adherents were none the less subject to the socio-political conditions obtaining at the time. Traditional values held sway, at both local and national level, and by and large those who obtained social advancement were still absorbed into the older cultural milieu of the German, Russian or Polish upper class.

But in 1918 these inhibiting factors were all swept away. As a result, the two decades of Baltic independence saw a great upsurge in the educational and cultural activities of the three Baltic peoples, whose final emancipation was achieved during this period. The real basis of this new development was the educational system, which was expanded at all levels by a combination of state and private initiatives.

In Estonia the duration of compulsory school attendance was extended from three to six years, and a standardised system of education was adopted, which enabled Estonian children to go straight through from primary school to university. The number of illiterates, most of whom lived in the eastern border areas, was reduced from 5·6 per cent of the total population in 1922 to 3·9 per cent in 1934. Conversely, the number of schools was greatly increased. By 1937 Estonia had 1,224 primary schools, which catered for 107,000 pupils. Many new middle or secondary schools were opened in both rural and urban areas. By 1927 there were 18,400 middle school pupils in Estonia.

The University of Tartu (Dorpat) was founded by Gustavus Adolphus in 1632 as a Swedish establishment with a Latin curriculum, and was closed down some seventy years later, only to be re-founded by Tsar Alexander I in 1802 as a German institute. Towards the end of the nineteenth century it was taken over by the tsarist authorities under the terms of their russification programme, and during the First World War a number of the university faculties were evacuated to Voronezh in Central Russia. Finally, the university was reopened as an Estonian foundation on 1 December 1919. Initially, the vast majority of the teaching staff were Baltic German or Russian professors, such as A. von Bulmerincq, H. Seesemann and H. Frey of the theological faculty, E. Masing and M. Bresowsky of the medical faculty, Tjutrjumov and Kurchinsky of the faculty of law, and W. Anderson, the professor of folklore. Subsequently, Finnish, Swedish and even Hungarian, Swiss and German scholars were appointed to the teaching staff. In the fullness of time, however, the Estonians provided their own university teachers, and by 1934, 85 per cent of all lectures were given in Estonian. The most celebrated Estonian scholars associated with the university included the neuropathologist L. Puusepp, the dermatologist A. Paldrock, the chemist P. Kogerman, the geographers E. Kant and A. F. Tammekann, the folklorist M. I. Eisen, the philologists J. Aavik, A. Saareste and J. Mark, the jurists J. Uluots, N. Maim and N. Kaasik, and the theologians P. Põld and J. Kõpp. The departments of archaeology and history were established by two Finnish scholars, A. M. Tallgren and A. R. Cederberg. Subsequently, H. Moora also made an important contribution to archaeological studies at Tartu while H. Kruus, P. Tarvel and H. Sepp helped develop historical studies. In 1919, the foundation year of the Estonian University, there were 347 students at Tartu. By 1926 there were 4,651, which meant that one Estonian in every 280 attended university in that year. This was a very high proportion indeed by comparision with Germany (one in 610) or Sweden and Finland (one in 645). Between 1919 and 1939 5,689 students graduated from Tartu.

Meanwhile, the School of Engineering in Tallinn was expanded and given university status as a College of Technology in 1937. Tallinn also had a military academy and a conservatoire, while Tartu had an academy of art and was the seat of the Estonian Learned Society and the Est?nian Literary Society, which had been founded in the nineteenth century. An Estonian folk museum was set up in the Castle of Raadi near Tartu, which had once belonged to the von Liphart family; and at the very end of the period of independent rule, in 1938, an Estonian academy of sciences was founded.

Not surprisingly, Tallinn and Tartu also became the focal points of artistic and literary life in Estonia. It was there that the writers gathered, the men of the older generation, such as E. Wilde and I. Kitzberg, being joined by representatives of the new wave, such as A. H. Tammsaare, M. Metsanurk, H. Raudsepp, O. Luts, G. Suits, Marie Under, F. Tuglas, H. Visnapuu, A. Mälk, Betti Alver and A. Gailit (whose novel *Toomas Nippernaat* was translated into numerous languages). Of course, the new wave was not restricted to writers. The graphic artist E. Viiralt, the painter N. Triik, the sculptor J. Koort, the conductors E. Tubin, Miina Härma and M. Saar, and the composers M. Lüdig and H. Eller are just a few of the talented young artists and musicians who made their début during the period of independence. The choral festivals, which had played such an important part in the development of a sense of national identity, were staged every five years. They were great national occasions, in which upwards of 10,000 performers often took part. In 1932 there were celebrations to mark the 300th anniversary of the University of Tartu, while three years later further celebrations were held in honour of the first Estonian book, which was printed in 1535.

The Estonians' determined efforts to improve their educational facilties soon brought results. For example, the number of qualified doctors in the republic rose from 370 in 1921 to just under 1,000 in 1932. At the same time, the number of hospitals, clinics and surgeries also increased.

But although the results of this educational programme were beneficial in the medical sphere, where they led to a reduction in mortality rates, in other areas of Estonian public life it soon became apparent that the schools and universities were turning out too many graduates. Changes had to be made, and an educational reform was introduced in 1934, which had the effect of reducing the pupil and student bodies. Thus, by 1937 the number of senior middle school pupils was cut back to 12,808, while the number of full-time university students dropped to 3,241 in 1934 and 2,689 in 1939. Under the terms of the 1934 reform English replaced German as the principal foreign language in the Estonian middle school curriculum.

In the Latvian Republic the number of primary schools rose from 864 in 1920 to 2,057 in 1933, and the number of secondary schools from thirty-six in 1920 to ninety-six in 1933. Different kinds of technical schools were also established. A statistical report prepared for the Latvian Government revealed that the teacher–pupil ratio in primary schools was 9,000 to 244,700 and in secondary schools 2,371 to 24,928. Latvia spent 15 per cent of her budget on education at a time when the average European expenditure was 12 per cent.

There was no specifically Latvian university before 1919. Under Russian rule Tartu was the only university in the Baltic area, and as such served the needs of all three Baltic provinces. The focal point of the Latvian student fraternity was the Lettonia Student Association, which was founded in 1870 and formed a pendant to the Estonian Vironia Student Association, which was founded in Riga in 1900 and subsequently transferred to Tartu. In July 1917 a Latvian Teachers' Conference which met in Tartu recommended that the Latvian Polytechnic, which had been established in Riga in 1862, should be expanded and given full university status. This recommendation was endorsed by the Latvian Government during the War of Liberation, and on 28 September 1919 the new Latvian State University was officially opened by the Minister of Education K. Kasparson. In its first year the new university had 940 students and 110 teachers. By 1921 the student intake had risen to 4,000, and by 1933 the teacher–

student ratio stood at 383 to 8,509, which was considerably higher than the authorities would have wished. Over the next six years, however, the situation gradually improved, and in 1939 the ratio was 446 to 7,347.

As in Tartu, so too in Riga, a large proportion of the academic chairs were held in the first instance by non-Latvian professors – Germans, Russian and Jews – but were subsequently taken over by Latvians. The most celebrated of the Latvian scholars associated with the University of Riga included the anatomist Prismanis, the jurist J. Kārkliņš, the chemist U. Fišers, the engineers P. Depners and G. Taube, the writer J. Lautenbachs, the philologist J. Endzelins, the archaeologist F. Balodis, the historians A. Švabe, A. Tentelis and A. Spekke, and the ecclesiastical historian L. Adamovics. In July the agricultural faculty was removed from the university at the instigation of K. Ulmanis and re-established in the Castle of Jelgava as an indepedent Academy of Agriculture. Meanwhile, a Catholic theological faculty was opened in 1938. Riga University was an important academic foundation, and between 1919 and 1939 it produced 6,841 graduates. In 1936 an historical institute was established in Riga, which was commissioned by the government to investigate the history of the Baltic area from the point of view of the Latvian people.

Riga was also the seat of a musical conservatoire and an academy of the fine arts. There were many celebrated Latvian musicians and artists in the 1920s and 1930s, not least the composer and conductor J. Vitols, the choirmaster T. Reiters and the landscape painter V. Purvits. The musical life of Latvia was fully integrated into the musical life of Europe; opera and ballet productions were of a very high standard. Latvian writers were also extremely active during the period of independence. Jānis Rainis-Pliekšans (1869–1929) and his wife Elsa Pliekšane ('Aspazija') were the foremost poets and Anna Brigadere, K. Krūza, E. Wirza and Veronika Strēlerte the foremost novelists of the new republic, which produced more books than any other European country save Denmark. All in all, Latvia made immense progress in the cultural and educational spheres during the inter-war years, and by the end of the 1930s the Latvian professional class numbered some

8,000 people. Of these about 1,800 were engineers, 1,600 doctors and 1,400 lawyers.

Meanwhile, the Lithuanians also made considerable headway with their educational programme. In 1913 there were 875 primary schools in this territory with 1,022 teachers and 31,212 pupils; in 1919 there were 1,036 primary schools with 1,232 teachers and 45,540 pupils; and in 1931/2 there were 2,292 primary schools with 4,120 teachers and 222,594 pupils, as well as 113 technical schools. Immediately following the proclamation of independence steps were taken to combat illiteracy, and over the years this campaign was extremely successful. In 1923 32·6 per cent of the population were still unable to read or write, but with the gradual expansion of the schools programme and, finally, the introduction of compulsory education on 1 November 1931, this unacceptably high figure was greatly reduced. In proportional terms Lithuanian education made even greater progress than Latvian or Estonian. Thus, in 1931/2 116 per thousand of the Lithuanian population were attending school compared with 111 per thousand in Latvia and 105 per thousand in Estonia. If we consider that in 1913 only 15 per thousand had attended school in Lithuania we see just how successful the educational programme had been.

It is true that in qualitative terms Lithuanian education was inferior to that provided in Latvia and Estonia. But the level of education in the Baltic region as a whole was much higher than in either Poland or the Soviet Union. Although the Soviet Russians made great progress in their campaign to counter illiteracy, 49 per cent of the Soviet Russian population were still illiterate in 1926 compared with 14·3 per cent of the Latvian and 5 per cent of the Estonian population in that year.

When the ancient Lithuanian University of Vilnius, which was founded in 1579, was taken over by the Poles following Żeligowski's coup in October 1921, the Lithuanians were forced to set up an alternative foundation. This new university, which contained seven faculties, was opened in Kaunas on 16 February 1922. In 1930, the 500th anniversary of the death of Grand Prince Vitold (Vytautas), it was officially named the Vitold University. In 1927 the university had 134 lecturers and 3,064 students, and in 1931/2 330 lecturers and 4,721 students. In 1924 an Agricultural Academy was established in Kaunas which provided all agricultural training from then onwards. In 1927 68·5 per cent of the student body in Kaunas were Lithuanian nationals, 27 per cent were Jews, 2·1 per cent were Poles and 1 per cent Russians. Lithuania produced many eminent native scholars including the theologian P. Būčys, the philologists A. Salys, J. Basanavicius (who worked in Vilna) and K. Būga, the philosophers P. Dovydaitis and S. Šalkauskis, the literary historians M. Biržiška and V. Mykolaitis-Putinas, the historians A. Šapoka and Z. Ivinskis, the mathematician Z. Žemaitis and the physicist V. Cepinskis, the expert on constitutional law M. Römer, the legal historian A. Janulaitis, the social scientist and author V. Krèvè-Mickevičius, and the technologists J. Šimkus and M. Tomašauskas.

The principal members of the older generation of Lithuanian writers were A. Vienuolis (1882–1957), J. Tumas-Vaižgantas (1869–1933) and L. Gira (1884–1946), while the younger generation was led by B. Sruoga, P. Cvirka, P. Vaičiūnas and J. Savickis. Following the Vilnius coup in 1920, Kaunas became the musical and theatrical centre of the new republic. It was there that the compositions of M. K. Čiurlionis (1875–1911) received full recognition and S. Šimkus made his name as a conductor. Like the Latvians, the Lithuanians were very gifted dancers, and at the International Folk Dance Festival, held in London in 1935, the Lithuanian troupe won the first prize.

The various national groups also contributed to the intellectual and cultural life of the Baltic States. For the most part, it is true, these manifestations of minority art were restricted in their effect by the language barrier. But on occasions this barrier was transcended, particularly in Riga, the most cosmopolitan of the Baltic cities. There the Russian theatre, with its world-famous actors, was an extremely potent artistic force, as were the indigenous musical troupes which, true to the tsarist tradition, employed many Russian, Jewish and Baltic German artists. A number of college courses were held in Riga, and several important Russian émigré scholars found employment there. (The Herder Institute, which operated as a private college in the Latvian Republic, is referred to below.) Riga also produced two well-known newspapers: the German-language *Rigasche Rundschau* and the Russian-language *Segodnja*.

There was a German theatre in Riga with counterparts in Tallinn and Tartu. This Baltic German theatrical movement had a long local tradition, and maintained close links with the living theatre in Germany. There were similar Russian and Jewish initiatives in Tallinn and Tartu. For example, a Jewish school of music was opened in Tartu under E. I. Schkljar, but it had little success until it moved to Riga.

6. *The Cultural Autonomy of the Minorities*

In 1917–18 the Baltic minority groups suddenly found themselves in a completely new situation. The change was greatest for the Germans and Russians. The Germans, after all, had formed the traditional upper class in the Baltic territories and consequently had been largely responsible for local government, while the Russians, although holding no administrative posts, had been members of the ruling race.

With the capitulation of the German Army, the Baltic German gentry lost their political power, and with the introduction of the agrarian reforms they also lost their estates. At first they fought against the new dispensation, but eventually wiser counsels prevailed and they recognised that if they wished to remain in the Baltic area they would have to accept minority status.

The question of guarantees for the rights of the minorities was first raised at the various constituent assemblies when the new constitutional laws were discussed. In the event, this question was never debated by the parliamentary delegates because their constitutions all contained a general statement to the effect that no citizen was to be victimised on account of his nationality, beliefs or race. In the Estonian constitution the rights of the minorities were dealt with in no less than six paragraphs. Thus, in Paragraph 6 all citizens were granted equal rights irrespective of their nationality, and in Paragraph 12 all national groups were given the right to establish their own schools and teach their children in their mother-tongue.

Under the terms of Paragraph 20 all citizens were allowed to determine their own nationality, while Paragraphs 22 and 23 authorised the use of vernacular languages for administrative purposes. Finally, Paragraph 21 established the principle of cultural self-government.

In the first draft of their constitution bill the Latvians also spelled out the rights that were to be enjoyed by their minorities. Thus, after establishing the general principle of equality before the law, this document specifically authorised the different national groups to use their own languages, for both speech and writing, and to set up autonomous corporations.

When they joined the League of Nations all three Baltic States were obliged to give additional guarantees to their minorities. Thus, on 15 September 1920, the League called upon the Latvian Government to give an explicit assurance that it would protect the interests of the minority groups within its territorial borders. The discussions which were then instituted dragged on for a considerable time, but in July 1923 the Latvian representative finally gave the requisite undertaking to the League of Nations Council, and on 1 September 1923 the League assumed responsibility for the welfare of the minority groups in Latvia. The undertaking given by the Latvian Government contained a proviso to the effect that any legislation enacted for the protection of the minorities would have to conform to the constitution and could not be allowed to prejudice the requirements of Latvian sovereignty or the social needs of the majority group. On the other hand, the League of Nations Council was authorised to deal with any complaints lodged by the minorities. A minorities convention was also concluded on 11 December 1923 between the League of Nations and Lithuania. But this followed the Polish rather than the Latvian or Estonian model.

It was in the parliamentary assemblies that the minorities fought to obtain, and preserve, their rights. They had been granted political representation under the electoral laws of all three Baltic States, and consequently German, Russian, Jewish, Polish and Swedish parliamentary factions were to be found in all three Baltic capitals. Baltic German parliamentary activity was particularly strong in Latvia, where six separate political parties emerged in the late 1910s. In 1920 these six parties formed a joint committee, and from then onwards acted in concert wherever possible. Later, a seventh party joined the committee. The leading lights of the Baltic German community in Latvia at this time were Baron W. Fircks, the leader of the Conservative People's Party, and Paul Schiemann (1876–1944), the chief editor of the *Rigasche Rundschau* and leader of the Democratic Party, who headed the joint party committee from 1922 onwards. During the first ten years of Latvian independence Baltic German delegates served in various governments. The government comptroller in Ulmanis's first cabinet (1918–19) was a Baltic German, as were the Ministers of Justice and Finance in Ulmanis's second cabinet (1919) and in the 1928–9 cabinet. Between 1920 and 1934 the head of the Baltic German Educational Service had a permanent seat in the cabinet, and was consulted on all questions relating to his professional sphere. The officers commanding both the Latvian and the Estonian navies were Baltic Germans: Admiral Count Keyserling and Admiral Baron Saltza. This kind of collaboration continued until the early 1930s, when it became impossible due to the upsurge of nationalist feeling in the Baltic States.

Unlike their compatriots in Latvia, the Baltic Germans in Estonia produced only one political party, which was led from 1926 onwards by Axel de Vries, editor of the *Revaler Bote*. Baltic German interests were represented in the Estonian parliament by several delegates, chief among them Werner Hasselblatt. However, in Estonia, the minority delegates played only a limited role in the executive. In the Provisional Government of 1918 one Baltic German, one Russian and one Swede were given seats in the cabinet, but they were relieved of their posts when the People's Secretariat was established, and from then onwards all Estonian cabinet seats were held by members of the majority group. The situation in Lithuania was quite different: three Jewish and three White Russian representatives were co-opted into the *Taryba* in November 1918, and in both the Provisional Government of 1918 and all subsequent governments there were special ministers for Jewish and Russian affairs.

The number of minority delegates in the Baltic parliaments was never very great. In Estonia the Germans sent three delegates to the Constituent Assembly, while the Russians and Swedes sent one each; and in the three following parliamentary assemblies – between 1921 and 1929 – the Germans were represented by four, then three, and finally two delegates, and the Russians by one, then four, and finally three, while the Swedes were not represented at all. In the elections to the fourth Estonian parliament, which ran from 1929 to 1932, the Russians won two seats while the Germans and Swedes, who stood on a joint platform, won three. The most important Russian delegates in Estonia were A. Sorokin, P. Baranin and M. A. Kurčinskij (who lectured on the national economy at Tartu University). In Latvia the minorities were slightly better represented. Thus, at the Constituent Assembly the Germans had six delegates, the Jews had six (one of whom was the celebrated jurist Professor Mintz), and the Russians had four, while in the four following parliamentary assemblies – between 1922 and 1934 – the Germans had six, five, six and six delegates respectively, the Jews had six, five, five and three, and the Russians three, five, six and six. In Lithuania the number of Jewish delegates fluctuated – up till 1926 – between three and six, the number of Polish delegates between two and four, and the number of German delegates between one and two. In 1926, when the people of the Klaipeda/Memel territory were enfranchised, a further five (Memel-)German delegates were returned. The Russian community in Lithuania won only one parliamentary seat, in 1923.

There was a certain amount of parliamentary collaboration between the delegates of the different minority groups, and although this trend was not developed as fully as it might have been, it was not without some significance. In 1920, for example, the Baltic German, Jewish and Russian parties in Latvia set up a Minorities Committee, which opened its own information centre and formed a parliamentary faction. However, this united front did not survive very long. Then, in 1921, Schiemann persuaded the editors of the minority newspapers and magazines in all three Baltic States to send representatives to a Journalists' Conference in Kaunas. In January 1926 he organised a further conference in Riga, which was also attended by representatives of the minority groups in all three territories. However, the outcome was disappointing, for the only lasting benefit to come from this initiative was a closer liaison between the Baltic German delegates in Estonia and Latvia. What Schiemann had hoped for was the establishment of a parliamentary bloc embracing all sixteen minority delegates in the *Saeima*. He continued to pursue this conciliatory project even after the Riga Conference, but was obliged to abandon it when he realised that, for the time being at least, the differences between the various political factions within the minorities were irreconcilable. This was demonstrated later the same year when a number of left-wing Jewish, Russian and Polish delegates formed a tripartite bloc, which then supported Skujenieks' government. It was only when the Latvian Minister of Education, A. Keniņš, introduced his violently nationalistic policies that the minorities were reminded of their common interests.

In Estonia the German and Russian minorities formed an electoral alliance in 1926, which they abandoned once the elections were over. But three years later the Baltic Germans and the Swedes formed a similar alliance, from which both groups benefited and which led to the formation of a permanent German–Swedish coalition in the Estonian parliament. On occasions the Russians also joined forces with the Germans and Swedes, thus creating a tripartite bloc.

The parliamentary activities of the minority delegates were not restricted to matters of direct interest to the members of their national groups. Many of them also played an active part in the legislative processes of parliament, both on the floor of the house and in committee. The German–Swedish faction in Tallinn was very heavily involved in this kind of work, and at one point its members were sitting on no less than seven parliamentary commissions. As far as their own nationals were concerned, the Baltic German delegates sought first to oppose the agrarian reforms and subsequently to mitigate their effects. Other problems to which they devoted their energies, especially in the late 1920s and the 1930s, were those of cultural autonomy and the use of the German language in Baltic German schools.

In a manifesto published on 24 February 1918 – i.e. before the founding of the republic – the Estonian political leadership gave its assent to the principle of autonomy for minority groups. Subsequently, the constitution of 1920 condemned discrimination on grounds of nationality in Paragraph 6, and expressly authorised the minorities to set up autonomous social and cultural institutions in Paragraph 21.

The educational legislation drafted by the Estonian parliament allowed for the foundation of schools for the children of the minority groups, in which tuition would be given in the vernacular tongue of the particular group concerned, while the Estonian language would simply form a normal part of the 'curriculum.

Traditionally, Estonian education had been controlled and co-ordinated by private societies, and when the new republic was established in 1918 this tradition was continued. It was not long before a Baltic German society – *Gesellschaft Deutsche Schulhilfe* – was set up in Tallinn, and in 1920 this society was incorporated into the Union of German Societies in Estonia.

But the minorities had to wait several years before they were granted cultural autonomy. The peoples most interested in this development were the Germans and the Jews, both of whom were distributed over large areas of Estonia. Unlike the Russians in the eastern border district and the Swedes on the north-western coastal strip and the offshore islands, they had not developed as corporate and close-knit communities, and so were unable to achieve their cultural goals by taking action at local authority level.

Starting in 1921, the Baltic Germans introduced various bills in the Estonian parliament, which were designed to obtain cultural autonomy for the minorities. The last and most important of these was drafted by the Baltic German delegate Werner Hasselblatt (1890–1958), and subsequently revised by E. Maddison and O. Angelus, who held civil service posts in the Ministry of Internal Affairs. The presentation of this bill posed considerable problems, for it broke entirely new legal ground, and there were some who had misgivings on this account. Konstantin Päts made an important contribution to the bill. It was he who suggested that the composition of the new cultural authorities should be modelled on that of the existing local authorities. But the fact that Hasselblatt's bill was approved by parliament on 5 February 1925 was not due, in the first instance, to the personalities who sought to promote it. What finally tipped the scales in its favour was the Communist *putsch* of 1 December 1924, which impressed on Estonians generally the need to muster support among all sections of the community interested in the maintenance of the young republic.

The law of 5 February 1925 was a skeleton law. Under its terms all national groups in Estonia of more than 3,000 persons were entitled, if they so wished, to set themselves up as public corporations and to establish their own cultural institutions. The fact that, unlike the existing local authorities, these new cultural authorities were not based on territorial criteria was almost certainly due to the influence of the Austrian Socialists O. Bauer and K. Renner, who had been arguing ever since the turn of the century that questions affecting minority groups in multinational states should be determined by the numerical size of those groups and not, as advocated by Lenin and Stalin, by the amount of territory they occupied. Päts doubtless heard of this controversy during his early years, for H. Pantenius, who worked as a headmaster and was actively engaged in local politics in Tartu, had drawn attention to it. As for Hasselblatt, he was fully informed on this matter by Professor Laun, the Hamburg expert on international law.

The members of national groups seeking to establish their cultural authorities had to present themselves at the national land commission, where their names were entered in the national land register. Once established, these cultural authorities were entitled to promulgate decrees and raise public taxes within their own particular sphere, which embraced the building, administration and supervision of minority schools, and the foundation and administration of cultural institutions.

After Hasselblatt's bill was passed into law the Baltic Germans held elections to determine the composition of the Baltic German Cultural Council, which had its first meeting on 1 November 1925. This council then elected a six-man executive which was headed by the parliamentary delegate Harry Koch (1880–1939) from 1925 to 1932. The routine work of the council was carried out by five separate departments.

Subsequently, special managerial boards were established in the larger towns to supervise cultural developments in urban areas. As a result of the cultural autonomy granted to the Baltic German minority group, all Baltic German schools were placed under the jurisdiction of the Baltic German cultural authority in 1925. The cost of state education was borne either by the central government or by the local authorities. As soon as possible the Baltic Germans introduced a standard curriculum in all their schools, which in 1928 provided tuition for 3,456 pupils.

The Germans were the first minority group to ask for their own cultural authority. The Jews were the second. The decrees establishing the Jewish authority were promulgated in 1925, and on 6 June 1926 the Jewish Cultural Council held its first meeting in Tallinn.

These cultural authorities soon proved their worth, and the Estonian Government was able to claim, with every justification that it had found an exemplary solution to the problem of its minorities.

In 1931, just six years after his great parliamentary success with the Estonian cultural authorities bill, Hasselblatt undertook a new task in an international setting. Like Paul Schiemann, he had played a leading part in the European Nationalities Congresses (which had been inspired by another Baltic German politician, Ewald Ammende from Pärnu), and as a result he was appointed President of the Association of German National Groups in Europe, which had its headquarters in Berlin.

In Latvia the first call for Baltic German autonomy took the form of a memorandum, drafted in the spring of 1918, to the German occupation authorities. On 8 December the following year, when the Latvian National Council passed educational legislation to cater for the needs of its minorities, the non-Latvian nationalities were allowed to establish and administer their own schools. In the course of the 1920s no less than five minorities – the Russians, Germans, Jews, Poles and White Russians – availed themselves of this opportunity by setting up their own educational administrations under the auspices of the Latvian Ministry of Culture. The heads of these administrations, who were nominated by the minority factions in the Latvian parliament, were given civil servant status. The German administration was headed by Pastor Karl Keller (1868–1939), who had already been appointed Secretary of State in the Ministry of Culture on 3 December 1918 and who led the successful parliamentary campaign for German autonomy from 1919 onwards. In 1929 Keller was succeeded by his deputy Dr. Wolfgang Wachtsmuth (1876–1964). The number of German schools rose from 45 in 1919/20 to 112 in 1927/8, while the number of German schoolchildren rose from 8,192 in 1919 to 12,168 in 1923, only to drop back again to around the 11,000 mark later in the decade.

Shortly after the proclamation of the Latvian Republic, the Baltic Germans living in Latvia began to press for the establishment of German university courses. As a result, courses of further education were introduced in 1920, which led on to the founding in 1921 of the Herder Society, named after J. G. Herder, the renowned leader of the German Enlightenment, who was a pastor in Riga during the 1760s. Subsequently this society set up its own private German university – the Herder Institute – which was recognised by the Latvian Government in 1927 and given autonomous status. In 1930 the Institute acquired its own buildings, and by 1936 it had developed three faculties – Evangelical Theology, Jurisprudence and Political Science, and Philosophy – which between them employed a staff of forty-four lecturers. From 1926 onwards the Rector of the Herder Institute was Dr. W. Klumberg.

After the Estonians had granted cultural autonomy to their minority groups in February 1925, the Latvians had to make up their minds whether to emulate them. In the event, and despite the pressure brought to bear by the Jewish and German communities, the Latvian Government decided not to do so. With their Social Democratic learnings, which had already found expression in the Jewish League, the Latvian Jews were particularly conscious of the need to establish themselves as a national community. This need was also recognised – and at a very early stage – by a number of Baltic Germans, who took their lead from Paul Schiemann. Various attempts were made to extend the 1919 Act so as to enable the minority groups to set up their own cultural authorities. In 1925 a bill was drafted along these lines, but although it received the backing of the parliamentary commission appointed to deal with minority affairs, it was subsequently withdrawn because there was no hope of its receiving majority support in the full assembly. Faced with this impasse, the Baltic Germans sought to achieve their objective by establishing an unofficial Baltic German cultural authority. Thus, in 1920, a German Parents' Association was set up, which subsequently reformed the whole of the educational programme for Baltic German schools, and made up any deficit in the funds provided by the Latvian state or the local authorities. In 1923 this association merged with all the other Baltic German cultural associations in Latvia to form the Centre for Baltic German Work, which had its headquarters in Riga. Three years later this Centre introduced a system of voluntary taxation, whereby all Baltic German nationals living in Latvia were asked to contribute a regular monthly tithe of between 0·5 and 3 per cent of their income. As a result, the Baltic German community was able to amass very considerable financial resources. The last step in this gradual process of cultural and administrative centralisation was taken in 1928 when the Centre in Riga was transformed into the Baltic German National Community in Latvia. This was a completely representative body which had its own elective diet and whose business affairs were conducted by a central committee. In fact, the unofficial Baltic German National Community in Latvia, which worked in close collaboration with the Baltic German political parties in the *Saeima* (national assembly), fulfilled the same functions as the official Baltic German cultural authorities in Estonia.

Up to 1931 the Latvian Ministry of Education was run by intelligent politicians, who were sympathetic to the needs of the minority communities. But with the growth of nationalist influence in the Latvian political parties, especially the Democratic Centre, serious inroads were made on the educational rights granted to the minorities under the terms of the 1919 Act. The worst period was from 1931 to 1933, when A. Keniņš was Minister of Education. Keniņš arbitrarily revised the curriculum established for use in Baltic German schools, reduced their grants, accused the Baltic German educationalists of disloyalty to the Latvian state, and generally made life as difficult as possible for the members of this community.

But Keniņš' educational policy was so disruptive that it was eventually repudiated by a majority of Latvian politicians, and so led to the overthrow of the Skujenieks administration in February 1933.

CHAPTER IV

NEW DEVELOPMENTS IN THE 1930s

1. *The Parliamentary Crisis*

By the late 1920s it was apparent that under the Estonian (1920) and Latvian (1921) constitutions there was an inbuilt tendency for governments to change very frequently, thus frustrating any attempt at long-term planning. The average life of Estonian governments between 1919 and 1933 was eight months and twenty days.

During this period coalitions were rare, due to the fact that both Estonia and Latvia produced such a large number of political parties, all of them relatively small. Consequently, before a coalition government could be set up, at least three – and probably four or five – parties had to agree on a common policy. In the 1923 elections in Estonia, twenty-six parties put up candidates, and fourteen had members returned, whilst in the Latvian elections of 1931 there were no less than 103 candidacies, and twenty-seven political parties or groups were represented in the ensuing parliament. Of these, twelve had only one member, and only two had more than ten members.

The Estonians were not slow to recognise the implications of this problem, and in 1926 they tried to reduce the number of parties by stipulating that political organisations putting up candidates in future elections should pay a deposit, which would be forfeited is they won less than two seats. By 1929 the number of parties had been reduced to eleven, due partly to the effect of this new measure, and partly to the continuing trend towards alliances between political parties. Thus, after the Social Democrats and Independent Socialists had joined forces in 1923 to form a Socialist Workers' Party, the Peoples' Party and the Christian Peoples' Party followed suit in 1931, to be joined in the following year by both the Workers' Party and the House Owners' Party, thus creating a quadripartite alliance, which paved the way for the formation of the National Centre

Party in the following year. In 1932 the Farmers' Union and
the Settlers also united under the banner of the United Agrarian Party, an ill-fated venture which collapsed within months.
The basic tendency during this period was that the clear-cut
distinction between the right and the left, which had been the
cornerstone of Estonian politics in the early years of the republic, was progressively eroded. The Settlers moved to the
right, and the Christian People's Party to the left. Even more
important, the electoral trend in Estonia showed a steady increase in support for the bourgeois camp. Thus the Farmers'
Union, which had won 6·5 per cent of the popular vote in
1919, won 40 per cent in 1925. Moreover, the Social Democrats began to display nationalist tendencies, which by 1934
had become so marked that three of their parliamentary
delegates broke away from the party to become Marxist
socialists.

Meanwhile, the socialist share of the vote also dropped in
Lithuania: from 38·7 per cent in 1920 to 19 per cent in 1931.
There, too, the socialist camp was weakened by the defection
of small groups on the extreme left.

One of the major problems arising out of the proliferation of
the political parties in the Baltic States was the length of time
it took to form a cabinet. Estonia was particularly vulnerable
on this account: it took fifty-nine days in 1923 before a new
government could be appointed, and thirty-one days in 1926.

The weakness of the parliamentary system in the Baltic
States undermined the stability of these territories. There was
a real danger that parliamentary democracy might degenerate
into a kind of partisan dogfight. Meanwhile, the political parties
lost their ideological appeal, and by the early 1930s their
actions seemed to be dictated purely by economic or sectional
considerations. In Estonia no less than 11 per cent of the parliamentary delegates either changed their allegiance or became independent members in 1933.

The parliamentary crisis of 1933/4 was triggered by the
international economic crisis, which led, in all three Baltic
States, to a drop in exports, especially of agricultural products,
and from 1929 onwards brought great distress to the country-
dwellers, who still accounted for the major part of the population. The drop in exports was accompanied by the with-

drawal of foreign capital, and a rise in unemployment. In 1931 the crisis was aggravated still further in Estonia and Latvia by the collapse of the German banks and the devaluation of the pound sterling. By 1934 unemployment in Estonia stood at the record level of 32,000. Of course, Estonia had been hit particularly hard when Britain went off the gold standard, for the Estonian currency had lost one-third of its securities at a stroke. On 28 June, 1933 the Estonian Government was forced to devalue the kroon by 35 per cent and to emulate the Scandinavians in joining the sterling bloc.

It seemed doubtful whether Estonian parliamentary democracy – which, as we have just seen, had already been seriously weakened in the course of the 1920s – could survive this economic crisis. The demands for constitutional reforms designed to increase the power of the executive grew more insistent. The Farmers' Union had proposed a bill along these lines in 1926, and in 1929, after merging with the People's Party, it reintroduced its bill. In August 1932 this proposal was put to the people in a referendum, and was rejected by a small majority (345,000 votes to 334,000). In a second referendum held in June 1933 the majority against the proposal was much bigger (330,000 to 160,000).

In the circumstances it is hardly surprising that the *Vabadussõjalaste Liit* – the Association of Estonian Freedom Fighters – should have come to the fore at that time. This association, whose founder-members had been recruited from the veterans of the 1918–20 War of Liberation, came into being in 1929, when a number of smaller provincial societies – the first of which was established in Tallinn in 1926 – were amalgamated. In the following year the association held its first congress which, unlike later congresses, was a non-political assembly. Subsequently it launched its own magazine *Võitlus* (Struggle). The Estonian Association of Freedom Fighters was a patriotic, nationalistic association with strong anti-communist and anti-parliamentarian tendencies. It was undoubtedly modelled on a Finnish association, which came to be known as the Lapua Movement after its members held a meeting in that town in 1929 and which created a considerable furore with its anti-communist terror tactics, and with its opposition, not only to the Finnish Social Democrats, but to parliamentary democracy as such. By 1932 the Lapua Movement had become such a threat to the democratic order in Finland that it was forcibly disbanded. Its members then founded a legitimate political party, the Patriotic People's Movement (*Isänmaallinen Kansanliike*); but although it subsequently held fourteen seats in the Finnish parliament, it was no longer a force to be reckoned with.

However, the Lapua Movement continued to inspire the Estonian Association of Freedom Fighters which, after shedding a number of its non-political military members in 1932, ceased to be a veterans' association, and quickly developed fascist characteristics that found expression in anti-Marxist, anti-Liberal and anti-parliamentarian activities. After General Laidoner had failed to live up to their expectations, the Freedom Fighters turned to Major-General Andres Larka, who had been deputy Minister of War from 1918 to 1925 and had subsequently retired from public life for health reasons. But Larka was President in name only. The true driving force behind the association was Artur Sirk, an ambitious lawyer with a marked gift for demagogy. Under his guidance the Freedom Fighters were organised in companies and sections, and were issued with para-military uniforms: grey-green shirts with black-and-white arm bands bearing the insignia of the association – a hand grasping a sword and the dates '1918–1920'. In its manifesto the association called upon its members to oppose party rule, to eradicate the 'spirit of Marxism', to fight for a generous resettlement programme, and to work for the establishment of a united workers' front. In its new form the association attracted support from various sources: the unemployed, members of the lower middle class and political adventurers.

After the failure of the two referenda instigated by the Farmers' Union and the People's Party in August 1932 and June 1933 respectively with a view to increasing the power of the executive, the Freedom Fighters put forward their proposals for constitutional reform, which were presented to the electorate in a third referendum in October 1933. The result of this referendum, which was preceded by violent agitation, was 416,879 for to 156,000 against. The turn-out was unusually high: 75 per cent. Up till October 1933 Estonia had had no President of the Republic. But this office was created under the terms of the new constitution, which also authorised the transfer of the executive power from parliament to the President. The President was to be elected by popular vote for a five-year term, and his authority was to be virtually absolute. Among other things, he would be able to dissolve parliament, issue decrees, appoint and dismiss governments, and declare states of emergency.

Meanwhile, the Estonian people were growing more and more restive. The devaluation of the kroon carried out by Tõnisson, whose government held office from May to October 1933, was a necessary measure and one destined to have beneficial long-term effects. However, its immediate effect was to exacerbate the economic situation, which was already bad. Fearing civil disturbance, parliament approved the declaration of a state of emergency which made it possible to proceed against both the left- and the right-wing radical organisations, including the Freedom Fighters. At this point Tõnisson's government, which was supported by the National Centre and the Settlers, stepped down, and on 21 October, 1933 Konstantin Päts formed his fifth cabinet, which depended for its parliamentary majority on a far from reliable alliance.

On 24 January, 1934 the revised constitution passed into law, and elections were called to find a new government, and to decide who was to become the first President of the Estonian Republic. The candidates in the presidential election were Päts, General Laidoner, Rei (the Socialist leader) and General Larka (the President of the Association of Freedom Fighters). During this pre-election period the agitation of the Freedom Fighters became even more violent, and on occasions – for example, when their propaganda squads drove from town to town in convoys of lorries – they seemed to be flaunting their strength in open defiance of the executive. In the local government elections at the beginning of 1934 they won an absolute majority in the three biggest towns – Tallinn, Tartu and Narva – and there was every reason to believe that they might obtain majority support in the general election or, failing this, try to seize power by force.

Faced with this threat, Päts decided to take pre-emptive action. On 12 March, 1934 he appointed General Laidoner Commander-in-Chief of the Army with special powers to maintain law and order. The Association of Freedom Fighters was then forcibly disbanded on the grounds that it posed 'a threat to the security of the state', and its leaders were arrested. By mid-March 425 people had been detained, including a group of industrialists who had supported the association financially. A number of people who had established liaison between the Association of Estonian Freedom Fighters and similar organisations in Germany and Finland were also detained, while K. R. Pusta, the Estonian envoy to Sweden and one of the country's most senior diplomats, was recalled from Stockholm because he had been designated by the Freedom Fighters as their Foreign Minister elect. The state tried, but failed, to produce evidence of a plot to overthrow the government, and in the trials which followed the detentions only thirty-seven of the accused were found guilty. They received prison sentences of up to two years for having threatened the security of the state. Meanwhile, all political assemblies were banned, and after it had unanimously approved the emergency legislation on 16 March the Estonian parliament was prorogued. A decree promulgated on 19 March then deferred the presidential elections indefinitely. But when parliament was reconvened for a short session the following September, a number of delegates called for the revocation of the emergency legislation and the announcement of a new election timetable. Päts responded by dissolving parliament and ruling by decree with the help of a compliant cabinet headed by Kaarel Eenpalu, who acted as deputy Prime Minister and Minister of the Interior.

Although essentially similar, the political developments in Lativa at this time differed in certain respects from those in Estonia. For example, while the anti-parliamentarian forces in Estonia took their lead from Finland, their Latvian counterparts followed the example set by the Lithuanians. The Latvians started their campaign back in 1926 when a nationalist mass meeting was staged in Riga to protest against the 'demagogy of the leftists'. In the course of this mass meeting several speakers expressed their sympathy with Mussolini's political aims.

Later, the Latvian anti-parliamentarians were greatly encouraged by the parliamentary crisis in Germany. As a result, the Nationalist Association – which was a relatively insignificant right-wing party – put forward proposals for a new constitution designed to strengthen the position of the President of the Republic. Other associations and groups then advanced alternative ideas. A general debate ensued, and gradually two quite distinct patterns of criticism of the existing order began to emerge. This is an important point, for although these anti-parliamentarian factions were at one in their desire to increase the power of the President, their motivations were very different. Basically, they were a fascist camp and an anti-fascist camp. The National Revolutionary Work Force was one of the fascist groups. It called for the persecution of Communists, Socialists and Jews, and for the introduction of a planned economy. Štelmachers's Latvian National Socialist Party was also opposed to the minorities, and – despite Štelmachers's great admiration for Hitler – was anti-German to boot. Karlsons, who led the Economic Centre, was another admirer of Hitler; he dressed his youthful followers, most of them from the lower middle class, in brown shirts. A fourth fascist group was the Association of Legionnaires, which was organised along Polish lines and was composed largely of former officers. Its leader was Lieutenant-Colonel Ozols.

But of the various fascist organisations in Latvia, the one most closely aligned to the Estonian Association of Freedom Fighters was the Fire Cross (*Ugunkrusts*), which was founded in 1933 by Gustav Celmiņš, who fought as a volunteer in a Students' Company during the War of Liberation. This organisation was promptly proscribed by the Latvian Government but reappeared almost immediately under the name Thunder Cross (*Pērkonkrusts*). The members of the Thunder Cross wore grey shirts and black berets, and adopted the Nazi salute and the near-Nazi greeting of '*Cīnai sveiks*' ('*Kampf Heil*'). But although extremely nationalistic and anti-semitic, they were also anti-German. With their simplistic slogan 'Latvia for the Latvians', they glorified their national heritage, subscribed to romantic notions of the simple life, and on occasions even went so far as to call for a pure Latvian religion. However, despite its members' great love for things rural, this movement was restricted primarily to the urban areas of the country, where it gained wide support from the students. At its peak the Thunder Cross Association had a membership of almost 6,000. Its propaganda was directed partly against the minorities and partly against the democratic Latvian politicians. The minorities – especially the Germans and the Jews – were vilified for having allegedly usurped control of large areas of the Latvian economy, while the politicians were accused of corruption.

Although few Latvians were prepared to admit it, the establishment of Hitler's National Socialist regime in Germany gave a considerable boost to the Latvian fascist movement, for it encouraged the right-wing radicals in their anti-Jewish and anti-Communist activities, and reinforced their nationalist feelings, which were then vented – ironically enough – on the local Baltic German community. Moreover, when Hitler stripped the Reichstag of its powers by setting up as a dictator, he undoubtedly stoked the anti-parliamentarian fires in the Latvian Republic.

But, as I have already indicated, there was another side to this anti-parliamentarian movement. The fact of the matter was that the major political parties also felt the need for constitutional changes, not least because without such changes there was no possible way of proceeding against the right-wing radicals. The clearest warnings of the fascist threat were given by the Social Democrats. In this connection Skujenieks pointed to the example of Germany, where the Weimar constitution – on which the original Latvian constitution had been modelled – had led to the emergence of a highly dangerous situation, and he insisted that Latvia must set a new course in order to avoid a similar fate. In August 1933 Ulmanis, who had just returned from a visit to Hitler's Germany, presented reform proposals to the Latvian parliament in his capacity as leader of the Peasant League. But he failed to obtain sufficient support among the bourgeois delegates to introduce a bill effecting constitutional changes. The delegates from Latgale refused to co-operate. So too did the Social Democrats, who had been alarmed by the Socialist uprising in Austria in February 1934 and were loth to support provocative legislation. But this provocation was given in any case, for seven Communist delegates to the *Saeima* were arrested without any comparable action being taken against the members of the Thunder Cross Association. It was then that Ulmanis made his move.

Ulmanis had been asked to form a new government, and

F*

did so on 16 March, 1934. Apart from acting as Premier, he also served as Foreign Minister, while General Balodis assumed responsibility for the Ministries of War and Justice.

At the same time – i.e. on the night of 15/16 March – Ulmanis declared a state of emergency. Although he claimed to have uncovered a Communist plot to overthrow the government, he can hardly have been uninfluenced by the events of 12 March in Tallinn. At all events, he suspended parliament, banned party political activity, made a number of arrests, and proscribed the Thunder Cross Association. There was little or no resistance. And so, like the Estonians, the Latvians came to be governed by an authoritarian regime, which insisted that it had assumed absolute power in defence of democracy. On 18 May Ulmanis set up a special government committee – a sort of inner cabinet – to deal with legislation, and this new committee was eventually approved by the President of the Republic, Kviesis, on 8 June. Kviesis remained in office until the expiry of his six-year term in April 1936. He was succeeded by Ulmanis, who then combined the office of Premier with that of President of the Republic.

2. Authoritarian Democracy in Estonia and Latvia

The authoritarian regimes established by Päts and Ulmanis in March and May 1934 respectively were strengthened by subsequent legislation, and as a result both proved extremely durable. Of course, they were not by any means identical. Their constitutional structures differed, and so too did their long-term objectives.

Nonetheless, there were certain things that all three of the Baltic States had in common. For example, the reorganisation of these territories along authoritarian lines was initiated, not by an entirely new race of demagogues, but by the men who had brought them independence in 1918. All of the new leaders came from peasant stock, and all were born in the 1870s. Moreover, their governments all had the same power-base – namely, the army – and their closest advisers were senior army officers who had played leading roles in the War of Liberation. As in Finland, so too in the Baltic States, the regular armies were strengthened during the 1930s by the formation of para-military organisations, such as the Estonian *Kaitseliit* and the Latvian *Aizsargi* (both words mean 'defence league').

Päts and Ulmanis both ruled by decree, and both suspended parliament during the initial phase of their new government. The old freedoms, including the freedom of speech, were restricted, but not completely denied; and although the political parties in Estonia and Latvia were forcibly disbanded in 1935, many of their leaders continued to support the government.

As to the question of foreign influence, it is significant that as early as 16 March, 1934 General Laidoner referred to the authoritarian policies being pursued by Chancellor Dollfuss in Austria with obvious approval. Later, after Hitler had acquired absolute power in Germany following the death of Hindenburg and the elimination of his political rivals, and after Dollfuss had been assassinated, Laidoner just as obviously dissociated himself from the principle of totalitarian government. According to A. Bērziņs, the Latvian Minister for Public Affairs and the only Latvian minister to escape in 1940, Ulmanis was also opposed to totalitarian methods. On one occasion Bērziņs – who was commonly referred to by his opponents as 'the President's evil genius' – observed that neither 'Mussolini's poses nor Hitler's martial music had struck a responsive chord in Ulmanis'. This was perfectly true. Ulmanis did not give his assent to either of these dictatorial figures, even though he himself was not entirely free from the vanity to which they were so prone. For example, when he compared himself with Oliver Cromwell, he was surely striking a pose. On the face of it, such a comparison was ludicrous: where, after all, were his Ironsides? And what sort of Puritan was he?

Päts and Ulmanis both revealed an obvious liking for professional bodies, and both consciously sought to develop nationalist ideas. In Estonia a Chamber of Labour was established, which took over certain functions formerly fulfilled by the trade unions, the activities of which were restricted from 1934 onwards. All in all, fifteen such bodies were created, including a Chamber of Commerce and a Chamber of Culture. This kind of development, which ran counter to the egalitarian principles of parliamentary democracy, was carried still further in Latvia, where Ulmanis based his new administrative structures on Italian fascist models. Thus, the members of the Latvian chambers, who acted in a purely advisory capacity, were appointed by the leadership. The Latvians also set up a National Economic Council and National Cultural Council to supervise the activities of their different chambers, and it has been suggested by many observers that these two institutions were intended to pave the way for the creation of an upper house.

By restructuring the administration in this way the Latvian Government was able to develop the public sector of the economy at the expense of the private sector. Thus the Minister of Finance was given special powers to investigate all private companies and order then to go into liquidation if he considered this to be in the national interest. As a result, numerous private banks were taken over by the newly-founded Latvian Loan Bank, and there was a growing movement towards nationalisation in every branch of industry. Free competition was also restricted by the introduction of a system of special privileges for state-controlled companies.

This new economic policy had political repercussions, for the movement towards greater centralisation had a particularly adverse effect on German companies. Under Ulmanis, Latvian nationalism was no less aggressive than it had been in the heyday of the right-wing radicals and the Democratic Centre, and it was especially antagonistic to the minority communities. In practical terms, the slogan 'Latvia for the Latvians' meant that a determined attempt was made to 'latvianise' the economic, educational and cultural life of the country. It also led to a marked increase in the use of administrative methods. By comparison, Estonian nationalism was far less aggressive. What the Estonians wanted was to establish their national identity. Consequently, typical of the nationalist activities in which they engaged was a project for the propagation of Estonian Christian names and surnames, many of which had been adopted in the period following the abolition of serfdom and so frequently revealed Germanic forms.

In this respect as in many others, the application of authoritarian rule was very different in the two territories.

On 17 January 1935 Päts announced that the Estonian constitution would have to be amended because in its existing form it was conducive to the emergence of dictatorial practices. A commission was then set up, and was charged with the task of drafting a new constitution. In February 1935 a further innovation took place when the old political parties were dissolved and a new corporate body – the *Isamaaliit* or National Association – was formed to take their place. The president of this new body was the celebrated constitutional lawyer from Tartu, Professor Jüri Uluots.

In the course of 1935 it became apparent that the Estonian Freedom Fighters had formed an underground organisation and were continuing their activities unabated. In November 1934 Sirk had escaped from prison and fled to Finland via Riga and Ventspils. In his absence Sirk's place was taken by an Estonian businessman and reservist named Holland, who used the money and weapons privided by Finnish sympathisers to form a fighting force of some 600 to 800 crack troops, who were ready to move at a moment's notice. It was decided that this force was to act on 8 December, when the National Association held its congress in Tallinn. Holland proposed to arrest and try the members of the government, and to replace parliament by a People's Congress of Freedom Fighters. By issuing bogus orders to the Tallinn garrison it was hoped to stage a speedy and successful coup. Sirk was subsequently to return from Finland to take charge of the government. But thanks to his intelligence reports, the Minister for Internal affairs Eenpalu was informed of the Plot, and on 7 December twenty of the leading conspirators were picked up by the security police in a house on the outskirts of Tallinn. They were then charged before a military court with having sought to overthrow the government by force of arms, found guilty and sentenced in May 1936 to long terms of imprisonment. Sirk remained in exile until he died, probably by his own hand, in Luxembourg in 1937.

With this successful action behind him, Päts decided that the time had come to legalise his authoritarian regime by appealing to the nation. Accordingly, he held a referendum in February 1936, in which the Estonian people were asked to approve the convention of a national assembly and the drafting of a new constitution. The result was 474,218 votes in favour of the proposals and 148,834 against, i.e. a majority for Päts of 62·5 per cent. But whether Päts could truthfully claim to enjoy popular support following this referendum is doubtful. In the first place, he rejected a request submitted by four former

premiers – Tõnisson, Teemant, Piip and Kukk – who wanted
the elections to the National Assembly conducted along parliamentary lines by properly constituted political parties, insisting that the candidates must be nominated by the so-called
Social Committees, which in the majority of cases meant
either the National Association or the police. And in the second
place, when the results of the elections were published in
September 1936, it was readily apparent that the turn-out had
been very low. In the urban areas no more than 30 to 35 per
cent of the electorate had recorded their vote.

The National Assembly, which was officially opened on
18 February, 1937, ratified the draft constitution drawn up by
the government. Under the terms of this new constitution,
which took effect from 1 January, 1938, the authority vested
in the President by the 1933 Act was reduced. However, the
reduction was purely marginal, and the presidency remained
the key position in the republic. From 1938 onwards the President was elected by a special electoral chamber composed of
parliamentary delegates and local government representatives.
The new parliament consisted of two chambers: the State
Assembly (*Riigivolikogu*), whose eighty delegates were elected
by the people, and the Council of State (*Riiginõukogu*), whose
forty members were either appointed by the President or
delegated by administrative departments, professional bodies,
and ecclesiastical and secular organisations. All new legislation had to be ratified by the President. In the new parliamentary elections the system of proportional representation,
which had been used in the past, was dropped in favour of a
straight majority system, which virtually denied parliamentary representation to the minority communities as far as the
State Assembly was concerned. On the other hand, those
national communities which had set up cultural authorities
– i.e. the Germans and the Jews – were allowed to delegate
a joint representative to the Council of State. The President
was empowered to appoint and dismiss the government. The
government, for its part, was both accountable to parliament
and dependent on the President. If the government lost the
confidence of parliament, the President could either dismiss it
or dissolve parliament and order new elections. The first
parliament elected under the new constitution was opened

on 21 April, 1938, and a few days later the special chamber set up to elect the President confirmed Päts in office; thus he attained his objective. The authoritarian regime which he had arbitrarily imposed in 1934 had become the legitimate government of the republic.

There was no lack of opposition in the State Assembly. On the left were the Socialists, and in the centre was Tõnisson's Liberal Democratic Party, with its roots in the university city of Tartu, whose intellectuals were well known for their liberal attitudes (so much so that the phrase *Tartu vaim* [the Tartu spirit] was commonly used as a synonym for liberalism). Of course, the opposition groups held only seventeen of the eighty seats in the lower chamber. Nonetheless, by the end of 1938 there was a growing expectation that the state of emergency would soon be brought to an end. Nor was this idle speculation, for there were many indications that the government really did intend to restore democratic rights. Admittedly, the Päts regime drew the major part of its support from the farmers and the urban bourgeoisie. But it was also quite clearly conscious of its responsibilities towards the whole of the Estonian population.

In Latvia party political activities were also suspended during the period immediately following the 1934 coup. Thus the Peasants' League was forcibly dissolved, and the Thunder Cross Association proscribed. But unlike the Estonians and Lithuanians, the Latvians did not create a new all-embracing party organisation, from which it clearly follows that those who accuse Ulmanis of having run a one-party state are in error. On the other hand, Ulmanis, who combined the offices of Premier and President of the Republic from 1936 onwards, was certainly the most powerful politician in the country, and was able to appoint his collaborators without consultation with anybody. Moreover, a considerable number of eminent party politicians were prepared to serve under him, including Bergs of the Nationalist Association and Skujenieks of the Progressive Association, while the members of the Democratic Centre, the New Settlers and the representatives from Latgale made no attempt to oppose him. But perhaps the most remarkable testimony to Ulmanis' powers as a peacemaker was the fact that he was able to come to terms with the

Social Democrats and acquire the services of high-ranking Social Democratic officials. From the summer of 1936 onwards two of Ulmanis' associates began to play a more significant role in the affairs of the country. They were General Balodis and the new Foreign Minister Munters, who had been the guiding light in the Foreign Ministry ever since his appointment as General Secretary in 1933. The state of emergency which Ulmanis had declared in 1934 did not continue throughout the remaining life of the republic. It was brought to an end on 11 February 1938 when a new law was passed governing the security of the state.

It is quite possible that if Ulmanis had held a referendum he would have gained popular backing for his government, but he chose not to do so. Whether he ever considered the advisability of such a step is a matter for conjecture. There are those who argue that Skujeniek's resignation from the post of deputy Premier in February 1938 was linked with the question of a referendum; this argument is not unpersuasive. Moreover, General Balodis, who resigned in 1940, also seems to have pressed for a new constitution.

There was virtually no active opposition to Ulmanis, although there was certainly latent discontent among the intelligentsia, and it also looked as if the workers might eventually press their socialist demands rather more forcibly than the Social Democrats had done on their behalf. Meanwhile, however, the regime continued to absorb any right-wing radical tendencies while the Communist sympathies of the left wing remained largely inactive until the summer of 1940.

During this period both the Estonian and Latvian governments achieved a considerable measure of economic and political stability, and it is for this reason that Päts and Ulmanis are still regarded by Estonian and Latvian *émigrés* of all political persuasions as the leading representatives of their respective periods of national independence. In the economic sphere the depression of the late 1920s and early 1930s was successfully overcome during their ministries. Unemployment, which had reached record levels, was progressively reduced. In Latvia the number of industrial workers rose from 94,000 in 1935 to 120,000 in 1939. In fact, industrial expansion was so great that Polish migrant workers had to be recruited by the Latvian

Government. Latvian exports, which had reached an extremely low ebb by 1933, also showed a constant upward trend during the six years of authoritarian rule. By 1938 they were worth 454 million lats compared with 103 million in 1921. During the same period the value of Estonian exports rose from 71·6 to 211 million kroons. In 1938 two-thirds of Latvian and Estonian exports went to Britain and Germany.

See p. 120 for 1926 Coup.

3. The Lithuanian Presidential Regime

Even in the 1930s the political conditions obtaining in Lithuania were rather different from those found in Latvia or Estonia. Following the introduction of the 1928 constitution the _Tautininkai_ began to assert themselves as the dominant political party in the Republic. The leading figure in this party was Voldemaras, who was responsible for both the internal and external policies of the Latvian state up to 1929. But although Voldemaras' foreign policy initiatives appeared extremely promising, his handling of Lithuania's internal affairs caused alarm. While the activities of the traditional political parties were subjected to stringent restrictions during his ministry, a new organisation, whose very name – _Gelezinis Vilkas_ (Iron Wolf) – betrayed its fascist allegiance, was allowed to flourish. But this was hardly surprising since it was led by Voldemaras and numbered President Smetona among its honorary members.

Lith fascists

The late 1920s brought growing opposition to Voldemaras' policies in conservative ecclesiastical circles. On 6 May 1929 three Lithuanian students mounted an assassination attempt, in which Voldemaras' adjutant was mortally wounded and which had the effect of strengthening the Premier's dictatorial attitudes. Subsequently, he applied himself wholeheartedly to the expansion of the Iron Wolf Association, neglecting government business in the process. By September 1929 the situation had become completely untenable, and President Smetona asked Voldemaras to resign. When Voldemaras refused, he was arrested and sent to live in the provinces under police supervision. The new Premier was J. Tūbelis, Smetona's brother-in-law, who remained in office until 1939, thus providing a period of relatively stable internal government from 1930 to 1938, based on the authoritarian powers vested in the

President. Of course, even during this period there were tensions between the nationalist *Tautininkai* and the Catholic Church, whose clergy tended to sympathise with the Christian Democratic Party. The concordat concluded in 1927 failed to prevent this conflict, which reached its peak in 1931, when the papal nuncio Bartolini was expelled from Lithuania, and which was not resolved until 1937.

During the early 1930s the *Tautininkai* built up their party machine with the aid of the *Šauliu Sajunga* (Light Infantry Association). In its original form this association had been composed entirely of Lithuanian veterans. But from 1930 onwards it expanded by incorporating the older members of the youth organisations, thus creating an armed force comparable to Mussolini's fascist militia, much to the annoyance of the regular army. As for the members of the *Tautininkai* youth organisation (*Jaunoji Lietuva* [Young Lithuania]), they were fed a diet of blatant nationalism. Meanwhile, a new electoral law was passed, establishing an indirect voting procedure for all future presidential elections. This law, which took effect shortly before Smetona was returned to office in 1931, gave extensive powers to the *Tautininkai*, who virtually decided the outcome of the election.

The year 1932 also brought Lithuania up against the problems triggered off by the world economic crisis. The distress of the populace, especially in the rural areas, steadily grew. The establishment of normal trading relations with Germany would have brought considerable relief, not only to the Klaipeda territory but to the whole of Lithuania. But far from improving, relations between the German and Lithuanian governments became more inflexible then ever from 1933 onwards. As a result, conditions within Lithuania deteriorated rapidly, and on 8 February 1934 the government passed a law 'for the protection of the state and the nation', which imposed extremely harsh penalties for crimes against the Republic.

These measures had the effect of stiffening the resistance of all political parties opposed to the *Tautininkai*. Encouraged by recent events in Latvia and Estonia, and no doubt conscious of the transformation wrought in Germany in the previous year, a group of Voldemaras' followers, composed primarily of officers from the Kaunas garrison and members of the Iron

Wolf Association, mounted a *putsch* with a view to restoring the former Premier to power. The *putsch* failed. Voldemaras, who had been flown to Kaunas from his place of banishment in Zarasai, was arrested and sentenced to a long term of imprisonment. He was released in 1938 under the terms of an amnesty, on condition that he left the country, whereupon he settled in the South of France. Voldemaras was an intelligent and highly cultured man with considerable diplomatic gifts. But his judgement was easily distorted by subjective reactions; and this, combined with a lack of moderation and a power-lust which made him challenge Smetona, brought about his downfall.

Meanwhile, the government remained very much in control. In the summer of 1934 there were peasant revolts, especially in the southern and eastern districts, which appear to have been encouraged by both right- and left-wing agitators. But the government took radical action to halt this wave of unrest: it banned all political parties except the *Tautininkai* and confiscated their funds; and at the same time it made concessions to the rural population by agreeing to the election of a new legislative assembly. However, this was a hollow victory for the advocates of parliamentary democracy, for on 13 May 1935 – i.e. before the elections to the assembly took place – a new law was passed reserving for the government the right to nominate all electoral candidates. With the composition of the assembly a foregone conclusion, it comes as no surprise to learn that the turn-out was very low.

On 11 February, 1936 a new draft constitution was submitted to the legislative assembly, which was, of course, a purely advisory institution. This new constitution – the fifth since the founding of the Republic – vested still greater powers in the President, and authorised the establishment of professional chambers, which suggested that Smetona proposed to bring large areas of the economy under state control. State registry offices for the solemnisation of marriages, as envisaged by Slezevičius back in 1926, were also to be established under the terms of this constitution, thus separating the Lithuanian state from the Roman Catholic Church. Finally, there was a special provision repealing the minorities legislation of 1920.

In the closing years of the inter-war period the *Tautininkai* strengthened their position still further. In 1939 the youth organisations formed by the other political parties were incorporated into the offshoot of the *Tautininkai*, called Young Lithuania. The minority educational systems were progressively undermined by a series of laws from 1935 onwards; and in 1935 and 1936 new laws were passed restricting the right of assembly and the freedom of the press. Although no attempt was made to reduce the powers of the local government authorities during this period, these had, of course, already been brought under pretty strict central control by the Local Government Act of 1931.

As a result of these measures Lithuania had virtually become an authoritarian one-party state. President Smetona was addressed as *Tautos Vadas* (Leader of the People), and there were frequent celebrations designed to glorify Lithuania's past and revive the spirit of her great mediaeval period.

After the constitutionally elected Böttcher provincial government was deposed in 1932, conditions in the Klaipeda territory became particulary oppressive. The International Court of Justice in The Hague gave a ruling on the territory in 1932 but failed to achieve a lasting settlement. During the elections to the legislative assembly the indigenous inhabitants of the Klaipeda territory were in an extremely belligerent mood, for they regarded the government's decision to give several thousand Lithuanians Klaipeda citizenship as an attempt to influence the election results. The new provincial government, which was headed by Dr. Ottomar Schreiber and consisted of twenty-four Memel-German and five Lithuanian delegates, was soon faced with a difficult situation. In the spring of 1933 Pastor von Sass founded his Christian Social Workers' Community, which was in all essentials a National Socialist Party, whereupon all the other parties in the Klaipeda territory joined forces under Ernst Neumann and formed a Socialist People's Community in order to offer concerted resistance. Eventually, both of these factions came under the sway of party offices in Königsberg and Berlin, thus provoking the Lithuanian authorities, who could hardly be expected to tolerate such foreign influences and were bound to intervene sooner or later. The special legislation passed on 8 February, 1934 to maintain the security of the state was clearly designed to counter precisely this kind of development.

By then, of course, the Hitler–Pilsudski pact of January 1934 had posed an additional threat to Lithuanian and, more particularly, Klaipeda security, so in June 1934 the Governor of the territory took further action. Numerous arrests were made, von Sass's and Neumann's parties were both banned, and the directoire was deposed. On 3 April 1935, eighty-four persons, who had been charged with treason before a military court in Kaunas, were sent to prison; and shortly afterwards the Legislative Assembly in the Klaipeda territory was suspended. With this, German–Lithuanian relations reached their lowest ebb: trade was broken off, and the frontier was all but closed.

But it was not long before the Lithuanians relented. In September 1935 elections were held for a new legislative assembly, in which the ratio of Memel–German to Lithuanian delegates remained almost unaltered. The new President of the provincial government, a Memel–German named Baldschus, announced that his ultimate political objective was the restoration of full local self-government. Negotiations were then initiated between Kaunas and Berlin, and these led to a temporary *détente* and the conclusion of a new trade agreement in 1936, from which the Lithuanian farmers derived considerable benefit.

4. *Development of the Baltic German Community*

Although the minority communities in Estonia and Latvia accounted for a not inconsiderable part of the total population, they exerted little or no political influence in the inter-war years. But, of course, during the earlier period of Baltic history – from the thirteenth century to the War of Liberation – the German community had played a major political role; and in view of the historical importance of this particular minority, it is perhaps not without interest to trace its development during the period of independence.

In the course of the 1920s the Baltic Germans had to come to terms with a completely different set of socio-political conditions. This was no easy task, for it presupposed a total reorientation from their previous role as members of the indigenous upper class to their new role as members of a national minority. While 22·5 per cent of the Estonian Baltic German community worked on the land in 1922, only 15·6 per cent did so in 1930. By 1936 as many as 24 per cent of this minority group were engaged in academic pursuits. By 1930 the drift from the land, which had been the principal feature of Baltic German life in the first decade of independence, had been halted.

During the same period, of course, there had been a decline in the Baltic German population in both Latvia and Estonia. According to the official returns, the Latvian Baltic German population fell from 70,964 in 1925 to 69,815 in 1930, and the Estonian from 18,319 to 16,346. In both communities there was a drop in the birth rate (except among the agricultural settlers), both had a relatively high proportion of older people, and both had a surplus of women. In the nineteenth century, Latvians or Estonians who married Baltic Germans were almost invariably integrated into the German community. From 1918 onwards, however, this process was reversed, thus further increasing the indigenous, and depleting the Baltic German, population. The Baltic German educational system was also cut back during the 1920s. At the beginning of the period of independence there had been an almost complete network of German schools. But the number of these schools was soon reduced. In Tartu, for example, the three privately-owned German schools were merged in 1925, and thus effectively reduced to one.

The members of the rising generation of Baltic Germans also discovered that certain professions were closed to them. Civil service and army careers were particularly difficult, especially in the 1930s. Not surprisingly, many of the young Baltic German students who attended universities in Germany decided to emigrate there. Despite the inflation, and despite the economic crisis, Germany offered them far greater professional and cultural opportunities than their Baltic homeland, which had become for them a stagnant backwater.

Preoccupied as they were with the need to assert their own political and social rights, the Baltic German minorities in Latvia and Estonia were less than enthusiastic about the system of parliamentary democracy which had been adopted after the War of Liberation. It comes as no surprise to find, therefore, that the demands for a new socio-political system which were advanced in Germany during the 1920s were echoed by Baltic German politicians. Wittram has rightly observed in this connection that the political ideas emanating from Germany at that time – which were grounded in an essentially romantic and idealistic view of the world – were taken over quite indiscriminately by the Baltic Germans. Everything calculated to promote a German revival – National Socialism included – was considered beneficial. By observing the tenets of Christianity in private and public life, and by insisting on the sanctity of their national community, the Baltic Germans sought to overcome the adversities to which they had been exposed.

A conservative and Christian form of the new revival movement was developed in the esoteric and élitist circles of the Baltic Fraternity, an association founded in Germany by Otto von Kursell, whose members sought to preserve the old feudal ideas of the Teutonic Order. There was also a Liberal Democratic trend, which was represented by the *Volksnationale Vereinigung*, an association founded in Tallinn in 1934 by Siegmund Klau, and the Baltic National Party, a Latvian association founded in Riga in 1933 by Helmuth Stegman. And, of course, there was a fascist trend, which was represented by a number of groups that had first come to the fore in 1932 and whose ideas were based on National Socialist ideology. Incidentally, in Latvia and Estonia the groups most strongly influenced by the Nazis accepted one another as natural allies and called themselves '*Die Bewegung*' (The Movement).

Despite their common interests, the Latvian and Estonian groups nonetheless developed different characteristics, due to the different socio-political conditions in which they found themselves. In Latvia the National Socialist movement was headed by Erhard Kroeger (born 1905), and in Estonia by Viktor von zur Mühlen (1879–1950), who had served as a captain with the tsarist cavalry and who already proved his loyalty to the Estonian state in the War of Liberation in 1918. In November 1933 von zur Mühlen tried to take over the Baltic German party leadership in Tallinn, and to this end openly expressed his solidarity with the Estonian Freedom Fighters. This was a bold but costly move. There was an immediate public outcry, the Freedom Fighters were forced to dissociate themselves from von zur Mühlen, and the government acted against both his movement and the Baltic Fraternity, which was also suspected of disloyalty. A number of people were banished from the capital, while others were arrested and brought to trial in October and November 1934, when they received minimal terms of imprisonment.

Meanwhile, in January 1934 a few Baltic Germans had been arrested in Latvia and accused of maintaining subversive contacts with Königsberg. In Latvia the National Socialist movement had also been inspired by Hitler's accession to make a bid for the political leadership of the Baltic German community. But although Paul Schiemann was forced to relinquish his post as editor of the *Rigasche Rundschau* and W. von Rüdiger (1874–1960) had to step down as President of the German National Community, it was not until 1938–9 that the Latvian movement was able to achieve its objective.

In both Latvia and Estonia the movement concentrated on community work. In other words, it tried to promote a sense of solidarity and muster active support, both in the main body of the Baltic German minority and also in peripheral groups such as the small settlers, most of whom had come to the Baltic region in the early years of the twentieth century. The neighbourhood organisation set up in Riga in 1933 was subsequently expanded to provide much more intensive cultural and social services after the Transylvanian pattern; efforts were made to revive Baltic German craftsmanship, which had fallen into a decline at the turn of the century; and the Baltic German youth organisations opened special camps for young people in the countryside, where they performed voluntary work on German farms and residual estates.

In view of the growing importance of the National Socialist element in the Baltic German community one might have expected the relations between this minority and the Latvian and Estonian governments to have improved in 1934, when Päts and Ulmanis established their authoritarian regimes. In fact, they deteriorated, especially in Latvia, where the government exploited the state of emergency in order to keep its minorities under strict surveillance. Back in 1931, when Keniņš became the Latvian Minister of Education, a determined attempt had been made to undermine minority rights in the educational sphere with a view to 'latvianising' the minority schools. In 1934 this process was carried one step further under the terms of the Education Act of 18 July, which enabled the Latvian Government to bring the Baltic German educational authority under its control. From then onwards the Baltic German official attached to the Latvian Ministry of Education acted in a purely advisory capacity. Meanwhile, the special educational authority responsible for the administration of Baltic German schools in Estonia was disbanded, and despite the cultural autonomy granted to the Baltic German community its powers were transferred to the Estonian Minister of Education. Legislation was also introduced in both Latvia and Estonia governing the nationality of the children of mixed marriages. Under its terms such children in Latvia were registered as Latvians, while in Estonia they took the nationality of their fathers. The net result in both countries was to reduce the number of Baltic German schoolchildren and consequently the number of Baltic German schools.

In 1934–5 special language laws were passed in both Latvia and Estonia prohibiting the use of German place-names on street signs and public notice boards. The Latvian law also stipulated that the names in passports and on identity cards had to be written in Latvian; the original German spelling could be added in parentheses. No new measures were taken against the minorities in the ecclesiastical sphere, for this had already been dealt with by the Lavian and Estonian governments prior to 1934. The Estonians expropriated Tallinn Cathedral in 1927, while the Latvians did the same to the Church of St. James, Riga, in 1923 and Riga Cathedral in 1931. The Latvian Archbishop Irbe protested against this intrusion into the religious life of the Baltic German communities, but to no avail. A number of Russian Orthodox churches were also taken over by the state.

The churches were not the only Baltic German institutions to suffer from the centralisation policy pursued by the Latvian Government. Various commercial firms, factories and banks were forced out of business as a direct result of this development. In the spring of 1935, for example, the Baltic German agricultural associations were closed down and had their funds confiscated, following the creation of a Latvian Chamber of

Agriculture. In the autumn and summer of the same year the Baltic German banks were nationalised, as were the archives and exhibits owned by the Baltic German associations and museums. Finally, at the end of 1935, the medieval Baltic German guilds were closed and their property, which included numerous historic buildings and sites, was taken over by the state. This measure, which was effected under the terms of the so-called New Year Laws, was bitterly resented.

With the suspension of parliamentary activity, the Baltic German political parties and politicians were no longer able to represent the interests of their community. In Latvia this responsibility passed to the praesidium of the Baltic German National Association. In Estonia the situation was somewhat easier, for there Baron Wilhelm Wrangell, one of the leading members of the Baltic German community, was invited to join the Council of State, i.e. the Estonian upper house, as the joint representative of the Baltic German and Jewish cultural autonomies following the introduction of the new constitution in 1937.

The fact that the Latvian and Estonian Baltic German communities followed different paths of development was due only in part to the difference between the socio-political conditions in which they found themselves, but also to some extent to the way in which they reacted to those conditions. In Estonia, where the centralisation measures were less stringent than in Latvia, the Baltic Germans were, not unnaturally, more willing to co-operate with the government. On 26 January 1934 the Baltic German delegate Baron Carl Schilling – who, like Baron Wrangell, had the ear of President Päts – gave a speech in Tallinn to the local Baltic German party association in which he appealed to all Baltic Germans to remain loyal to the Estonian state and defend it against its enemies. This appeal reflected the official policy of the Baltic German leadership. But four years later, on 7 October 1938, Baron Wrangell, who was President of the Baltic German cultural administration from 1933 to 1938, informed the German envoy in Tallinn that he was very much afraid that the Baltic German youth, who had been influenced by the Nazis, might disregard Estonian neutrality if war should break out. This assessment of Wrangell's was prompted by the development of the Nazi movement in Estonia. In May 1935 a radical faction had broken away from the main body of the movement and adopted the extremist line already being pursued by the whole of the Latvian movement. In the ensuing struggle for power it soon became apparent that the new militant faction was a force to be reckoned with, and when it rejoined the movement in May 1939, there was every reason to fear that it would soon come to dominate it. But despite the threat posed by the movement, the political leadership of the Baltic German community – which in 1938–9 was headed by Hellmuth Weiss, a library director and the last president of the Baltic German cultural administration – managed to maintain its independent status. This was not easy, for the community was dependent on the German Government for the financing of its educational and cultural programme, which meant that Berlin was able to bring pressure to bear. Needless to say, the German Nazi Party regarded the Baltic movement as its chosen instrument, and gradually tried to eliminate the official leadership of the Baltic German community.

Of course, Hitler's political design for the Baltic area was to be revealed, step by step, in the late 1930s.

5. The International Status of the Baltic States from 1930 onwards

Towards the end of the 1920s the Baltic States were obliged to revise their foreign policies, not for internal or local reasons but because international pressures were being brought to bear on them. After first rejecting the peace pact, which was initiated by the American Secretary of State Kellogg and the French Foreign Minister Briand, and signed by various European states in August 1927, the Soviet Union came to regard it as a possible basis for the creation of an extended system of alliances in Eastern Europe that would provide an effective counter to the Western Locarno system and would also serve to frustrate Polish attempts to create a new Eastern bloc centred on Warsaw. The man responsible for this change of course was Chicherin's deputy Maxim Litvinov, who had taken charge of foreign affairs when the Commissar was taken ill.

At first the Russians approached only the Lithuanians and Poles, but subsequently, at the request of the Polish Government, they also invited the Estonians and Latvians to take part in talks, which led eventually to the conclusion of the Litvinov protocol. The signatories to this agreement, which was reached in Moscow on 9 February 1929, were the three Baltic States, Poland, Rumania and the Soviet Union. The special relationship between the Soviet Union and Lithuania found tangible expression in the appointment of V. A. Antonov-Ovseënko, one of the early Bolsheviks and a man of great eminence in the Communist world, as the Soviet envoy to Kaunas.

To some extent, of course, this Soviet initiative was prompted by Moscow's desire to secure its western front so as to be free to deal with any threat to its Far Eastern frontier from the Japanese. But it also had the effect of establishing a new system of alliances, which embraced all the states on Russia's western borders, and gave a fresh impetus to the development of Soviet–Baltic relations. Thus on 17 May 1927 the Soviet Union signed a trade agreement with Estonia similar to that concluded with Latvia in 1927.

What had persuaded the Baltic States to lay aside the reticence which had characterised their attitude to the Soviet Union until well into the second half of the 1920s? Clearly, they felt that the political situation was less dangerous in 1929 than it had been two years before. The Kellogg pact had created what appeared to be a more reliable and secure framework, within which it seemed reasonable to enter into closer agreements with their great eastern neighbour. Nobody appears to have realised at that time that, sooner or later, this new eastern pact was likely to be dominated by Moscow, in which case the weaker members would undoubtedly become subservient to Bolshevik interests.

It is possible that the Estonians – who had always been particularly suspicious of Soviet intentions – had sensed this danger, for while negotiating their part in the new alliance, they also strengthened their cultural bonds with Finland and the Scandinavian countries. Finno–Estonian relations were, of course, already extremely close, due to the linguistic and ethnic links between these two peoples. But in the late 1920s this traditional affinity with the Nordic region was further reinforced when the Swedes launched a propaganda campaign in Estonia to promote the Swedish way of life by invoking memories of the 'good old days of Swedish rule'. Premier Tõnisson's visit to Stockholm in 1928 and King Gustav V's return visit to Tallinn in 1929 were both designed to improve relations between Sweden and Estonia. So too were the presence of the Swedish Crown Prince at the 300th anniversary of the University of Tartu, which had been founded by Gustavus Adolphus in 1632, and the erection of a public monument in 1936 commemorating Charles XII's victory at the Battle of Narva. Meanwhile, in October 1929, an article by W. Hasselblatt appeared in the *Baltische Monatsschrift* under the title 'Baltic Policy', which appealed to the Swedish Government to represent the interests of the Baltic States *vis-à-vis* the western powers and to press for the consolidation of the Baltic area into a power bloc. Hasselblatt argued that if the Soviets were to launch a new offensive, the Baltic territories might well be conquered, and their peoples displaced by Soviet settlers. Like the Swedish geographer, R. Essén, he also advocated friendly relations with Germany. However, the Swedish Government did not respond to Hasselblatt's appeal and was decidedly sceptical about any initiatives that might impinge on Sweden's neutral status. Thus, when the Swedish Riksdag delegate Lindhagen advocated the formation of a Scandinavian–Baltic bloc (which, unlike Hasselblatt's bloc, would have included Poland), his proposal was widely acclaimed in the Baltic States but received little support in Sweden. Basically, the Swedes were not prepared to enter into political commitments towards the Baltic peoples. They valued their neutrality far too highly to put it at risk in this way.

Thus in political terms there was clearly no substance whatever in the Soviet charge that ever since 1929 there had been a concerted attempt to set up an anti-Soviet northern bloc. On the other hand, there were definite indications that the Comintern and the Red Army were taking a keen interest in the internal affairs of the Baltic States. In 1930 an illegal Communist organisation was discovered in Estonia, and the Estonian Government was forced to protest about the violation of its air space by Soviet reconnaissance planes. There was no need to remind the Baltic peoples of the need to safeguard their frontiers; the Soviet threat was readily apparent.

Towards the end of 1931 the Soviet Union decided that the time had come to establish still closer relations with the East European states. Litvinov – who by then had replaced Chicherin as People's Commissar for External Affairs – first approached Poland and Finland, and eventually concluded non-aggression pacts with these two states on 22 July and 25 July 1932 respectively. Meanwhile, an approach had also been made to Latvia and Estonia, and on 5 February 1932 Skujenieks concluded a similar pact on behalf of the Latvian people. In Estonia the government crisis which led to Päts' temporary removal from the premiership delayed matters, but on 4 May 1932 the incoming premier, Teemant, also gave his approval. All four pacts were to run for a three-year period. As originally drafted, they were admittedly imperfect instruments, for they failed to spell out what was meant by the concept of non-aggression. However, this defect was made good by the London Convention of 3 July 1933.

What the Baltic States gained from their non-aggression pacts was confirmation of the western borders established for the Soviet Union in the peace treaties of 1920. What the Soviet Union gained was greater stability. Thus, on 23 February 1933, Molotov was able to report to the Central Executive Committee in Moscow that the international position of the Soviet Union was very much stronger that it had ever been before. This was perfectly true. Between them, these four pacts and the Soviet–Lithuanian pact of 1926 had enabled the Soviet Union to establish a system of alliances embracing the whole of Eastern Europe.

In concluding the non-aggression pacts of 1932 the Kremlin was pursuing both a general and a particular objective. In general terms, these pacts were meant to prove to the world at large that the Soviet Union was intent on peaceful policies. They paved the way for the treaty with France, which led on to a *rapprochement* with the other western powers and to Soviet membership of the League of Nations. France had previously pursued an anti-Bolshevik policy in the east, based on the maintenance of a *cordon sanitaire* in which Poland had been the vital link. But with the conclusion of the Franco–Soviet treaty this anti-Bolshevik policy was abandoned, and from then onwards Moscow played an important part in French plans for Western Europe. Meanwhile the Kremlin had also been intent on disproving the Polish contention that the Soviet Union had aggressive intentions towards the Border States. The principal question here was whether the governments of the Baltic States could be persuaded to believe that in the new era of 'socialism' the Bolsheviks had really abjured their original goal of world revolution, or whether, despite its peaceful overtures, the Kremlin was still determined to achieve that gaol.

Although the need to establish a *rapprochement* with the western powers and the desire for friendlier relations with the Border States were important factors, the principal motivation was undoubtedly provided by the changes then taking place in Germany. During the 1920s and the beginning of the 1930s the Soviets had often supported the Germans in their attempts to throw off the restrictions imposed on them by the Treaty of Versailles. The treaties of Rapallo and Berlin had stabilised Soviet–German relations in the same way as the Locarno Pact had stabilised Franco–German relations. If the Germans had attempted to assert their influence in the Baltic area prior to 1932, Moscow would doubtless have regarded such a development as a welcome counter to the activities of the western powers. At that time, the friction between the Germans and the Poles precluded any possibility of their forming an anti-Soviet front; and, of course, Soviet–German trade was improving rapidly. But when the Nazis emerged as the dominant force in German politics the situation was very different. The internal changes wrought in Germany in 1932, the authoritarian course pursued by von Papen's cabinet and, finally, the accession of Hitler in 1933 persuaded the Soviets that Germany would soon adopt a more belligerent eastern policy. Thus the territories of Eastern and Central Europe acquired a new significance in terms of international politics. From being buffer states for the western powers, they gradually became a political arena in which the Germans and Russians vied with one another for supremacy. Considered in this light, the non-aggression pacts concluded by the Kremlin in 1932 appear as an attempt to test the ground for a possible Soviet take-over, thus pre-empting any subsequent initiative by Hitler.

On the face of it, it seems most unlikely that in 1933 Hitler harboured any aggressive intentions towards Poland or the Baltic States. After all, he had then yet to establish his New Order in Germany. It was only after successfully annexing Austria and Czechoslovakia that Hitler was able to evolve a detailed eastern policy. Of course, the people of Eastern Europe knew the nature of the National Socialist programme, and so, understandably, a wave of apprehension swept through the Border States immediately after Hitler's coming to power. Some Baltic politicians anticipated the event. The former Latvian Foreign Minister Cielēns, for example, called for the creation of a Latvian–Polish–Soviet bloc in 1932. Not many were prepared to advocate such extreme measures, but subsequently alternative ideas were put forward in the Estonian press, including suggestions for a *rapprochement* with Poland, and for the adoption of neutral status along Swiss lines with guarantees from the great powers. In the end, a sense of deep insecurity set in with the realisation that the Baltic States were in danger of being crushed by their two great totalitarian neighbours.

At the end of 1933 Litinov considered that the time had come to exploit this insecurity. He persuaded Poland to join with the Soviet Union in undertaking to guarantee the frontiers of the Baltic States and Finland, and in December 1933 an offer was made along these lines to the governments concerned. At the same time, Litvinov impressed on the Central Executive Committee the danger to the Soviet Union of German aggression in the Border States area. Finland was the first to reject the Soviet–Polish offer, on the grounds that her borders were already adequately guaranteed under the terms of the Soviet–Finnish non-aggression pact of July 1932. As for the Baltic States, they made no attempt to conceal their mistrust, and deliberately slowed down the discussions, with the result that British newspapers got wind of the plan and leaked the story. The Soviet Union was then obliged to issue a denial and drop the whole project.

One of the cornerstones of the *pax Sovietica* of 1932–4 was the hostility which marked Polish–German relations. This was confidently regarded as one of the fixed points in an otherwise fluid situation, and for this reason the agreement reached by Hitler and Pilsudski on 2 January 1934 must have come as an even greater blow to the Soviet Union than the election of the German National Socialist Government in the previous year. The Hitler–Pilsudski pact destroyed the whole basis of Soviet foreign policy in the Baltic area and impressed on the Kremlin the need to take new initiatives urgently. It was by no means unintelligent of the Polish Government to send Foreign Minister Beck to Moscow immediately following the conclusion of the agreement with Hitler in order to extend the Soviet–Polish non-aggression pact and arrange for an exchange of ambassadors to replace the existing diplomatic missions. But Soviet fears were not to be allayed by soothing gestures. Thus the Soviet Government decided to seize the bull by the horns. On 28 March 1934 a note was handed to the German Government in Berlin containing proposals for a protocol to be signed by both Germany and the Soviet Union that would guarantee the independence of the three Baltic States. Without waiting for a reply, the Soviet Union extended its non-aggression pacts with the Baltic States until 31 December 1945.

On 14 April Hitler rejected the Soviet proposals on the grounds that there was no call for such a guarantee; hence yet another attempt to decide the fate of the Baltic States behind their backs was frustrated. Following this rebuff, the Kremlin looked around for some other means of safeguarding Soviet interests in the new situation created by the Hilter–Pilsudski agreement. An opportunity was provided by the French Foreign Minister Barthou, who had worked out a scheme for an East European pact, which the Kremlin hoped to exploit in much the same way as it had exploited the Kellogg Pact in 1929.

Basically, Barthou's plan called for the creation of a treaty system for Eastern Europe corresponding more or less to the Western Locarno system. By persuading Germany and the Soviet Union, Poland, Czechoslovakia and the Baltic States to conclude a general agreement, he hoped to prevent conflict between these states. France was prepared to guarantee such an agreement. After a fruitless visit to Warsaw Barthou went to Prague, where he had a more favourable reception. But his first real success came on 29 May 1934, when Litvinov pledged the support of the Soviet Union for the proposed general treaty system, which would, of course, have engulfed and so effectively undermined the bilateral German–Polish pact. With Moscow having come out in favour of Barthou's scheme, it was up to the Baltic States to make a move on their own. After visiting Warsaw in the spring, the Estonian Foreign Minister J. Seljamaa – who, as a former envoy to Moscow, was well versed in Soviet affairs, and was reputed to be vaguely sympathetic to the Soviet cause – went to Moscow in June 1934. In a speech which he delivered at the brilliant reception held in the Kremlin in Seljamaa's honour, Litvinov dwelled at length on the untroubled relations enjoyed by Estonia and the Soviet Union over a fourteen-year period. Subsequently, Seljamaa discussed the treaty proposals with the Latvian envoy in Moscow, A. Bīlmanis, and suggested certain modifications to the text of the Russian draft. It would appear that Litvinov was not unduly concerned on this account for, according to the American Ambassador Bullitt, he regarded his talks with Seljamaa as completely successful. Shortly afterwards the Lithuanian Foreign Minister, S. Lozoraitis, appeared in Moscow.

While the Soviets played host to the foreign ministers of Estonia and Lithuania, the Polish Foreign Minister Beck visited the Baltic States to assess the political climate and determine the attitude of the various Baltic governments to Polish policies. In Riga Beck's reception was decidedly cool and, although he fared rather better in Tallinn, by and large his tour of inspection was a disaster, for it showed that Polish influence in the Baltic area was virtually non-existent. By then Estonia and Latvia had established much closer links with Lithuania, whose relations with Poland were still unsettled, thus creating an entirely new situation in eastern Europe, which was not conducive to the revival of the kind of quadripartite bloc that had been a feature of the 1920s.

In 1934 the only relevant question was whether Litvinov's initiatives would actually acquire for the Soviet Union the military and political supremacy to which Poland had vainly aspired. The Baltic States adopted an extremely cautious attitude to the Soviet proposals for an eastern Locarno pact, refusing to commit themselves until they discovered how Germany and Poland had reacted. Then on 8 September 1934 the German Government announced that it was unable to participate in the Soviet pact because under its terms Germany might have been embroiled, against her will, in conflicts between other member-states. Berlin in fact regarded Litvinov's proposals as an anti-German plot pure and simple. Subsequently, Poland also declined on the grounds that she had already concluded pacts with both the Soviet Union (1932) and Germany (1934). Warsaw feared that if the treaty conditions were ever invoked, Poland might well find foreign troops marching through her territory. A little later the Baltic States were to entertain similar fears.

The major difference between the Franco–Soviet proposals for a new eastern pact and the bilateral pacts of 1932 was that the principle of neutrality was replaced by one of mutual aid, including military intervention if necessary. Not surprisingly, there were many who regarded this new commitment as a threat to peace rather than a safeguard.

When Barthou was assassinated in Marseilles in 1934 he was succeeded by Laval, who continued to work for the conclusion of an eastern pact. On 5 December 1934 the French and Soviet governments signed a protocol in Geneva, in which both countries undertook to guarantee both the Locarno Pact and the proposed eastern pact. But by then the Baltic States were even more concerned over the growing power of Hitler's Germany, and were loth to give offence in Berlin, where a decision to participate in the new pact might well have been construed as an unfriendly act. Moreover, participation would also have meant abandoning the policy of strict neutrality which Baltic politicians had come to regard as an absolute prerequisite of survival. Consequently, the commentaries in the Latvian and Estonian press in February and March 1935, which were based on government hand-outs, were more devious than ever. Ulmanis and Seljamaa could hardly be blamed for adopting such a cautious approach, for by then Germany had openly declared her intention to re-arm.

After the British representatives, Sir John Simon and Anthony Eden, had visited Berlin, Warsaw and Prague in the spring of 1935 it became quite clear that Germany and Poland were not prepared to join the proposed eastern pact under any circumstances. Litvinov then tried a new tack.

On 6 April his representatives asked the three Baltic governments in Tallinn, Riga and Kaunas whether they would be willing to conclude addtional bilateral agreements with the Soviet Union instead of a general eastern pact. He received his answer on 6 May, when a conference of Baltic foreign ministers was held in Kaunas. The communiqué issued by the conference stated that there was no need for such special agreements, and recommended that the Baltic States should pursue a policy of strict neutrality, and refuse to join any power group. It is possible that this final rejection of the Barthou–Litvinov initiative was prompted by Polish pressures. But even without such pressures there was good reason to avoid entering into an agreement with the Soviet Union involving mutual aid.

On 18 September 1934 the Soviet Union became a member of the League of Nations, and in May 1935 concluded treaties with France and Czechoslovakia, thus greatly strengthening its own position and making it still less likely that the Baltic States would decide to join the Franco–Soviet defensive system. And when the Baltic foreign ministers met again in May 1936 to consider whether their governments should follow the example set by Czechoslovakia in the previous year, they decided that such a course was far too dangerous, since it was bound to antagonise Germany and Poland.

At the same time, the Baltic States were equally loth to enter into binding agreements with Germany, although they certainly wanted to maintain friendly relations. The Baltic press, admittedly, was inclined to express its opposition to the Third Reich in no uncertain terms, but the governments of these three territories had adopted a neutral policy and were determined to remain on a friendly footing with both Germany and Russia at all costs. It was an eminently reasonable policy. But whether, in view of the geographical position of the Baltic States, it could be maintained for any length of time was another matter.

6. The Baltic Entente

The close contact established by the Estonian and Latvian governments over the Litvinov proposals led to a revival of interest in the project for the creation of a joint commission to co-ordinate foreign policy decisions. This project, which had first been mooted following the declaration of independence, was dropped after the conclusion of the Latvian–Estonian alliance in 1923. In view of the mounting threat from the Soviet Union and Nazi Germany, its revival was of course a logical step.

A further threat to the security of the Baltic States was represented by the Hitler–Pilsudski pact of 26 January 1934, which repaired German–Polish relations and so created a completely new situation in the Baltic area. The Lithuanian left-wing newspaper *Lietuvos Žinios* reacted violently to this development, declaring that Germany had postponed her onslaught on Poland for ten years in order to invade the Baltic States and use them as a springboard for an attack on the Soviet Union, and although this alarmist attitude was not shared by the government departments in Tallinn and Riga, they were sufficiently disturbed by the changes that had taken place to opt for much closer collaboration over foreign affairs. Accordingly, they concluded a bilateral treaty on 17 February 1934, which constituted both a renewal and an extension of the Latvian–Estonian defensive alliance of 1 November 1923. Under the terms of this new treaty they undertook to send joint delegates to represent their interests at all international conferences; they also agreed to hold regular talks at foreign minister level, and to set up a mixed commission to co-ordinate their legislative, political and economic affairs. Finally, Latvia and Estonia left the door open for other states to join them if they so wished.

In making this last resolution they were, of course, thinking primarily of Lithuania. In 1923 the Lithuanian Government had remained aloof; in 1934 it opted for participation. On 25 April Kaunas enquired officially in Tallinn and Riga whether Lithuania might join the new community and was invited to take part in discussions to this end. These tripartite discussions were held up for several months, due partly to the ramifications of the Lithuanian officers' *coup* in the summer of 1934, and partly to the fact that in both Tallinn and Riga the authorities suddenly realised that they must first take steps to ensure they were not drawn into disputes with Germany or

Poland over the Klaipeda and Vilnius questions. But once these matters had been dealt with, negotiations quickly got under way, and agreement was reached in the autumn. As a result, the foreign ministers of the three Baltic States – Julius Seljamaa, Vilhelms Munters and Stasys Lozoraitis – met in Geneva on 12 September 1934 and signed a consultative treaty which came to be known as the Baltic entente.

This treaty provided for collaboration in foreign affairs, for mutual diplomatic support in all international questions, and for the convention of periodic conferences at foreign minister level. A special clause excluded both the Vilnius and Klaipeda questions from the treaty, which was to run for a period of ten years.

The first pan-Baltic foreign ministers' conference was held in September 1934, immediately following the signing ceremony in Geneva. In 1935 a special bureau was set up to evolve ways and means of strengthening the alliance. It was concerned primarily with the planning of joint cultural and economic projects and the convention of congresses and conferences. A trilingual periodical – the *Baltic Review* – was to be published. But the first issue of this publication, which was based on a similar review dating from 1918–19, did not appear until February 1940.

From December 1934 onwards the foreign ministerial conferences were held at regular intervals, and as a result the three Baltic States were able to evolve a more or less unified foreign policy. International recognition of this new bloc came in October 1936 when Latvia was asked to represent the Baltic States in Geneva as a non-permanent member of the League of Nations Council. Prior to this, in April 1936, Voroshilov invited the chiefs of the general staff of the Latvian, Lithuanian and Estonian armies to attend the May Day Parade in Moscow, which meant that the Soviet Union was also prepared to accept the reality of the Baltic entente.

This constituted a new but by no means unintelligent departure on the part of the Kremlin, whose principal preoccupation at that time was with the growing power of Germany. Prior to the establishment of the Nazi regime, alliances between the Border States were regarded by Moscow as a direct threat to the Soviet Union, but from 1933 onwards the Kremlin welcomed them as a first line of defence against Hitler. Thus, despite the emergence of authoritarian governments in Estonia and Latvia in March and May 1934 – a development that was represented in Moscow as a victory for the forces of fascism – the Soviets sought to use the Baltic entente as a means of opposing the German fascists. According to K. Tofer, the Estonian envoy to Moscow, they also welcomed it because it provided them with an opportunity of extending their influence to Tallinn via their contacts in Kaunas and Riga.

In the summer of 1936 both the Estonian and the Latvian foreign ministers were replaced. In Tallinn, Seljamaa stood down in favour of Dr. F. Akel, who had already served as foreign minister and premier in 1923 and whose pro-Scandinavian bias was viewed with distaste in Moscow. Meanwhile, Vilhelms Munters, the long-standing general secretary of the Latvian Foreign Ministry, assumed full responsibility for foreign affairs in Riga. Munters (1898–1967), who had been brought into the Foreign Ministry in 1920 on the recommendation of his school friend Meierovics, was a man of high intelligence but somewhat unstable character. He had a certain amount of influence on Ulmanis, and his phenomenal powers as a linguist stood him in good stead both at foreign conferences and in his dealings with foreign diplomats.

But with the passage of time it became apparent that the high hopes placed in the Baltic entente were doomed to disappointment. Economically, it was undermined by the predominantly agrarian structure of all three member-states. Estonia and Latvia had admittedly achieved a considerable degree of success in the development of their native industries. But unfortunately, they found themselves in competition with one another in the export market, and when the so-called Baltic Clause which had regulated Latvian–Estonian trade was scrapped as a result of the Finno–Estonian trade agreement of 1937, relations between Tallinn and Riga became decidedly strained. From then onwards there was no further mention of the customs union that had been envisaged in the early days of the entente.

Although it had been hoped that the political *rapprochement* between the three Baltic States would lead to closer cultural ties, the results were disappointing. The Estonians, who were essentially a level-headed people, did not take kindly to the chauvinism engendered in Latvia by the Ulmanis regime. Not that Päts and his colleagues were averse to drumming up nationalist fervour; but on the other hand they did not hesitate to eliminate the Freedom Fighters when it became apparent that this radical right-wing association posed a threat to state security. The Estonians always retained a certain capacity for self-criticism which the Latvians, who were much more volatile and easily swayed by their emotions, seldom displayed. The romanticised accounts of early Latvian history published in Riga were not taken at all seriously in Tallinn, much to the annoyance of Latvian historians. And when O. Loorits, the Professor of Folklore at the University of Tartu, was expelled from Latvia for publishing 'false' accounts of the relationship between the Latvians and their Livonian kinsfolk on the occasion of the Congress of Baltic Historians, an extremely lavish affair staged at Riga in 1937, a great deal of bad blood was caused in Estonia, especially at Tartu, which was the intellectual and cultural centre of the country. Not surprisingly, the plan for a joint Academy of Sciences, which had been mooted from time to time, was quietly dropped after this debacle. One of the major difficulties inhibiting the development of closer cultural bonds was caused by the language barrier. Various proposals were put forward with a view to resolving this problem. One group advocated the use of French or English as a common language, but although this proposal received considerable support from abroad, it made little headway because neither the Estonians nor the Latvians had any knowledge of either language. Russian was much less alien but was ruled out by political considerations. There were also objections to the use of German, especially among the older people who remembered the period of German hegemony. But their resentment was not always shared by the members of the younger generation, who frequently resorted to German for the simple reason that it provided them with an effective means of communication.

Finding that they were unable to establish a close relationship with the Latvians, the Estonians began to renew their old links with Poland. Estonian politicians visited Warsaw and

Polish politicians visited Tallinn, while Päts suddenly found it necessary to take the cure in Polish spas. Cultural relations between the two countries were also intensified. Meanwhile, relations between the three Baltic States steadily deteriorated. In May 1936, after the publication of a particularly colourless communiqué at the end of the fourth Baltic Conference in Tallinn, General Laidoner gave a lecture to the Polish–Estonian Society in which he made no attempt to conceal his scepticism regarding the Baltic entente. His comments provide a pointer to the mood of the Estonian officer corps at that time.

The friendly relations cultivated with Poland by the Estonian Government were particularly resented in Lithuania, for the Estonian press was not averse to recommending solutions for the Vilnius problem that were more or less in line with Polish policy. The Polish press was also very free with its advice, and on a number of occasions referred to the Baltic entente as one of the less positive aspects of the international situation. And so, once again, it became apparent that the problems which Lozoraitis had failed to solve at his meeting with the Polish Foreign Minister Beck at Geneva in 1935 still imposed a considerable burden on the Baltic entente.

Meanwhile, the Latvian Foreign Minister Munters was trying hard to persuade the League of Nations to take a more active interest in the Baltic area. In 1934 Riga had begun to pursue a good neighbour policy towards Lithuania by expanding Latvian–Lithuanian trade (within the general framework of the trade agreement concluded on 15 December 1930), and by establishing contacts between the Latvian and Lithuanian general staffs. But it was not long before Poland started to play a more dominant role in Latvia, whose relations with Lithuania suffered as a result. Curiously enough, the Latvians also fell out with the Lithuanians over a minority group: the Courlanders (Kuren) of the Lithuanian coastal strip near Polangen. A congress held in Kaunas in September 1936 to promote friendship between the Latvian and Lithuanian peoples was marred by a dispute over the arrangements for a joint commemorative event.

The pro-Polish factions in Estonia and Latvia had failed to realise that Poland's status in international politics had been greatly reduced. In the 1920s, when she had been seeking to

G*

assert her authority in the Baltic area, she had been a force to be reckoned with, and at that time had undoubtedly posed a threat to the Baltic States. But by the mid-1930s Poland was fast becoming a pawn in the power game being played out by her two great neighbours, Germany and Russia. This new situation was far more dangerous for the Baltic States, for if they allowed themselves to be drawn into the whirlpool then developing in Eastern Europe there could be no hope for them.

The advocates in Estonia of a pro-Polish policy were to be found primarily in the town of Tallinn and in the army. This group was opposed by a pro-Scandinavian faction concentrated in Tartu, the ancient university town and home of Jaan Tõnisson, the Liberal leader and former premier who had pleaded for a *rapprochement* with the northern states of Europe as early as 1917. Tõnisson's ideas were revived in the mid-1930s. In 1936 his son Ilmar published an article in a new students' magazine, in which Baltic policies were subjected to a searching critique, and which created a great furore at the time. After rejecting both military pacts and reliance on the League of Nations as ineffectual, Ilmar Tõnisson pointed to the cultural differences between the Estonians and their southern neighbours, and called for a complete reorientation of Estonian policy based on a northern alliance. As was only to be expected, this exposé by one of the younger generation of Estonians was taken very much amiss in both Latvia and Lithuania.

It is perhaps significant that shortly after the publication of this article the Nordic countries seemed prepared, for the very first time, to come to grips with the problems of Baltic politics. In February 1937 the Finnish Foreign Minister Holsti caused a stir in European political circles by visiting Moscow. This was the first visit by a senior Finnish politician to the Soviet Union and was interpreted at the time as the harbinger of a more active period of Finnish diplomacy. In the summer of the same year the Swedish Foreign Minister R. H. Sandler prompted further speculation when, after visiting Berlin, Warsaw and Moscow, he suddenly appeared in the Baltic capitals. It was soon being put about that he hoped to negotiate a solution to the Vilnius problem.

But the rumours soon died down, as did the hopes entertained in Estonia for a Scandinavian commitment to the Baltic area.

Holsti's visit to Moscow produced no tangible results, and at the next conference of Scandinavian foreign ministers, convened in Helsinki, it was stated categorically that the Scandinavian nations would not consider entering into commitments of any kind south of the Gulf of Finland. Subsequently the Danish Foreign Minister Munch reaffirmed this statement through the Danish press. Meanwhile a number of Estonian politicians, all Socialists, had also expressed doubts on the advisability of concluding a political alliance with the Scandinavian countries. Following the Foreign Ministers' Conference of May 1936, the Estonian Foreign Minister Seljamaa had rejected the idea of a united Balto–Scandinavian front, insisting that in view of the different geographical and political situations of these two groups of nations, such a project was impractical. In Seljamaa's view, the pro-Scandinavian faction was as misguided as the pro-Polish faction; what he wanted to see was a policy of total non-alignment, in other words a policy which would enable the Baltic States to maintain friendly relations with all foreign states. In July 1937 the Estonian deputy Foreign Minister A. Rei, who went to Moscow shortly afterwards as Estonian envoy to the Soviet Union, took a similar line in an interview which he gave to a Polish news agency. Although he advocated closer cultural and economic links with Scandinavia, Rei was opposed to any form of Balto-Scandinavian political collaboration, save under the auspices of the League of Nations. He also pointed out that if, as he believed they should, the Baltic States refused to join any international power bloc and did not form a power bloc of their own, they would automatically provide a neutral zone between Germany and the Soviet Union. In saying this he was, of course, trying to allay Soviet misgivings.

In the summer of 1936 Britain also took a more active interest in Baltic affairs. Lord Plymouth, the Under-Secretary for Foreign Affairs, visited both Tallinn and Riga; and it suddenly seemed as if this north-eastern corner of Europe was to become a focal point of international politics. At the same time the Baltic States redoubled their efforts to secure British support. The coronation of King George VI in May 1937 provided an excellent opportunity for informal but intensive contacts in London, which the Baltic diplomats, including Munters, the

Latvian Foreign Minister, put to good use. It was probably in London that Munters came to realise that no diplomatic moves, however well conceived, could help the Baltic States unless they took due account of the reality of Nazi Germany.

In the speech which Munters delivered at the Foreign Ministers' Conference at Riga in December 1936, in which he pledged his support for the League of Nations and agreed to accept neutral status for the Baltic States on the Scandinavian pattern, it is possible to detect a note of deep pessimism. This is hardly surprising, for the League of Nations had been quite powerless to solve the two really crucial problems of Baltic politics: the questions of Vilnius and Klaipeda. Meanwhile, however, the growing dynamism of the Third Reich was forcing Munters to consider the wishes, not only of Moscow, Geneva and London, but also of Berlin.

In a speech a few months later in April 1937, Munters stressed the importance of maintaining good relations with both Germany and the Soviet Union, and called for freedom of navigation in the Baltic. At the Foreign Ministers' Conference in Tallinn in December the same year, he insisted that if the Baltic nations were to survive as a cultural entity, they must remain aloof from the ideological struggle then being waged in Europe. His visits to Berlin no doubt reinforced him in this conviction. But it seems that they also left him with the definite impression that Nazism posed the greater threat to Baltic sovereignty, and that to some extent he underestimated the aggressive nature of Soviet policy.

The major question facing the Baltic politicians in 1937 was whether a loose association of small nation states could hope to hold the balance between Nazism and Bolshevism. Had the Baltic entente created a sufficient degree of integration to make neutrality a viable policy?

CHAPTER V

THE BALTIC STATES AND THE TWO GREAT POWER BLOCS

1. Harbingers of the Storm

From 1935 onwards the foreign policies pursued by the Baltic States were influenced to an ever-increasing extent by the rivalry between Germany and the Soviet Union.

In a speech delivered to the Soviet Congress on 28 January 1935, Molotov quoted at length from Hitler's *Mein Kampf* in order to demonstrate the aggressive tendencies inherent in Germany's *Ostpolitik*. On 31 March the same year, *Pravda* published an article by Marshal Tukhachevsky drawing attention to the threat posed by the German rearmament programme. Tukhachevsky maintained that by the end of the year the German Reichswehr would achieve parity with the Red Army, although the territory it had to defend was only one-tenth the size of the Soviet Union, and suggested that in these circumstances there was a distinct danger that the Soviet Union's western borders might come under attack. Following this propaganda exercise, Litvinov approached the Estonian, Latvian and Lithuanian governments on 6 April 1935 to ask if they were prepared to conclude bilateral pacts with the Soviet Union providing for mutual aid in the event of aggression by a third party. (It is significant that Lithuania was approached, even though she had no common frontier with the Soviet Union.) A month later, on 6 May, Moscow received its answer in the form of a resolution passed at the Foreign Ministers' Conference in Riga, which stated that all three Baltic States would maintain a policy of strict neutrality and refuse to enter into special agreements with individual great powers.

Almost immediately Germany tried a similar approach. On 25 May Hitler announced that he was prepared to conclude non-aggression pacts with all European states except Lithuania, and shortly afterwards it was rumoured that Berlin had secretly offered to include the Lithuanians in this arrangement provided they renounced their claim to the Klaipeda territory.

That Germany should have been concerned about Lithuanian affairs was natural enough in view of the Klaipeda dispute. But during the closing years of the decade it became apparent that she was also taking an active interest in developments in Estonia and Latvia, especially when they affected the local Baltic German communities or trade between the Baltic States and Germany. Relatively little was exported by Germany to the Baltic States, but she imported a considerable quantity of foodstuffs and other agricultural products, and from 1935 onwards the German Navy purchased a large proportion of the oil produced in Estonia by the oil shale industry. In the course of the 1930s Germany's relations with Estonia were much more friendly than her relations with Latvia. According to Baron Wrangell, one of the principal reasons for this was the fact that the Estonian Government and the leaders of the Baltic German community in Estonia had collaborated with one another from the outset, which had mitigated the psychological problems created by the socio-political changes following the War of Liberation.

For various reasons there was no such collaboration between the Latvian Government and the Baltic German community in Latvia. In the first place, the tsarist 'russification' campaign had been much more effective in Latvia than in Estonia, with the result that educated Latvians tended to feel a greater affinity with Russian culture and so had little interest in German affairs. Moreover, the Latvians had suffered far more, and for far longer, than the Estonians at the hands of the German occupation forces during the First World War; they had also had to contend with the activities of the 'Baltische Landeswehr'; and they were much closer to Germany and consequently that much more vulnerable to any political or military threat. For all of these reasons, the Latvians were extremely reserved, if not hostile, in their attitude to things German. From 1934 onwards Ulmanis introduced special laws which bore heavily on the minority communities, and which were bitterly resented, not only by the Baltic German community in Latvia, but also by the German Government in Berlin. When Munters visited the *Wilhelmstrasse* in November 1937 and May 1938, he was taken to task on this account. On the second occasion he left Berlin 'in a very pensive mood'.

The interest taken by the Germans in the internal affairs of the Baltic States was viewed with considerable suspicion in Moscow. On 29 November 1936 this suspicion was voiced in no uncertain terms by A. A. Zhdanov, the Leningrad Party Secretary, in a passionate speech given at the 8th Soviet Congress in Moscow. As a Leningrader, Zhdanov was particularly sensitive to the German threat, which he painted in lurid colours, insisting that from the vantage point of his native city, which Peter the Great had so aptly described as a 'window on Europe', it was only too apparent that the fascist beasts were preparing to attack the Soviet Union. He then went on to remind the governments of the small states bordering on the Leningrad district, states such as Finland, that if they succumbed to the blandishments of political adventurers and allowed fascist armies to pass through their territories, they would live to regret it. After urging these governments not to embark on such a foolhardy venture he concluded his speech by threatening 'the fascists' with massive retaliation.

Zhdanov's remarks produced a sharp reaction, not only in the Finnish press, but also in the 1 December issue of the Latvian army newspaper *Latvijas Kareivis*; subsequently other Latvian journals and the Estonian press also repudiated Zhdanov's suggestion that their territory would be opened up to foreign armies. On 2 December Brodovsky, the Soviet envoy in Riga, told the Latvian Foreign Minister Munters that the newspaper reports of Zhdanov's speech had been inaccurate and that none of the threats made by Zhdanov had been directed against the Baltic States. At the same time the TASS news agency issued the text of an official statement correcting the false reports published in the foreign press, in which it was again emphasised that Zhdanov's threatening tones had been directed against 'fascism', not against the Baltic States. This may have been the case. Certainly the version of the speech printed in the official Soviet publications (*Pravda*, 1 December 1936) was completely in line with the statement subsequently put out by TASS. But it is also possible that this version had been doctored, and that the threats made by Zhdanov really were intended to intimidate the border territories. According to one Baltic commentator, Zhdanov said that the small border states should beware lest the Soviet Union opened the 'window on Europe' and sent out the Red Army to see what was happening on the other side of the border.

Assuming that Zhdanov actually did comment on the border states, it is significant that he restricted his remarks to Finland, Latvia and Estonia. As always, Lithuania was treated as a special case. Far from being censured by Zhdanov, the Lithuanian Government was told yet again by the Soviet envoy in Kaunas that the friendship between the Soviet Union and Lithuania was the one really effective guarantee of peace, and that only the Soviet Union could protect the Baltic States from external enemies.

Although Moscow's special concern for Lithuania at this time would seem to suggest that the Kremlin was reverting to the policy it had pursued in the 1920s, when it had actively sought to undermine Baltic solidarity, in fact the Soviets went to great lengths to avoid alienating Estonia and Latvia. In 1937 they still regarded the three Baltic States as a tightly-knit community, and so continued to adopt a more or less common policy towards them. This was effectively demonstrated by the Zhdanov affair, which led to an exchange of visits between Moscow and the three Baltic capitals, all designed to allay Baltic apprehensions. Thus Marshal Egorov, the Chief of the General Staff of the Red Army, travelled to Kaunas, Riga and Tallinn in February 1937 to return the visits made to Moscow in the previous year by the Chiefs of the Baltic General Staffs. The Soviet cruiser *Marat* also put in at the ports of Riga and Tallinn, and shortly afterwards a group of Soviet journalists toured the Baltic States. By 1937 the Soviet leaders had come to regard Munters as the key figure in Baltic politics, and in June that year they invited him to Moscow.

Munters arrived in the Soviet capital on 15 June, just three days after the execution of Marshal Tukhachevsky and a group of high-ranking officers who had fallen foul of Stalin. This was the time of the great purges. It would be interesting to know Munters' reaction to the macabre atmosphere of the show trials and executions, but he appears to have kept his own counsel in this respect. Litvinov welcomed his Latvian guest with a cordial speech, in which he reminded him, as he had reminded Seljamaa three years before, of the friendly relations that had always existed between the Soviet Union and the Baltic States, and assured him that the Soviet Government would continue to take a keen interest in the independence of the Latvian republic, not least on account of its geographical position. The Soviet press paid a great deal of attention to Munters, and at a banquet given in his honour on 16 June Stalin himself conducted an animated discussion with him on the political issues of the day. This was a great distinction, for it was a rare thing for Stalin to attend such functions, and even more rare for him to engage a foreign diplomat in a political discussion.

The American ambassador Davies, who was accredited to Moscow during this period and was basically sympathetic to the Soviet Union, provided some interesting observations on the Baltic States, which he visited in July and August 1937. In Estonia Davies noted the predominance of British influence and in Riga strong sympathy for the Poles. As for Lithuania, he considered that the general mood of the country was essentially pro-Soviet, largely because the Soviet Union offered the best safeguard against the double threat posed by Germany and Poland.

In Riga Munters told Davies about a conversation he had had a few months before with the British Prime Minister Neville Chamberlain. It seems that Chamberlain acquainted Munters with the details of a comprehensive plan for the peaceful solution of the problems facing the countries of Eastern Europe. This plan envisaged a system of bilateral treaties between Germany on the one hand and Poland, Rumania and the Baltic States on the other, which would have provided an effective counterpoise to the system of alliances already established with these countries by the Soviet Union. It was an ingenious proposal, for it exploited the hostility between Germany and the Soviet Union as a means of safeguarding the interests of the smaller eastern states. But it was of course entirely dependent on that hostility, and would lose all meaning if this were ever resolved.

For the keen observer of Baltic politics the two-year period 1936–8 must have been harrowing. After being a virtual backwater for a decade and a half, the Baltic States suddenly found that they had become a focal point of international politics. High-ranking foreign diplomats visited Kaunas, Riga and Tallinn, new political alignments were proposed, and astonishing vistas were opened up.

From 1925 to 1936 the eastern border districts, i.e. the area east of Rezekne and Narva and south of Lake Peipus, had lived in almost perfect peace. Although ships of the Soviet fleet used to anchor a few miles off shore at Narva-Jõesuu every summer, no Estonian regarded them in those halcyon days as a threat to national security; they had a certain curiosity value for the local population and the holiday visitors, but that was all. Up till 1936 the border territories lived in a state of blissful ignorance, refusing even to contemplate the possibility of Soviet aggression. But then came the rude awakening. In February 1936 Soviet planes flew over Tartu. The Estonian Government protested to the Kremlin, and many a carefree Estonian felt an initial twinge of apprehension, which was to be exacerbated the following November by the Zhdanov affair. From 1937 onwards, despite Holsti's visit to Moscow, there were repeated infringements of Finnish air space by Soviet aircraft and numerous frontier incidents involving Soviet and Finnish troops. In January 1937 there was also a serious frontier incident on Lake Peipus, where Soviet frontier guards tried to kidnap a group of Estonian fishermen; shots were exchanged across the frontier and two Soviet soldiers were killed. In February the Soviets again attempted to kidnap a group of Estonians, and on this occasion they succeeded; three Estonian citizens were seized near Lake Peipus, carried over the frontier and killed; their countrymen were deeply shocked. Meanwhile spy trials were held in Tallinn, which furnished extensive evidence of Communist intrigue.

Between 1929 and 1932 the Soviet Union had already strengthened its military position on the Estonian and Latvian borders by laying new railway lines both to and along the frontier, and by building strong-points, airfields and artillery installations. Towards the end of 1937 this military build-up was continued, several villages between Narva and Jamburg being depopulated and taken over by the Red Army. Work was also started on three new railway lines running parallel to one another and linking the main Soviet network with military railheads on the border with Latgale. These new supply routes, the strategic importance of which could hardly be overestimated, were completed by the beginning of 1939. Meanwhile, the Soviet Government had extensive areas of forest land, chiefly along the Finnish border, burnt to the ground to facilitate the supervision of its western frontiers. Throughout the summer months of 1938 and 1939 thick clouds of smoke drifted across the Baltic as far as Sweden. These were ominous portents, for they showed beyond any doubt that the Kremlin had designs on the Baltic territories.

But the worsening political situation in the Baltic States was not due entirely to the stepping up of Soviet military activity along the border. There were also other factors, which arose out of developments in the sphere of international politics. Thus, the events of the Spanish Civil War served to heighten the ideological conflict between Germany and the Soviet Union in the two-year period of 1936–8, while the Austrian *Anschluss*, which the western powers accepted without demur, strengthened Hitler's position in Central Europe and paved the way for German–Polish operations in the Baltic area. True, these were not combined operations in the customary sense of the word, but they were agreed beforehand and their timing was fixed after consultation between Berlin and Warsaw.

Following a minor incident on the demarcation line in the Vilnius territory, Poland gave Lithuania a 48-hour ultimatum on 17 March 1938 which called for the restoration of normal diplomatic relations between Warsaw and Kaunas. The ultimatum, which was expressed in the strongest possible terms, was backed up by Polish troop concentrations on the border. The Lithuanian diplomats in the west were immediately instructed to ask the great powers to negotiate a settlement. But nothing came of this initiative, and Lithuania was forced to accept the Polish *Diktat* and agree to the establishment of diplomatic missions in Warsaw and Kaunas by 31 March.

As a result of this débâcle Tubelis, who had held the office of premier ever since 1929, was forced to resign. Lozoraitis also offered his resignation to President Smetona, but was asked to continue in office until the end of the year. A new cabinet was formed by V. Mironas, the head chaplain to the Lithuanian Army and a former member of the *Taryba*, who chose every one of his ministers from the ranks of the *Tautininkai*. Although the new government announced that there would be no change of policy in either home or foreign affairs, it also expressed its intention of improving Lithuania's relations with Poland. It then took measures to re-establish direct rail and postal communications with Poland, and to open the Nemunas/ Memel River for the transportation of Polish timber.

If Lithuania had rejected the Polish ultimatum she would undoubtedly have been invaded, not only by the Polish Army in the east, but also by the German Wehrmacht in the west. In an order sent to the German Army Command on 18 March, Hitler laid down that if Kaunas failed to comply with the Polish directive, German troops were to occupy the Klaipeda territory together with an additional, and much larger, area extending as far as Siauliai (all in all some 15,000 sq. km., of which the Klaipeda territory accounted for only 2,600). Moreover, arrangements had already been made in Berlin to provide Lithuania with economic aid following the take-over of the Klaipeda territory.

In the event, of course, the Lithuanians bowed to the inevitable, and this, together with the growing urgency of the Sudetenland question, forced the Germans to postpone any further initiatives in respect of Lithuania. Subsequently, after Hitler had forced the western powers, literally at gunpoint, to agree to the transfer of the Sudetenland to Germany at the Munich Conference in September 1938, the Germans and Poles collaborated even more closely in the implementation of their expansionist policies. As a result, Poland acquired the district of Teschen. But that was the last time she received support from Germany, for by then German-Polish collabora-tion had run its course.

In Estonia and Latvia the pressure brought to bear on Lithuania was viewed with regret but produced no tangible reaction. In both these countries, but more especially in Estonia, the sense of solidarity that had once united the three Baltic States had long since been superseded by a pro-Polish attitude. Moreover, in Tallinn, although not in Riga, the government also tended to pay rather more attention to the wishes of Berlin.

After the Munich Conference Hitler announced that he would make no further territorial claims in Europe. And yet before the year was out the British were convinced that Lithuania would be unable to prevent Germany from gaining control of the Klaipeda territory. Since 1935 the friction between the German and Lithuanian national communities in the territory had been greatly increased, due to the expropriation of minority estates, the curtailment of minority rights, and the high incidence of civil disturbances in the harbour district. Towards the end of 1938 the Lithuanian Government decided that the time had come to establish a *rapprochement* with Berlin. Foreign Minister Lozoraitis approached the German Government and offered to negotiate a settlement of all outstanding problems. Urbšys, who succeeded Lozoraitis as foreign minister when a new cabinet was formed on 5 December, repeated this offer, giving explicit assurances that Lithuania was prepared to accommodate Germany in respect of the Klaipeda territory. Then, on 11 December, the elections to the provincial diet in the Klapieda territory produced an overwhelming majority for the German party led Dr. Neumann, which gained 87·2 per cent of the popular vote. As a result the Germans sent twenty-five delegates to the new diet, and the Lithuanians only four.

On 12 December Britain and France tried, but failed, to persuade Germany to respect the *status quo* established by the Klaipeda Convention. Although not unexpected, Germany's refusal was a bitter disappointment to the Lithuanian Government, which had instigated this France-British move. But on 22 December Lithuania was at least able to conclude a trade agreement with Poland, which was granted facilities for its transit trade in Klaipeda harbour and so acquired a vested interest in the maintenance of the Lithuanian position. Incidentally, the Polish Government knew that Berlin was hoping to settle the Klaipeda question at the negotiating table. Hitler himself informed Foreign Minister Beck that he intended to do so when he received him at Berchtesgaden on 5 January 1939.

German
Ultimatum
on
Klaipeda

But when the negotiations came, they took the Lithuanians completely unawares, for both the timing and the venue were highly unorthodox. When news of the Prague coup of 15 March 1939 reached Rome, where representatives from all the European states had gathered for the consecration of the new Pope, Foreign Minister Urbšys set off immediately for Kaunas to counter any possible repercussions. On his way he stopped off in Berlin for a conversation with von Ribbentrop, who suddenly presented him with an ultimatum from Hitler: Lithuania must cede the Klaipeda territory to Germany or German troops would move in and seize it forcibly. Although von Ribbentrop warned him not to seek help from foreign powers, Urbšys approached both the British ambassador and the Polish deputy foreign minister in Warsaw on the last leg of his journey. But he achieved no more than the Lithuanian envoy in London, who had to content himself with an assurance of deepest sympathy from the British Foreign Office. There were also numerous expressions of sympathy for Lithuania from members of the Polish parliament, but of course no offer of help from their government. Latvia and Estonia were an even less likely source of help, for the press in both these countries had welcomed the prospect of a 'peaceful' settlement of the Klaipeda question, since this would remove a long-standing trouble spot and enable the Baltic States to continue their traditional policy of strict neutrality. As for the Russians, they had made no attempt to intervene in Czechoslovakia either in September 1938 or in March 1939, and they had no intention of doing so over the Klaipeda issue. Of course, the Soviet Union had not been a signatory to the Klaipeda Convention, and so was able to justify its lack of interest on this ground. In the first instance, however, Litvinov simply made himself scarce; during the critical period of the German ultimatum he was not available when the Lithuanian envoy called at his office. Significantly, the Polish Government adopted a much more hostile attitude to the German proposals for the Klaipeda territory, which were communicated to Warsaw by Berlin at a later date.

The Lithuanian cabinet met on 21 March and after hearing Urbšys's report decided that it must bow to the inevitable and accept the German ultimatum. Later the same day the *Seimas* ratified this decision, and on 22 March a formal agreement was concluded in Berlin transferring the Klaipeda territory to the Third Reich. Six hours before the signing ceremony, units of the German fleet, with Hitler on board the flagship, arrived off Klaipeda, ready to take possession of the territory.

As a result of this action, Lithuania lost her only deep-sea harbour. True, she retained a free port area in Klaipeda, and Germany undertook to buy all her agricultural produce. But these were the only concessions which Hitler granted. In his memoirs the former German Secretary of State E. von Weizsäcker stated that Lithuania's decision to cede the Klaipeda territory to Germany had been 'partly voluntary and partly imposed', and suggested that when Urbšys left the negotiations he was both 'relieved and satisfied'. If this was the case, it seems strange that Lithuania should have tried so hard, and for so long, to maintain her supremacy in the territory.

The inability of the Lithuanian Government to obtain a satisfactory solution to either the Vilnius or the Klaipeda issue had internal repercussions. Although the opposition parties had been proscribed, they had continued to operate on a clandestine basis, and they now began to press for the formation of a broadly-based coalition capable of rallying the nation. As a result of this pressure a new cabinet was formed at the end of March 1939 under the premiership of J. Černius, until then Chief of the Lithuanian General Staff. The leader of the Christian Democratic Party, Dr. Bistras, representatives of the People's Socialists, and followers of Voldemaras all served in this cabinet, thus ending the long domination of the *Tautininkai*.

With a coalition government in power, and with the state of emergency already having been rescinded in October 1938, there was every reason to believe that democracy would soon be restored in Lithuania. But it was not to be, for in September 1939 the Second World War broke out and dashed all such hopes.

2. *Guarantees and Spheres of Interest*

No sooner had Hitler gained control of the Klaipeda territory than the Soviet Union attempted to redress the balance of power in the Baltic area by taking further diplomatic initiatives.

Thus on 28 March 1939 Litvinov sent identical notes to all three Baltic governments, in which he assured them that the Soviet Union took a special interest in the maintenance of their political and economic independence. This initiative was directed primarily at Estonia and Latvia, for following the transfer of the Klaipeda territory to Germany on 22 March, the Soviet Union regarded Lithuania as part of the German sphere of influence. When the text of the Soviet notes was published, many European observers protested against what they considered a direct threat to Baltic sovereignty. Ambassador Bullitt, who represented United States interests in Paris, was outspoken in his condemnation; he branded this initiative as a monstrous attempt to turn Estonia into a Soviet protectorate.

As for the Baltic States themselves, they were far from happy about Moscow's protestations of friendship. In Tallinn particularly, the 'special interest' evinced by the Soviet Union was viewed with great suspicion. Reports appeared in the national press stating that the Estonian Government would never agree to any curtailment of Estonian independence, no matter what pressures were brought to bear, and reserved the absolute right to decide for itself how best to fulfil its obligations vis-à-vis the European community of nations. On 18 April the Estonian Foreign Minister Kaarel Selter reaffirmed, in a speech to the Estonian parliament in Tallinn, that Estonia's relations with the Soviet Union would continue to be determined by the peace treaty of 1920, the non-aggression pact of 1932, and the long-established principle of neutrality vis-à-vis all foreign powers; Estonia, Selter said, would defend her independence and her neutral status against any aggressor. Two days later, the Soviet Baltic Fleet started its spring manoeuvres, which Zhdanov attended.

Although the Latvians shared the Estonians' apprehensions concerning this Soviet initiative, it seems that, for a variety of reasons, Riga was more frightened of Berlin than of Moscow, the reverse being the case with Tallinn. This is certainly implied by a series of documents dating from 1938 and 1939. As early as June 1938 the Estonian Foreign Minister Selter informed the German envoy in Tallinn that the Baltic States would not allow foreign troops to pass through their territories. In itself, of course, this was a perfectly innocuous remark, but it is apparent from a lengthy, confidential and extremely candid conversation which the Estonian Chief of the General Staff, General Reek, had with the German envoy in July 1938 that what the Estonians meant by 'foreign' troops was 'Soviet' troops. Reek assured the envoy that if the Red Army ever attempted to march through Estonian territory, his forces would fight to the bitter end, for nobody doubted that once Soviet troops entered the republic, Estonian independence would be at an end. In this connection Reek suggested that the Soviet Union might well think twice about engaging in an East European conflict once it realised that for the conquest of Estonia alone it would need a force of some 200,000 men. And if the Red Army did launch an offensive, he said, Estonia would certainly be able to hold out for a considerable time – although he hoped that Germany would come to her assistance, primarily with supplies of war materials. Reek then drew the envoy's attention to the need to protect the Estonian coastline, since the only way of transporting war materials from Germany would be by sea. Apart from mining the Gulf of Finland, which he regarded as an essential general measure, Reek also expressed his intention of improving and extending the military installations on the Estonian coast, for which heavy artillery would be needed. Having discussed his own country's attitude to the possibility of armed conflict in Eastern Europe, Reek went on to comment on the attitude of Finland and Latvia: although he was quite sure that the Finns would fight, he was much more sceptical about the Latvians. Above all, Reek left the envoy in no doubt that while the Estonians feared the Soviet Union, they did not fear Germany.

Two months later, in August 1939, Foreign Minister Selter told a German journalist, who had the ear of his government, that if it came to war between the Soviet Union and Estonia, his military advisers expected the Red Army to attack, not across the Estonian–Soviet frontier, but from the sea, thus disrupting communications with Finland. Like General Reek, Selter insisted that the Estonians would defend themselves, even if it meant fighting a long war of attrition, and he expressly asked that the Germans should not try to intervene on Estonia's behalf. The Estonian military attaché Colonel Jakobson also commented on the military situation to officials of the German Foreign Ministry immediately following the Munich Conference. He shared General Reek's concern over the more anti-German than anti-Soviet attitude of the Latvian Army, which he considered to be the single weak link in the Baltic line of defence. This view was echoed in a memorandum on the attitudes of the Baltic States during the Sudetenland crisis, which was drafted by the German Foreign Ministry on 8 November 1938. The authors of this report drew attention to the hostility of the Latvian press and people towards Germany, and suggested that in the event of a Soviet invasion, the Latvian forces in the border areas might possibly welcome the Red Army with open arms and that the Latvian Government might be unable, or unwilling, to organise a concerted defence of their territory. But perhaps the clearest demonstration of the different attitudes of the Estonians and Latvians at this time was given at the secret talks held in Valka in the early summer of 1939 between the Estonian and Latvian Chiefs of Staff. It seems that after General Reek had outlined his plans for the defence of Estonia against a possible Soviet attack, his Latvian ally informed him that he too had evolved contingency plans and that if war appeared imminent, he proposed to marshal his main force on Latvia's southern border to defend the country against the Wehrmacht.

It was because he regarded Germany as by far the greater threat that the Latvian Foreign Minister Munters tried so hard to obtain assurances from Berlin. When he visited the German capital in September 1938, he told his German hosts that Latvia would resist any attempt on the part of the Red Army to pass through her territory, and in return asked the German Government to guarantee the neutrality of the Baltic States. What Munters had in mind was an undertaking similar to that given to Belgium in October 1937. Hitler did not respond to this proposal, and when Munters asked for an interview with von Ribbentrop and Hitler he was told by the German Foreign Ministry that the time was not yet ripe for such a meeting. It is, of course, questionable whether a guarantee of this kind would have been of any real value.

As early as 21 June 1938, *Pravda* had insisted that the Baltic States were deluding themselves if they thought that by seeking refuge in neutrality they could avoid the dangers with which they would undoubtedly be confronted in the event of a Second World War. Not long before, the Soviets had been insisting on neutrality, but they now appeared to be asking for rather more. However, the Baltic States refused to be deflected from their course. At the IXth Foreign Ministers' Conference held in Kaunas at the beginning of February 1939, the three Baltic governments agreed that a policy of strict neutrality was in all their interests.

In March 1939 the question of Baltic security became a matter of active concern to the international community. As a result, President Roosevelt appealed to Hitler in early April to conclude non-aggression pacts with all those countries which felt themselves threatened by Germany's great military power. Since he could hardly afford to ignore the President of the United States, Hitler asked a number of European states, including the Baltic Republics, if Germany posed a threat to their sovereignty. Lithuania and Estonia said that she did not, but Latvia was less forthcoming: she gave Germany to understand that she would like to discuss the quesion, and promised to give her answer in the course of the talks, although she was careful to point out that she had no intention of departing from her traditional policy of strict neutrality.

Discussions were duly convened with both Latvia and Estonia, but although the Germans moved quickly on this matter, the Estonian Foreign Minister Selter still managed to have prior consultations with the British Foreign Office. At this time the British were arranging discussions of their own with the Soviets to try to settle the question of Baltic neutrality, but they had no objection to this parallel initiative. We have already seen that the Estonians were more afraid of the Soviet Union than of the Third Reich. It is hardly surprising, therefore, that a number of Estonian politicians should have advocated much closer links with Germany as the best means of defence against the Soviet menace. For them, a series of non-aggression pacts between Germany and the Baltic States would have been an ideal solution. In the discussions, which began on 4 May, the Estonian and Latvian representatives asked that the Latvian–Estonian alliance of 1923 should be maintained. To this, however, the German representatives were loth to agree, and in the end the Baltic representatives were obliged to compromise. In effecting this compromise, as in every other aspect of the negotiations, the Latvians and Estonians collaborated very closely, thus largely resolving the differences that had so obviously divided their two countries in the recent past. The German–Estonian and German–Latvian non-aggression pacts were finally signed in Berlin on 7 June 1939. On the following day Hitler received the Estonian and Latvian envoys, and in the course of these interviews stressed the importance of maintaining and strengthening the commercial links between Germany and the Baltic States.

This raises the question whether at that time Hitler regarded the Baltic States as trading partners pure and simple or whether he was already pursuing more ambitious goals. The Baltic States had always featured in Hitler's expansionist policies, although it must be conceded that in his early writings he tended to regard them as an adjunct of the Soviet Union. Thus, when he discussed Germany's alleged need for *Lebensraum* – living space – in *Mein Kampf*, he referred to 'Russia and the border states subject to Russia', while in his second book (1928) he spoke of the western border areas of Russia', a somewhat ambiguous phrase but one doubtless intended as a reference to the Baltic States. In this second book Hitler went on to say that the eastern coastline of the Baltic was as important for Germany as the Mediterranean was for Italy; and on 17 January 1938 Hitler assured the Jugoslav Premier Stojadinovich that he had no interest in the Adriatic or the Balkans since the North Sea and the Baltic were Germany's lifeline. A few months later, in April 1938, Hitler advised von Mackensen, the German ambassador in Rome, that once the Sudetenland issue was settled, the Baltic would be Germany's next objective.

Not for one moment did he doubt his ability to achieve this objective, for in an order signed on 11 April, in which he assessed the feasibility of a military campaign against Poland, the Wehrmacht was told that the attitude of the border states would be determined by one factor only: the overwhelming superiority of the German armed forces. According to Adjutant

Schmundt, Hitler made yet another reference to the Baltic area on 23 May 1939 in the course of a further discussion of the Polish question. On this occasion, we are told, he said that Germany's object was to gain more *Lebensraum* in the east, secure adequate food supplies, and solve the problem of the Baltic States. Apparently he hoped to obtain 'enormous surpluses' of food by establishing a 'really efficient German-style agricultural system'. In his Reichstag speech of 28 April, which was intended for publication, Hitler also stressed the importance of the Baltic States as trading partners, although he was careful to point out that for this very reason Germany wanted to see them develop as independent and well-organised national communities.

On the basis of these and other similar statements made by Hitler in the late 1930s, many observers have assumed that he was planning the annexation of the Baltic States. However, it would seem that at that time he was interested in the Baltic States only in so far as they were a factor in determining the balance of power in Eastern Europe. In 1939 Hitler's plans for the east depended almost entirely on the successful solution of the Polish question, which took priority over all other considerations. Not that the Germans entirely neglected the Baltic States; from time to time they would profess a special interest in this area, which they subsequently renounced in exchange for Soviet concessions in other spheres.

The fact that various high-ranking German officers visited the Baltic States in the late 1930s supports, rather than under-mines, the view that at that time Hitler was merely exploiting these territories as a means of establishing a temporary *modus vivendi* with the Soviet Union. It will be remembered that in 1937 General Reek, the Chief of the Estonian General Staff, visited Berlin. On 25 June 1938 General Halder, the Chief of the German General Staff, paid a return visit to Tallinn, accompanied by Major Krebs, the head of the operations division of the Wehrmacht. After landing at Tallinn airport, Halder had talks with the Estonian Commander-in-Chief Laidoner and Premier Eenpalu, visited military installations in the Tallinn district, and was received by President Päts in the Castle of Oru in Virumaa. He also asked to be shown the military installations on Estonia's eastern border, but Laidoner, who had no intention of provoking the Soviet authorities, rejected this request. On the morning of 29 June Halder left Tallinn for Helsinki. Although it was rumoured at the time that he had gone to Tallinn to discuss the establishment of a German naval base on the island of Saaremaa, it is in fact highly improbable that his visit, or the visit of the German battle-cruiser *Admiral Hipper* in July 1939, or the routine contacts maintained by Admiral Canaris, head of German Intelligence, with Estonian counter-espionage units had any real political significance.

However, even in the summer of 1939, the fate of the Baltic States was not being determined solely by the policy decisions of the two great totalitarian powers, Germany and the Soviet Union. By then the Baltic question had become an important issue in the negotiations being conducted by London, Paris and Moscow, and as such was clearly a matter of great international significance.

On 18 April the British Under-Secretary of State for Foreign Affairs, R. A. Butler, stated in answer to a question in the House of Commons (which had evidently been prompted by the guarantees offered to Poland on 31 March and Rumania on 13 April) that the British Government did not intend to guarantee the territorial integrity of the Baltic States. Yet a few days earlier Britain had approached the Soviet Union with a view to negotiating a system of defensive pacts that would ensure the security of Eastern Europe. Initially, notes were exchanged by the two governments, and talks were conducted at diplomatic level. In the course of these talks it soon became apparent that the Kremlin wanted to incorporate not only Poland and Rumania, but also the Baltic States into the proposed security system, even if these countries should refuse to participate voluntarily. Whether General Laidoner was aware of Moscow's intentions seems questionable, for at the critical time – between 17 and 24 April – he was paying an official visit to Poland, where he discussed Warsaw's plan for a Polish guarantee for the Baltic States. Even at that late hour the Poles were still clinging to their delusions of grandeur, which completely blinded them to the reality of their situation. The truth of the matter was, of course, that Poland was better qualified to receive international guarantees than to give them.

Laidoner, for his part, stressed both the interests and the dangers which the Baltic States shared with Poland.

But to return to the negotiations conducted by France and Britain with the Soviet Union, the Kremlin's insistence on guarantees for all East European states, with or without their approval, posed no great difficulties for the French, who accepted this provision on 22 April. By 22 May the British were also prepared to conclude a pact with the Soviets, but continued to take exception to the idea of imposing guarantees on third parties. Meanwhile, the reluctance of the British to commit themselves wholeheartedly to the Soviet proposals prompted Stalin to initiate secret talks at diplomatic level with the Germans. From then until the end of August, when his secret came out, Stalin played a double game. During this period – indeed, right up to the outbreak of the Second World War – the Polish question was, of course, Stalin's principal concern. At the same time, however, he continued to pay considerable attention to the problem of the Baltic States.

It seems highly probable that it was Stalin himself who first intimated – in his speech to the 18th Party Congress on 10 March 1939 – that the Soviet Union might consider entering into talks with Hitler. In April 1939 the Soviets and the Germans began to sound one another out in the course of low-level diplomatic talks, which were passed off as a continuation of the trade negotiations initiated earlier in the year. Meanwhile, the tripartite talks between the British, the French and the Russians began to move into a new phase, which culminated in the arrival of the Under-Secretary at the British Foreign Office, Strang, in Moscow in June. Within a fortnight, due to the pressure brought to bear by the French, the British withdrew their reservations, and on 1 July the French and British governments informed the Soviet Government that they were prepared to add a secret protocol to the projected pact guaranteeing the security of the Baltic States without the knowledge of their governments. One important feature of the negotiations in Moscow was Molotov's insistence that the political and military agreements entered into under the terms of the pact must be interdependent, and the fact that in discussing this issue he also introduced the concept of 'indirect aggression'. Although the British scarcely needed to be told about the dangers inherent in such a concept, they were in fact reminded of them by a memorandum sent to London on 10 July by the Estonian Government, which was extremely concerned lest the Soviet Union should claim the right to interfere in the internal affairs of the Baltic States. At the same time, Foreign Minister Selter intimated to the British commercial attaché that in his opinion Germany would not hesitate to sacrifice the Baltic States to the Soviet Union the moment it suited her to do so.

But despite these pleas from Tallinn, and despite its own misgivings, the British Government – which was under heavy pressure both from the French and from British public opinion – decided nonetheless to agree to the Soviet demand for a combined political and military pact, and on 22 July informed the Soviet Government to this effect. On 31 July, it is true, the deputy British Foreign Affairs minister, R. A. Butler, told the House of Commons that his government's principal concern in the negotiations with Moscow was to ensure that the independence of the Baltic States was not prejudiced in any way. But although this had originally been the case, by the end of July the British had been blown off course, and by that time were already preparing for the conference of military experts which was held in Moscow from 12 to 23 August. Significantly, the Soviet representatives at this conference immediately advanced concrete proposals that would have encroached on Baltic territorial rights. Among other things, they called for the occupation of all major harbours and the off-shore islands. This might well have become a major obstacle to agreement, had it not been overshadowed by Warsaw's refusal to allow Soviet troops to pass through Polish territory.

Meanwhile, the Soviet–German negotiations made rapid progress, and on 20 August Stalin finally acceded to Hitler's urgent requests for a non-aggression pact. On 23 August von Ribbentrop arrived in Moscow for the signing ceremony, which was completed before the day was out. And so this sensational pact between the two great ideological opponents of the 1930s was announced to an astonished world. But the protocol appended to it, which listed the Soviet and German spheres of interest in the Baltic area agreed upon in the course of the negotiations, was not made public; and this was the crucial part of the pact as far as the Baltic States were concerned.

At first the Germans had insisted that the territorial integrity of the Baltic States must be respected at all costs, and as late as 26 July the German negotiator was still putting this argument to his Soviet counterpart. But in a final attempt to win the Soviets over, they decided to make concessions in this sphere, and on 3 August the German ambassador to Moscow, Count Schulenburg, informed Molotov that Hitler was prepared to acknowledge 'vital Soviet interests in the Baltic area'.

On his first visit to Moscow, von Ribbentrop, acting on Hitler's instructions, suggested that the Daugava should be regarded as the demarcation line between the German and Soviet spheres of interest. But this proposal, which would have cut Latvia in two, thus recreating the old provincial borders established under the tsars, was not acceptable to the Russians. Stalin pressed for Soviet control of the ice-free ports of Ventspils and Liepāja in Kurzeme, and von Ribbentrop, conscious of the impatience with which Hitler was awaiting the conclusion of a German–Soviet pact, immediately telegraphed Berlin for permission to depart from his brief. This was promptly granted, and in Clause 1 of the secret protocol Finland, Estonia and Latvia were duly designated as Soviet spheres of interest and Lithuania as a German sphere, although a rider was added to the effect that consideration should be given to Lithuanian interests in the Vilnius territory.

During von Ribbentrop's second visit to Moscow in September 1939, i.e. after the subjugation of Poland, the Soviet spheres of interest were extended yet again. In the secret protocol appended to the German–Soviet Border and Friendship Agreement of 28 September, the Soviet Union renounced its claim to all Polish territory west of the 1919 Curzon Line in exchange for absolute control of Lithuania (save for a few districts around the town of Mariampol, which were retained by Germany in order to straighten out the so-called Suwalki salient). From then onwards the fate of all three Baltic States depended on the unpredictable whims of Stalin.

Thus the Germans and the Soviet Russians divided Eastern Europe into German and Soviet spheres of interest. But was this policy so very different from that pursued by the British

H

and French prior to 23 August during their negotiations with the Kremlin? They, after all, had also been prepared to recognise the Baltic States as a legitimate sphere of Soviet interest. Many historians consider that there was no difference at all, and it must be admitted that, as far as Soviet attitudes were concerned, their case is entirely convincing. Stalin's conception of a Soviet sphere of interest was not a variable quantity; it remained exactly the same whether he was dealing with a Franco-British or with a German team of negotiators. Yet there is an important distinction to be drawn here. Both Hitler and Stalin were dictators, and as such were impervious to altruistic considerations; the only criterion to which they attached any importance was that of self-interest. Consequently, Stalin could feel certain that Hitler would stand by the agreements concluded on 23 August and 28 September since they were of immediate benefit to his fascist state. But with the French and the British, with whom he had negotiated from June to August 1939, the situation had been far more ambiguous. Although they had agreed to recognise the Baltic States as a legitimate sphere of Soviet interest, they had done so unwillingly – Britain more unwillingly than France – and had certainly not been prepared to abandon the Baltic peoples to a Communist future. On the other hand, it could of course be argued that if the Anglo-French–Soviet pact had been concluded, then no matter how well disposed the British and French governments had been towards the Baltic States, they would have been quite powerless to prevent the Soviet Union from achieving its objective.

The Estonian, Latvian and Lithuanian governments were both surprised and perturbed when Moscow and Berlin announced that they had concluded a non-aggression pact. They would, of course, have been even more perturbed if the protocol appended to the pact had been made public. As it was, both the Germans and the Russians did their utmost to keep it secret for as long as possible. Even the German diplomats in the Baltic States were told very little at first. It was not until 7 October that von Ribbentrop thought it necessary to inform the German envoys to the three Baltic capitals of the arrangement whereby the Baltic area had been divided into spheres of German and Soviet interest. He did so in the course of personal interviews, and impressed on the envoys that they were to treat the matter as top secret.

Meanwhile the Soviet Union had exploited a minor incident that had occurred on 18 September as a means of taking the first step towards the realisation of its objectives in the Baltic area. This incident involved a Polish submarine which had sought refuge from the German Baltic Fleet in Tallinn harbour, where it had been interned by the Estonian authorities in accordance with international law. Shortly afterwards, however, the submarine slipped out of harbour and made its way to England. This was a heavensent opportunity for the Soviet Government, which brought massive pressure to bear on Estonia. Within twenty-four hours of the submarine's disappearance, Molotov informed the Estonian envoy that the Soviet Union had no faith in the ability of the Estonian Government to protect its coastline, and said that the Soviet Navy would forthwith assume responsibility for this task. Units of the Soviet fleet then entered Estonian territorial waters, and Soviet aircraft violated Estonian airspace. The Estonian Government was fully aware of the gravity of the situation. On 21 December it decided that any attempt to repel the Soviet forces by military means would be foolhardy in the extreme, and elected instead to make a direct approach to the Kremlin with a view to clarifying matters in high-level talks.

Accordingly, Foreign Minister Selter travelled to Moscow on 23 September. He was received by Molotov, who insisted that Estonia must conclude a military alliance with the Soviet Union and allow Soviet forces to man certain military bases, preferably in Tallinn and Pärnu. Selter then tried to extricate himself from this extremely difficult situation by pleading neutrality, whereupon Molotov reminded him that not only did the Soviet Union have a legitimate historical claim to large areas of the Baltic States, but that it also enjoyed the support of pro-Bolshevik elements within the Estonian population. Having subdued Selter with these thrusts, Molotov pointed out that Estonia could expect no help from either Britain or Germany, which were both fully engaged in the west, and then rounded off his harangue by threatening to seize military bases if the Estonian Government refused to cede them voluntarily.

Molotov's ultimatum was due to expire on 27 September, and on 26 September the Estonian Government decided to accept the Kremlin's conditions in principle but to resist to the utmost any attempt to establish a Soviet garrison in Tallinn. An Estonian delegation was then sent to Moscow to sign the military pact demanded by the Soviets, but discovered on its arrival that the Kremlin had stepped up its demands. According to Selter, the members of the delegation were told that another – no doubt fictitious – submarine of unknown origin had torpedoed a Soviet merchant ship off Narva and that in view of the new and highly dangerous situation that was evidently emerging, the Soviet Government had no option but to insist on placing Red Army garrisons in a number of inland bases as well. In the subsequent course of the negotiations this additional demand was quietly dropped, due presumably to von Ribbentrop's second visit to Moscow and Berlin's willingness to compromise over the Lithuanian issue.

The Soviet–Estonian pact was signed on 28 September. Under its terms Soviet bases were established on the islands of Saaremaa and Hiiumaa and in the harbour of Paldiski, the sites being leased to the Soviet Union. In all other respects, however, the Estonian Government retained full rights of sovereignty, and continued to control its own economy and draft its own laws.

Shortly afterwards the Soviet Government forced Latvia and Lithuania to conclude similar military alliances. On 2 and 3 October the Latvian Foreign Minister Munters was received in Moscow in this connection by both Molotov and Stalin. Munters, it will be remembered, had already been received by Stalin back in 1937, at a time when the Soviet leader rarely condescended to meet visiting politicians, and it was doubtless due to this earlier meeting that he was again singled out for a personal interview in 1939. During the interview Munters was reminded that the Baltic region was the Soviet Union's natural outlet to the Baltic; he was also told that all necessary measures must be taken to guard against a possible German invasion and that, if need be, the Soviet Union could provide sufficient manpower to occupy all three Baltic States.

Two days after this interview, on 5 October, the Soviet Union concluded an alliance with Latvia that was virtually identical with the Soviet–Estonian alliance of 28 September. Under its terms, Soviet naval bases were to be set up in Liepāja and Ventspils, and Soviet artillery positions established on the coast to protect the straits of Irben.

Meanwhile the Lithuanian Foreign Minister Urbšys had also flown into Moscow on 3 October. As always, the Kremlin accorded the Lithuanians special treatment; and so they used blandishments instead of threats in their dealings with Urbšys. By then the Vilnius territory had been occupied by Soviet troops, and since the Soviet leaders knew from diplomatic feelers put out in Kaunas that the Lithuanians were still very interested in this area, they offered to restore the town of Vilnius together with 6,665 sq. km. of land to them in return for a military alliance. Despite this concession, however, Urbšys was in no hurry to conclude an agreement. First he contacted Berlin to ask if Lithuania might count on German support if she resisted the Soviet demands. He did this even though Molotov had already told him that in the course of his negotiations with the Kremlin in the previous month Hitler had asked that the district of Mariampol should be ceded to Germany. But Germany was far too preoccupied with events in the west to consider coming to the aid of the Lithuanians, who were eventually forced to accept the Soviet offer. On 10 October the Lithuanian delegation signed a military pact with the Soviet Union which authorised the establishment of Soviet land and air bases on Lithuanian soil.

In a speech given before the Supreme Soviet on 31 October, Molotov announced the outcome of the negotiations with the Baltic States. After stressing the great importance of non-intervention as a principle of political life, he went on to say that the Soviet Union would carry out its obligations under the terms of the new pacts honestly and conscientiously, and would at all times respect the sovereign rights of the Baltic republics. The rumours of a Bolshevik plot to infiltrate and assume control of the Baltic territories were, he said, completely unfounded and had been put about by enemies of the Soviet and Baltic peoples, who hoped to exploit any dissension they were able to sow between them.

In point of fact, when units of the Red Army and the Soviet fleet occupied the bases allocated to them in the three Baltic

States the local populace and the civil authorities remained quite calm and behaved correctly at all times. There were no incidents of any kind.

Could the Baltic governments not have found a way out? Did they really have to comply with the Soviet demands? After all, the permanent presence of Soviet military units on Baltic soil was a prospect that must have struck a chill in Baltic hearts, and one would have expected the leaders of all three territories to have fought tooth and nail before mortgaging their hard-won independence. Following the two submarine episodes the Baltic leaders cannot possibly have harboured any illusions about Stalin's intentions. It would seem that in Estonian government circles there were those who seriously considered the feasibility of resisting the Soviet demands. But, of course, such resistance would inevitably have led to armed conflict, and for this reason Estonia was unable to obtain the support of either Latvia or Lithuania for such a policy. Between his first and second visits to Moscow, Selter had a consultation with the Latvian leaders but failed to win them over. Indeed, Riga was quite prepared to accept the terms laid down in the first Soviet proposal, which were far more exacting than those finally agreed. Incidentally, if Selter ever deluded himself into thinking that Germany would intervene to protect the sovereignty of the Baltic States – and this seems highly unlikely – he had certainly ceased to do so by August 1939. This is quite apparent from the conversation which he had with the German envoy in Tallinn on 25 September, and also from a conversation between Munters and the German envoy in Riga on 3 October, in which the Latvian foreign minister referred to Selter's pessimistic assessment of the situation. (At that time, the German diplomats attached to the Baltic territories had not yet been informed of the agreement between Berlin and Moscow to establish German and Soviet spheres of interest in Eastern Europe.)

If the Estonians had been seriously thinking of offering armed resistance to the Soviet Union, they would undoubtedly have considered the possibility of forming an alliance with the Finns. Whether they actually approached them in this connection is not known, although on balance it seems unlikely. They probably realised that the chances of conducting a successful campaign against the Red Army, even if they received the support of their Baltic neighbours, were too slim to justify the risk.

An alternative solution was being advocated in Estonian opposition circles during the early part of August 1939. At that time the tripartite talks between Britain, France and the Soviet Union were still in progress, and Jaan Tõnisson urged the government to abandon the traditional Estonian policy of strict neutrality and become a signatory to the guarantee pact then being negotiated in Moscow. It is thought that Tõnisson, Piip (the former Estonian foreign minister) and a number of Latvian representatives were put in touch with Soviet diplomats by Mrs. Vuolijokki, the Finnish politician, and conducted preliminary discussions with them. But then came the German–Soviet pact of 23 August, and this project collapsed overnight.

In this fateful period many Baltic politicians – especially those accustomed to thinking in historical terms – were deeply perturbed by another measure which was taken as a result of consultations between Moscow and Berlin. This involved the resettlement in Germany of the members of the Estonian and Latvian Baltic German communities, the evacuation being carried out under the terms of an Estonian–German, and a Latvian–German, protocol signed on 15 and 30 October.

After the conclusion of the German–Soviet pact, the Baltic German communities, which were also taken completely unawares by this development, were far more concerned than their Estonian or Latvian hosts about possible ramifications in the form of increased Soviet pressure. And when Himmler intimated that in the event of Soviet intervention he would take steps to evacuate any Baltic Germans of military age and those Baltic German politicians who had collaborated with German political units, chief among them E. Kroeger, they successfully pressed for the resettlement of the whole community.

Technically, the resettlement operation proceeded without a hitch. But for members of the older generation it was nonetheless a very painful process, for they were too old to benefit from the occupational opportunities offered by the German Third Reich, and they were leaving a homeland with a 700-year-old history to which they were deeply attached. The younger members of the Baltic German community were less preoccupied with the past, and had identified to a far greater extent than their elders with Hitler's Germany, which held out the prospect of new employment in interesting occupations, and whose suspect political, legal and moral values only became apparent at a later date. The Estonian and Latvian Baltic Germans were resettled in the western part of the territories taken from the Poles, i.e. in the former provinces of Posen (Poznan, now Wartheland) and West Prussia, where they were subsequently joined by their counterparts from Lithuania. The communal properties and real estate held by the Baltic German communities in Latvia and Estonia were sold to the Latvian and Estonian governments, the transaction being negotiated by the German Government.

After its success in Estonia, Latvia and Lithuania, the Soviet Government turned its attention to Finland, which had also been designated as a Soviet sphere of interest in the Soviet–German military pact. But unlike the Baltic States, Finland – which was both politically and geographically better placed than its southern neighbours – rejected the Kremlin's proposals, which were essentially the same as those made to the three Baltic governments. The Kremlin then renounced the Finno-Soviet non-aggression pact, broke off diplomatic relations with Helsinki, and on 30 November 1939 embarked on the campaign which came to be known as the Finno-Soviet Winter War. In human terms the Baltic peoples were deeply involved in this war, but politically their hands were tied. Consequently, the Xth Baltic Foreign Ministers' Conference, which was held in Tallinn on 7 and 8 December, passed a resolution recommending a policy of strict neutrality in respect of the Finno-Soviet conflict, and on 14 December the Baltic representatives in Geneva abstained when the League of Nations Council voted to exclude the Soviet Union from the League on account of its blatant act of aggression against Finland.

The outbreak of the Finno-Soviet war had immediate repercussions in Estonia, where further military bases were taken over by the Red Army, including the port and district of Haapsalu. There were good reasons why the Kremlin should have decided to embark on the final phase of its Baltic campaign by invoking the terms of the Soviet–Estonian military pact. In the first place, the Estonian coastal strip was an area of major strategic importance, both for the defence of Leningrad and for Soviet naval operations in the Baltic; and in the second place it was considered that, of the three Baltic States, Estonia was likely to prove the most troublesome.

Not surprisingly, the Finno-Soviet peace treaty of 12 March 1940 was welcomed by the Baltic leaders, who were greatly relieved to find that stability had returned to their corner of Europe. At the XIth Foreign Ministers' Conference, held in Riga on 14 and 15 March, a resolution was passed calling for the continuation of the traditional Baltic policy of strict neutrality and for closer economic and cultural links within the Baltic entente.

But this call for increased co-operation was viewed with suspicion by the Kremlin, all the more so since it coincided with a proposal then being mooted by the Finns for a defensive alliance with the Norwegians and Swedes. In a speech to the Supreme Soviet on 29 March 1940, Molotov made it clear that the Kremlin was opposed to any such proposal. At the same time, he spoke warmly of the military pacts concluded by the Soviet Union with the Baltic States, insisting that these had not impaired Baltic sovereignty in any way and had done much to improve Soviet–Baltic trade.

Clearly this statement of Molotov's did nothing to prevent the Baltic States from collaborating with one another, but it did impose the need for caution.

3. *The Attack on Baltic Sovereignty*

Although the Baltic entente was established in 1923, and considerably strengthened in 1934, it was not until the winter of 1939–40 that really intensive and systematic collaboration took place between Tallinn, Riga and Kaunas. This was one of the tragic ironies in the history of the Baltic area, for by then the balance of power in Europe was far more unfavourable for the Baltic States than it had ever been. In 1918 Germany had opposed the Kremlin's Baltic policy. But from August 1939 until Hitler embarked on his eastern campaign in 1941, she actively supported the Soviet Union in this area. In 1940 the hands of Britain and France, who had championed the cause

H*

of Baltic independence in 1918, opposing both the Germans and the Russians in the process, were tied.

It was primarily the success of the German *Blitzkrieg* in Northern and Western Europe that pesuaded the Kremlin to change its Baltic policy. An officially inspired article published in *Izvestia* on 16 May 1940, immediately after the occupation of Holland, Belgium and Luxembourg, predicted a similar fate for the three Baltic States if their neutrality were ever impugned. A further motive appears to have been provided by Germany's economic interest in the Baltic States, which showed no sign of flagging.

Following the conclusion of the Soviet–Baltic military pacts in August 1939 Professor Piip, who succeeded Selter as Estonian foreign minister, assured the German envoy in Tallinn that these were purely defensive alliances, and did not constitute an attempt to create a new power bloc. Nor, he insisted, did they affect Estonia's declared policy of neutrality in the Second World War. Of course, all three Baltic governments would have been realistic enough to have understood that for the time being there was no prospect of Berlin's taking an active political interest in their region. However, according to a statement made to one of his political confidants in April 1940, Päts was of the opinion that the Soviet Union and Germany would fall out with one another very quickly, and that hostilities would be opened by Setember 1940. (The factual basis of his assessment is not known, although it should be mentioned in this connection that Hitler's decision to attack the Soviet Union was not finalised until July 1940.) Meanwhile, it seems that during the period 1939–40 the Estonian Government – and perhaps the Latvian and Lithuanian governments also – were trying to establish a *modus vivendi* with the Soviet garrisons stationed in their territories in the hope of preserving their independence until such time as the general political situation improved.

They also hoped to further their cause by maintaining their trading relations with Germany, and in fact we find that trade between then was stepped up considerably following the outbreak of war. Agreements were concluded with Latvia on 15 December 1939, with Estonia on 6 March 1940, and with Lithuania on 17 April 1940, under the terms of which Germany took 70 per cent of all Baltic exports. As a result, the Baltic

States acquired considerable significance for Germany's war-time economy, and it seems logical to assume that this was one of the reasons why Moscow decided that the Soviet Union must gain absolute control of the Baltic region.

In trying to achieve this objective the Kremlin first brought pressure to bear on Lithuania by accusing the Lithuanian authorities of arresting Soviet soldiers and forcing them to betray military secrets. On 30 May the Lithuanian Government informed the Kremlin that Foreign Minister Urbšys was prepared to go to Moscow to help clarify the situation, only to be told that the Soviet Government considered that such a visit would serve no useful purpose. Sensing the impending catastrophe, President Smetona instructed all Lithuanian diplomatic missions to take charge of Lithuanian interests abroad, the general responsibility for this operation being given to Lozoraitis, the former Lithuanian foreign minister and then ambassador in Rome. Similar precautions were taken by the Estonian and Latvian Governments. Moscow's next move came on 7 June 1940, when Molotov took the Lithuanian Premier Merkys severely to task over the alleged incidents involving the arrest of Soviet soldiers, and also accused the Lithuanian Government of concluding a secret military alliance with Latvia and Estonia. This charge, which had no foundation in fact, was strenuously denied by Merkys, and a few days later the Lithuanian foreign minister, who had also been drawn into the Moscow talks, handed Molotov a statement drafted with the unanimous approval of the Lithuanian cabinet, which had met under the chairmanship of President Smetona on 10 June to consider the implications of Merkys' mission. In this statement the Lithuanians gave explicit assurances that they had at all times honoured the terms of the Soviet–Lithuanian military pact, and offered to set up exhaustive enquiries into the alleged incidents. Significantly, Molotov declined his offer.

At this point Merkys returned to Kaunas with absolutely nothing to show for his labours. Then, at midnight on 14 June, his foreign minister, who had stayed on in Moscow, was summoned by Molotov, who informed him of the conditions on which the Soviet Union was prepared to settle the issue. The principal Soviet demands were the arraignment of the Lithuanian Minister for Internal Affairs, the formation of a new Lithuanian cabinet, and immediate approval for the establishment of Soviet garrisons in the most important strategic centres in the republic. Before the night was out Smetona called a full cabinet meeting, at which it was eventually decided to accept the Soviet ultimatum. Initially, however, Smetona asked his colleagues to consider the feasibility of armed resistance. This they did, but quickly rejected the proposal when they were told that there could be no question of Germany's intervening on their behalf, the Lithuanian envoy in Berlin having reported to this effect the previous day after putting out feelers in the German Foreign Ministry. At that time Paris had just fallen, and the Wehrmacht was fully occupied with the final stages of its West European campaign.

After Premier Merkys had stood down in compliance with Soviet wishes, Smetona asked General Raštikis, the former Chief of the General Staff and Commander-in-Chief of the Lithuanian Army, to form a new cabinet, Raštikis' own military appointments having by that time been taken over by General Vitkauskas, a Soviet sympathiser. But Molotov rejected Raštikis as premier, and on 15 June he insisted that the special Soviet representative in Lithuania, V. E. Dekanosov, should supervise the formation of a new cabinet. For Smetona this was the last straw, and before the day was out he had fled the country, accompanied by a number of leading Lithuanian politicians and public men. Raštikis did not go with him, but remained in hiding until he too saw no other option than to slip quietly over the border. Meanwhile Smetona travelled via Germany to Switzerland, moving on from there to the United States, where he perished in a fire on 9 January 1944.

On 16 June, when units of the Red Army were moving in to take up their new positions in Lithuania, Molotov sent identical notes to the Estonian and Latvian envoys, in which he also brought accusations against their governments and demanded that Soviet troops be allowed to occupy further strategic positions in their territories. The time limit set for this ultimatum was eight hours. The principal charge brought by Molotov was that the Latvian and Estonian governments had broken the terms of their pacts with the Soviet Union – both the non-aggression pacts of 1932 and the military pacts of 1939 – by transforming the Latvian–Estonian Alliance of 1923 into a military alliance embracing all three Baltic States, and by approaching the Finns with the object of persuading them to join this subversive grouping. The only evidence advanced by Molotov in support of his allegations was a reference to the Baltic Foreign Ministers' Conferences of December 1939 and March 1940, and the founding of *the Baltic Review*, a joint Latvian–Estonian publication which appeared in English, French and German language editions from February 1940 onwards.

The Baltic governments had in fact made no attempt to conceal these Foreign Ministers' Conferences from the Soviet Union, and no proposals were advanced at them which could be considered remotely anti-Soviet. It is perfectly true that military contacts were maintained between Kaunas, Riga and Tallinn, but there were certainly no plans for a tripartite, let alone a quadripartite, military alliance.

Like the Lithuanians, the Estonians and Latvians also found themselves obliged to accept the Soviet ultimatum without demur. The Red Army began to move in on 17 June, and within a few days had occupied areas of strategic importance in both countries. Incidentally, during that critical period, on 17 and 18 June, Päts maintained informal but intensive contacts with the German legation in the hope of persuading Hitler to intervene on Estonia's behalf. But according to the reports sent to Berlin by the German envoy it would seem that once Estonia had accepted Molotov's ultimatum, the Soviet negotiators stepped up their demands. Among other things, they insisted on the immediate surrender of all the dockyards in Tallinn, the vast majority of the War Ministry and General Staff buildings, all barracks and airports, and numerous private houses; they also demanded the disbandment of the Estonian militia. Moreover, it was suggested that the administrative centre for the whole of the Soviet Baltic fleet should be transferred to Tallinn.

In the circumstances, it is quite obvious that Päts' attempt to gain the support of the German Government was doomed to failure. At that time Berlin was still intent on maintaining the *status quo* established with the Soviet Union in August 1939. Accordingly, Molotov kept the German ambassador to Moscow informed of Soviet policy in the Baltic area, and in this connection he told him that the Kremlin had been obliged to act decisively in order to stamp out the intrigues hatched by Britain and France with the object of sowing discord between the Soviet Union and Germany. As it happened, the British ambassador, Sir Stafford Cripps, had frequent talks with Molotov at that time and, according to the Estonian envoy to Moscow, the Soviet ultimatums of June 1940 were actually inspired by the British and French who, the envoy said, hoped to induce Hitler to remove troops from the western front for deployment in the east by raising the bogey of Soviet aggression.

In fact, of course, the Soviet Union needed no encouragement to interfere in the Baltic area, although it clearly suited Molotov to lay the blame for Soviet aggression at the door of the western Allies. By that time it was, of course, perfectly obvious to the Baltic politicians that they could expect no diplomatic help from the west.

Soon after the Soviet Union had presented its ultimatum to Estonia and Latvia, Molotov sent special representatives to supervise the conduct of affairs in those two countries: Zhdanov went to Tallinn and Vyshinsky to Riga, Dekanosov having already taken up a similar post in Kaunas some time before. Zhdanov, who also assumed the overall responsibility for the Baltic area, wasted no time in getting down to business in Estonia. But at his first meeting with Päts he encountered some resistance, for the Estonian President categorically denied the existence of a military pact with Latvia, and when Zhdanov asked if he had made any progress in forming a new government to replace Professor Uluots' administration (which had stood down after accepting the Soviet ultimatum), Päts reminded him that under the terms of the Estonian constitution he was only authorised to appoint the premier, who then formed his own cabinet. It would be better, Päts suggested, if Zhdanov were to discuss the composition of the new cabinet with the incoming premier. Finally, he informed Zhdanov that he proposed to invite A. Rei, the former Estonian envoy to Moscow, to form a government, and suggested that, if he should decline the invitation, Pung, the President of the Council of State, might be a suitable alternative.

Meanwhile Zhdanov had also met a number of the leading functionaries in the Estonian Communist Party, which had been legalised on 4 July, together with a group of non-Communist left-wing radicals. It was from their ranks that he intended to build his new administration. Completely ignoring Päts proposals, Zhdanov singled out Johannes Vares, the Estonian doctor and author, as premier-elect, and then contrived to sabotage Vares' attempt to contact the president for informal discussions. For the time being Päts remained in office, but he was no longer a force to be reckoned with. Living in his official residence, and making occasional visits to his country seat in Kose near Tallinn, he became progressively more isolated.

On 2 July Päts approached the German legation in Tallinn, and made one last appeal to the envoy. As on previous occasions, he reminded him of Germany's trading interests in the Baltic area, and urged him to recommend the immediate deployment of German troops to prevent the Soviet Union from taking over the Baltic States and transforming them into Soviet republics. His long-term assessment of the situation in Estonia was pessimistic, but he told the envoy that he would remain in office for as long as possible in the hope of keeping Zhdanov and, through him, Molotov at bay. Having given this undertaking, however, he went on to point out that although he had been assured of the loyal support of a broad cross-section of the Estonian people, there was always the distinct possibility that Zhdanov might force him to relinquish his post.

Meanwhile Zhdanov tried to persuade Päts to approve the cabinet appointments proposed by Vares, and when the president refused to comply with his wishes, he mounted a pro-Communist demonstration on the streets of Tallinn. On 21 June, protected by troops of the Soviet garrison, a crowd of Bolshevik sympathisers marched to the president's official residence. The political prisoners were released from the dungeons. Subsequently, the red flag was hoisted on the 'Lofty Hermann', one of the great historic monuments of the city. At one point there was a brief skirmish between the demonstrators and soldiers from a pioneer regiment, in which shots were fired, and it became abundantly clear that armed resistance was out of the question. In the face of such pressure Päts was forced to capitulate, and duly confirmed the Vares administration in office. Professor H. Kruus, the well-known Tartu historian, who had been a member of the Russian

Social Revolutionary Party, was then appointed deputy premier.

In Latvia Ulmanis also continued in office as president of the republic, although he resigned his post as premier immediately the Soviet ultimatum had been accepted. He too approached the German envoy with a request for arms before capitulating to Moscow, and asked for permission for the Latvian Army to withdraw into the Klaipeda territory if this should prove necessary. But, like President Päts of Estonia, he was refused military aid by Berlin. Pro-Soviet demonstrations were staged in Riga the moment the Soviet occupation troops entered the city, and when Ulmanis refused to confirm the list of cabinet appointments submitted to him by Vyshinsky on 9 June, further demonstrations were mounted by a group of some 200 former political prisoners stiffened by a hardcore of sailors from the Soviet battle-cruiser *Marat*. These led to bloody disturbances in the streets. But they served their purpose, for on 20 June the composition of the new 'Peoples Government' was announced.

In Lithuania the task of the Soviet Union's special representative was simplified by the flight of President Smetona. By bringing pressure to bear on Premier Merkys, Dekanosov forced him to undertake the duties of president, and to invite the pro-Bolshevik publicist Paleckis to form a new government. Shortly afterwards Paleckis replaced Merkys as president, while Professor V. Krèvè-Mickevičius, who had served as foreign minister and deputy premier until then, was appointed premier.

The first foreign policy initiatives taken by the new Baltic governments led to the dissolution of the Latvian–Estonian Alliance of 1923 and the Baltic entente of 1934. Meanwhile, statements were put out by the Estonian, Latvian and Lithuanian heads of government, which implied that the territorial integrity of their respective states had been completely safeguarded and that there was no question of establishing Soviet regimes.

Despite these disclaimers, however, it was readily apparent that the Communist parties in the three Baltic States, which took their orders from the Communist Party in the Soviet Union, intended to establish Soviet-type regimes in their countries. This was a source of concern to those new leaders who felt that the best way of preserving Baltic independence was by collaborating with the Soviet Union. Krèvè-Mickevičius was one of those leaders, and his conversation with Molotov in Moscow on 30 June showed that there was in fact good cause for such concern. Like Stalin at his meeting with Munters in 1939, Molotov made no secret of the fact that the Soviet Union was prepared to occupy the whole of the Baltic area in order to safeguard its own vital interests. In this connection he defended the Russian tsars who, he said, had tried to extend their empire westwards ever since the time of Ivan the Terrible, not out of personal vanity and a lust for power, but because they regarded this as a necessary step in the development of the Russian state. Having defended the Kremlin's expansionist policy in these broad historical terms, Molotov then informed the Lithuanian foreign minister that in the present state of international politics small nations were a complete anomaly, and that consequently the Baltic republics would soon be obliged to join the great family of Soviet republics, and so would be well advised to adopt a Soviet-style administration forthwith. When Krèvè-Mickevičius began to raise objections, Molotov brushed them aside and told him that the Baltic governments would be given an opportunity of voicing their opinions later in the manner prescribed for Soviet republics.

On 14 and 15 July parliamentary elections were held in the Baltic States. Both the turn-out and the results were extremely gratifying to the Kremlin: in Estonia 81·6 per cent of the electorate went to the polls, in Latvia 94·7 per cent, and in Lithuania 95·5 per cent; the Communist candidates received 92·9 per cent of the popular vote in Estonia, 97·6 per cent in Latvia, and 99·2 per cent in Lithuania.

The elections followed the same illegal course in all three territories. The electoral laws were changed by decree, a practice specifically prohibited under the terms of the respective constitutions; moreover, the electoral procedure was cut short, non-Communist candidacies were declared invalid, a number of electoral returns were fasified, and the principle of electoral secrecy was contravened. Thus by rigging the elections the Soviet representatives were able to exclude all the bourgeois candidates and ensure an overwhelming majority for the

Baltic Communist parties. Three days after the elections, on 18 July, Communist demonstrators appeared on the streets of Tallinn and called for the proclamation of a Soviet republic in Estonia and the incorporation of the territory into the Soviet Union. When they reached the Soviet legation, Zhdanov came out on the balcony to greet them.

On 21 July, when the new Estonian parliament met for its first session, it fulfilled the first of the demonstrators' demands by proclaiming a Socialist Soviet republic; and on the following day President Vares fulfilled their second demand when he proposed, in the presence of Zhdanov, that the new Estonian Soviet should apply for membership of the Soviet Union. On 23 July the parliamentary delegates passed a resolution calling for the nationalisation of all urban and rural property and of all industrial concerns.

Meanwhile, on 21 and 22 July, similar measures were taken in Riga and Kaunas. At the same time, Päts and Ulmanis were forced to resign, and were deported to Central Russia. Ulmanis was sent to Voroshilovsk in the Caucasus on 22 July, and Päts went to Ufa on 30 July after a last-minute appeal – made by relatives through the American envoy – that he be allowed to emigrate to the west, had been refused. Ulmanis and Päts both died in exile, although the precise dates of their deaths were never revealed. The former Lithuanian President Voldemaras shared their fate. He returned to Lithuania after it had been occupied by Soviet troops and was promptly arrested and deported to Russia, where he died shortly afterwards.*

On 1 August 1940, when the Supreme Soviet met in Moscow, Molotov opened the proceedings with a lengthy speech dealing with recent developments in Soviet foreign policy. Almost immediately afterwards, delegations from the Lithuanian, Latvian and Estonian Peoples' Parliaments applied on behalf of their governments for membership of the U.S.S.R. Meanwhile, the Soviet army of occupation in the Baltic territories

---

* Päts is supposed to have died in Siberia in 1956. Laidoner was deported to Pensa on 19 July 1940, but the date of his death is not known. Ulmanis probably died in 1942, while Skujenieks was probably shot in 1941. It is thought that Voldemaras died in 1944, and Mironas and Merkys in 1953. Stulginskis returned to Lithuania in 1956; Munters returned to Latvia in 1958, and died there in 1967.

was strengthened to ensure the smooth transition of the territories from independent to subject status. Thus, after rising from 53,000 at the end of 1939 to 57,000 in February 1940, the establishment of the Red Army contingents in the Baltic area shot up to 250,000 in the spring of 1941, and by the beginning of June 1941 had reached the massive total of 650,000.

By annexing the Baltic States the Soviet Union regained the Baltic provinces lost by Russia in the First World War, and with it access to the Baltic on a broad front. Its population was increased by six million.

In territorial terms, the Latvian and Estonian Soviet republics fared badly as a result of their incorporation into the U.S.S.R., but the new Lithuanian republic did rather well. In addition to the Vilnius territory, which had already been allocated to Lithuania in exchange for the military pact of June 1940, a number of districts with predominantly Lithuanian populations on the border of the White Russian Soviet Republic were placed under the jurisdiction of Kaunas. The Lithuanians also benefited from the fact that the Soviet Union went back on its agreement to cede the district of Mariampol to Germany, preferring to pay an indemnity of 7·5 million gold dollars.

As for the new Estonian and Latvian republics, both were obliged to relinquish control of large areas. In January Tallinn lost the Petseri and Trans-Narva district (2,449 sq. km. with a population of approximately 63,000), while Riga lost the district of Pytalovo in Latgale.

4. Final Attempts to Re-establish Baltic Independence

Once the Baltic States had been incorporated into the U.S.S.R., the Kremlin was able to proceed with the administrative, economic and cultural reorganisation of those territories, thus bringing them quickly into line with the rest of the Soviet Union. It was greatly helped in this task by a hard core of Baltic Communists, whose numbers were swelled by expatriate colleagues who had emigrated to the Soviet Union and were then returning to their native lands to claim their inheritance. Meanwhile the great mass of the population remained completely passive. There was nothing they could have done to prevent the Soviet take-over, and so, in order to survive, they adapted themselves to the new conditions of Communist life. A small group of Baltic leaders managed to escape to Finland, Sweden, Denmark or Germany.

In order to ensure that the will to resist was completely eradicated in the Baltic territories, Serov, the deputy head of Soviet Security, and Malenkov came to Riga in August 1940 to identify and list all 'class enemies'. After the interrogations had been completed, a considerable number of top Baltic economists, politicians and army officers were arrested, and many – including Laidoner, Jaan Tõnisson, Skujenieks, Balodis, Voldemaras, Mironas, Stulginskis, Merkys and Urbšys – were deported to Central Russia. According to Švabe, no less than 60,973 Estonians, 34,205 Latvians and 38,450 Lithuanians were deported in 1940–1 alone.

On 11 August 1940 the diplomatic missions and consular offices set up in foreign countries were withdrawn, and the foreign governments concerned were told that since the Baltic republics had joined the Soviet Union, they would be represented in future by the Soviet foreign service.

Two of the great powers – the U.S.A. and Great Britain – refused to recognise Moscow's authority over the Baltic States. Most other countries then followed suit. Indeed, the only exceptions were those allied with or – like France – subservient to Germany. As for Germany herself, she had ceased to play an active part in Baltic affairs in August 1939, and in a secret protocol dated 10 January 1941, dealing with the question of the German–Soviet border, she gave her tacit approval to Moscow's brutal intervention in the Baltic area.

During the first nine months of Soviet rule, from August 1940 to June 1941, it must have seemed to the Baltic peoples that their fate had been sealed. But then, on 22 June 1941, came Hitler's surprise attack on the Soviet Union, and with it new hope for the future. When the German troops marched into the towns and villages of the Baltic republics they were greeted as liberators by the vast majority of the indigenous population, and in all three territories there were spontaneous popular risings against the Soviet army of occupation. Blissfully ignorant of Hitler's imperialist ambitions, the surviving Estonian, Latvian and Lithuanian politicians were convinced that

Baltic sovereignty would soon be restored. In Lithuania the parliamentary deputy Ambrazevičius set up a provisional government; in Estonia Professor Uluots, the last president of the independent republic, sent a memorandum to the German occupation authorities in which he called for the establishment of an independent Estonian Government; and in Latvia the same demand was made by Latvian politicians.

But these high hopes were soon dashed by Hitler's totalitarian conception of the future role of the Baltic States, which he envisaged as a single territorial unit completely dependent on Germany and forming an integral part of the Third Reich or its immediate sphere of influence. Subsequently Hitler appointed Alfred Rosenberg *Reichskommissar* with special responsibility for all occupied territories in the east. But although Rosenberg, who was himself born in Estonia, spoke in terms of a protectorate, in fact his plans for the Baltic area were only marginally different from Hitler's, which he would in any case have been powerless to oppose. Incidentally, no provision was made for resettling the Baltic Germans, who had been evacuated in 1939, in their old homes; and it was only very rarely that members of this group were recruited for service with the German occupation forces.

The Baltic peoples, especially the Estonians and Latvians, regarded the second German occupation in 1941-4 with even greater bitterness than they did the first in 1915-18. They had had such high hopes of regaining their independence, and they would no doubt have accepted a limited sovereignty within some form of German protectorate as a perfectly reasonable arrangement, but they were completely disillusioned by Hitler's refusal to allow them even a vestige of freedom. They were also disillusioned, if not indeed repelled, by the arbitrary way in which the German race laws were implemented and abused (for example, in the formation of military units for service with the *Wehrmacht* and S.S.), by the inter-departmental rivalry in the German government service and in the Nazi Party, and by the apparent insouciance with which the German authorities were prepared to exhaust the economic reserves of the Baltic territories.

But at least the three majority groups in the territories were no longer subjected to the persecution which they had suffered during the previous nine months of Soviet rule. With very few exceptions – such as Professor A. T. Kliiman, the Tartu lawyer, who was wrongly accused of collaborating with the Soviet authorities and sentenced to death by a German court – they were treated with due consideration during the German occupation. This was not the case with one of the minority groups. The Baltic Jewish community, the size of which had been greatly increased by the influx of Jews from Germany, Poland and other occupied territories, was subjected to the full rigour of Hitler's inhuman race policy. As early as November 1941 the 'Final Solution' was initiated in Riga with the massacre of some 27,000 Jews. In the following month a further 32,000 were slaughtered in Vilnius. Those spared in the initial pogroms were concentrated in ghettos or work camps, where their numbers were progressively reduced. When the former Lithuanian President Grinius protested about the persecution of the Jews, he was ordered to leave Kaunas and live in the country. Of the 250,000 Jews living in the Baltic area when it was overrun by the German Army, probably no more than 50,000 survived the war.

The only members of the Baltic Swedish community to be evacuated by the Swedish Government prior to the German occupation were the inhabitants of the Estonian island of Rogö, which was handed over to the Soviets in 1940 as a military base. The Swedes living on the mainland stayed on, and their two leading representatives – N. Blees and M. Westerblom – were deported to the Soviet Union. But in 1942 these mainland Swedes began to leave Estonia and make their way to Sweden. Subsequently a combined operation was mounted by the Estonian, German and Swedish authorities, as a result of which almost the entire Baltic Swedish community – over 6,000 people in all – was evacuated and resettled in Sweden before the Red Army returned in 1944.

The refusal of the Nazi regime to grant any form of independence to the Baltic peoples led to the emergence of nationalist resistance organisations, whose members looked to the western Allies for support. Then in March 1944 – by which time the military initiative on the eastern front had passed to the Red Army – the Estonians formed a National Committee, which issued an appeal to the Estonian people on 23

June that was reported in the international press. Meanwhile the Soviet forces drew ever nearer to the Estonian border, and on 17 September the German Army Command informed the Estonian representatives in Tallinn that the Wehrmacht was about to withdraw from Estonian territory. At this, Professor Uluots – who had been more or less accepted by the Germans as the spokesman of the Estonian people, not least because he had urged his compatriots to fight side by side with the Wehrmacht in defence of their homeland in both February and August 1944 – arrogated to himself the powers vested in the president of the republic under the 1937 constitution and appointed the former Minister of Justice Otto Tief head of the Estonian provisional government. On 20 September Premier Tief then issued a proclamation, in which he demanded the withdrawal of all foreign troops and the restoration of full Estonian sovereignty. But two days later advanced units of the Red Army entered Tallinn, and by the end of November 1944 Soviet troops had occupied the whole of Estonia. Uluots managed to escape to Sweden, together with the members of the National Committee, who continued their activities there. Subsequently attempts were made to transform the Committee into a fully-fledged government in exile, but the members were unable to agree on its composition. Premier Tief did not go to Sweden; he disappeared in November 1944 and was never heard of again.

The Latvian resistance movement also formed a Central Committee as early as 1943, and in February 1944 its leaders issued a proclamation calling for the restoration of the old Latvian republic. The Latvians were encouraged by the fact that part of their territory – the province of Courland – remained in German hands right up to the capitulation of 9 May 1945, for they hoped that the western Allies would advance into Courland and subsequently provide part of the army of occupation for the whole of Latvia. In the event, of course, these hopes proved illusory. The Red Army exercised absolute control over the Baltic area. The Latvian Central Committee was reconstituted in England, and subsequently in the United States.

In Lithuania, where the Provisional Government had been disbanded on 5 August 1941 by the German Army Command, the Lithuanian Party and Resistance Organisations announced the formation of a Supreme Committee to co-ordinate their activities in 1943, and on 16 February 1944 this Committee set itself up as the Provisional Government of a new Lithuanian republic. The Germans promptly arrested most of the members of this government, whereupon the praesidium went underground. During the Soviet occupation a number of resistance groups continued to hold out in the Lithuanian forests for several years. There were similar groups in Latvia and Estonia, but their activities were on a much smaller scale.

Following the Soviet take-over, the Kremlin was able to set about the task of restoring Soviet rule in the Baltic territories. On this occasion it was much more radical, and in 1944–5 all the necessary measures were taken to bring the Baltic area completely into line with the Soviet Union. The leading politicians, educationists and industrialists had already been deported to the Soviet Union in 1940–1. Now it was the turn of the wealthy farmers. With their disappearance the resistance of the rural community to collectivisation was effectively broken and new administrative procedures were immediately introduced to place Baltic agriculture on a communal footing. Meanwhile, the Estonian, Latvian and Lithuanian Communists, who had assumed responsibility for the administration of their respective territories immediately following the German withdrawal, were gradually removed from their posts; their successors were then hand-picked by Moscow, and included a number of Soviet functionaries. During the subsequent reconstruction and expansion of Baltic industry, the Kremlin was able to change the demographic structure of the whole area by recruiting Soviet workers and technicians for permanent employment in the major industrial centres. It has been estimated (in 1970) that nearly 300,000 Soviet workers were resettled in Estonia, between 300,000 and 400,000 in Latvia, and between 120,000 and 270,000 in Lithuania. In Tallinn alone the Russian community grew from 5 per cent in 1939 to 35 per cent in 1945. During the war years, of course, the indigenous communities had also been depleted as a result of the deportations carried out at that time – which involved an estimated 140,000 Estonians, 155,000 Latvians and 300,000 Lithuanians.

But despite these many vicissitudes, and despite the complete sovietisation of all Baltic social and administrative institutions, the Baltic peoples have retained their national characteristics, and after nearly thirty years of Soviet rule they still possess a strong sense of national identity.

Although in the final analysis they were to prove illusory, the hopes placed in the western Allies by the Baltic leaders right up to 1944–5 were by no means unjustified. In a statement issued on 23 July 1940, the American Under-Secretary of State Sumner Welles protested against the annexation of the Baltic States; on 5 September Winston Churchill adopted a similar attitude in the House of Commons; and on 15 October President Roosevelt informed the members of a Lithuanian delegation that he too was opposed to the Kremlin's policies in their homeland. In 1941, when Stalin received Anthony Eden, then British Foreign Secretary, in Moscow and demanded British recognition of Soviet sovereignty in the Baltic area, Eden responded by calling for the restoration of Baltic independence; and from then onwards both the British and the Americans impressed their view on the Soviet Russians on every possible occasion. In January 1942 Churchill even went so far as to say that to surrender the Baltic peoples up to the Soviet Union against their will would contravene every principle for which the Allies were fighting. But then Roosevelt made a compromise proposal to the effect that any Estonians, Latvians or Lithuanians who objected to the *Anschluss* with the Soviet Union should be allowed to emigrate, and to take their personal assets with them. This entirely cynical solution reflected badly on Roosevelt's political acumen.

The Anglo-Soviet alliance of 2 May 1942 contained no reference to the Baltic question, which meant, of course, that the British Government had, in effect, abandoned its commitment. Shortly afterwards the Baltic envoys in London were told that their names had been removed from the list of diplomats accredited to the Court of St. James. The next move came on 16 March 1943 when Litvinov met Roosevelt's special adviser Harry Hopkins and argued that on both historical and security grounds, the Soviet Union had a just claim to the Baltic territories. A few months later, at the Teheran meeting of November 1943, Stalin stated unequivocally that the Baltic question was no longer a matter for discussion since the Baltic peoples had opted for membership of the Soviet Union in national referenda.

In fact, of course, the Soviet initiative in the Baltic area was a clear transgression of international law. Moscow's annexation of the Baltic States constituted both an act of 'direct aggresion', as defined by the Kremlin in the Baltic–Soviet non-aggression pacts of 1932, and an act of 'indirect aggression', as defined by the Soviet representatives in the secret negotiations with the French and British in the summer of 1939. Far from being a voluntary act of union, the incorporation of Estonia, Latvia and Lithuania into the Soviet Union was a blatant example of imperialism.

The legal arguments advanced by the Soviet Union in support of its Baltic policy have been analysed – and refuted – by Boris Meissner, a leading expert on the Soviet aspects of international law. First, Moscow maintained that the applications for membership of the U.S.S.R. submitted by the three Baltic governments in 1940 were a genuine pointer to the wishes of the Baltic peoples, and as such constituted an act of self-determination. Of course, they contravened the right of self-determination because they failed to reflect the true wishes of the Baltic peoples. Secondly, Moscow insisted that its intervention in the Baltic territories was justified by the need to protect the Soviet Union from invasion. But even assuming that the military bases ceded to the Soviet Union in 1939 were insufficient for such defensive purposes – and this is a large assumption – there was absolutely no reason why Baltic independence should not have been restored in 1945 after the capitulation of the German armed forces.

To this day the western powers have refused to give *de jure* recognition to the Soviet Union in the Baltic area. The British and French, it is true, have granted what amounts to *de facto* recognition, but the Americans have steadfastly refused to do so, and have remained quite uncompromising in this respect. Meanwhile, in terms of international law, the Baltic republics continue to exist as legally constituted states, which happen to be occupied at present by a foreign power.

CHAPTER VI

THE PAST AND THE FUTURE

If Marx and Engels had been called upon to assess the Baltic peoples, they would undoubtedly have lumped them together with the Czechs, Slovaks and Slovenes, whom they regarded as 'historically non-existent nations' who were incapable of building a state of their own because they lacked the basic requirements of independent nationhood. Like Hegel, they regarded such small communities as *Volkertrümmer* – so much racial debris – which served no useful purpose, and merely impeded the historical development of the great nation states.

This attitude, which had been developed by Marx and Engels in the 1860s in order to oppose both the nationalities concept advanced by Napoleon III and the anarchistic pan-Slavism of Bakunin, was later modified by the Russian Marxists as a result of the changes which took place in Europe during and after the First World War, when so many new nation states came into being. At that time Lenin and Stalin showed greater regard for the concept of self-determination, although they still insisted on the primacy of the proletarian class structure and the socialist ideology defined by the party leaders following the October Revolution.

Of course, the origins of the concept of self-determination go back considerably further than Hegel, let alone Marx and Engels. As far as the Baltic peoples are concerned, the prime source was undoubtedly Herder, whose searching enquiries into Baltic folklore, conducted in Riga between 1764 and 1769, paved the way for the emergence of the Baltic nationalist movements. Herder refuted his traditional idea that a nation's value depended on its size, and his view was subsequently endorsed by Jakob Burckhardt, who repeatedly drew attention to the importance of small states in European history. Later still, Herder's ideas were to re-emerge in the socialist ideology developed for the industrial societies of the twentieth century;

and in Austromarxist theory Bauer and Renner have evolved a new principle specifically designed to enable nations with widely dispersed populations to preserve their identity.

The Baltic nations have been fortunate in this respect, for over the past two centuries their peoples have lived as more as less self-contained communities in specific areas, where they have survived under successive foreign rulers, successfully resisting all attempts to absorb them into alien cultures. The Lithuanians, it is true, were able to look back to a period of nationhood in the medieval period, but from 1600 onwards they were in exactly the same position as the Latvians and Estonians, who somehow contrived to preserve their sense of community during the long pre-political phase of their development, when they were slowly moving towards a conscious realisation of their national identity. Far from being racial debris, these peoples were vigorous young saplings, drawing sustenance from their native soil and growing steadily upwards towards the light. By the late 1910s they had reached the light.

But why was their success so short-lived? Were the Baltic States simply too small to be politically viable? This can hardly have been the case, for they were larger than other European states which have survived and prospered. Estonia with 47,500 sq. km., Latvia with 55,700 and Lithuania with 65,800 compared favourably with Belgium (30,507), the Netherlands (32,400), Switzerland (41,288) and Denmark (42,936). Of course, the population and population density of the Baltic republics, their economic development and their living standards compared less favourably. On the other hand, their educational and cultural achievements during the period of independence were of a very high order, while the political sense and drive of their peoples were exceptional. The military élan which they displayed in the War of Liberation, the development of their economy and of a modern educational system, and the diplomatic skill with which they dealt with the great powers all testified to remarkable qualities. So too did their endeavours to establish a *modus vivendi* with the minorities living in their territories. True, these minorities suffered considerably as a result of the agrarian reforms introduced in the early 1920s and as a result of the nationalist fervour which swept the Baltic States a decade later. But they were allowed to maintain their cultural autonomy by establishing their own national infrastructures, a concession which was all the more remarkable if we consider the harsh treatment meted out to the minorities in other European countries at the time. The cultural autonomy granted by the Estonians was particularly generous, and before long the Estonian system was being advocated as a model by the international bodies working for the welfare of the European minorities. If – as Lord Acton once observed – 'the civilisation of a state is best measured by its respect for minorities', then Estonia was clearly a highly civilised state.

It is also perfectly clear, in view of the considerable progress they were able to make in their twenty years of independence, that there was no inherent reason why the Baltic States should not have been politically viable. But, of course, they were in an extremely vulnerable position; and it must be said – with all the advantages of hindsight – that Tallinn, Riga and Kaunas would have been better advised to create a Baltic federation and pursue common policies wherever possible.

Various attempts were made to promote much larger federal groupings – such as a Nordic Union, which would have embraced the three Scandinavian countries and the three Baltic States; and a Baltic Polish alliance, which would have revived the hegemony enjoyed by the old Polish state in the sixteenth and seventeenth centuries – but these proved utopian. A far more realistic project was that for the Baltic entente, which the Estonian Foreign Minister K. R. Pusta liked to refer to as the Baltic Commonwealth. But although extremely attractive, this description was misleading, for the Baltic entente had little in common with the British Commonwealth. First, it was far too small to merit such a title, and in the second place it had no unifying symbol remotely comparable to the British crown. Nor, for that matter, had the Baltic entente much in common with the Kalmar Union or with the Finno-Swedish Union before 1809, for it was based on the egalitarian principle of absolute parity. In fact, the only grouping to which it bore any resemblance was the contemporary Little entente in the Danube region.

The Baltic entente developed far too slowly. Looking back from our present vantage point, it is quite evident that it lacked the kind of forceful leadership that could have turned it into a cohesive and fruitful union. At one point it seemed as if the Latvian Foreign Minister Meierovics might provide the necessary drive, but this hope was dashed by his untimely death. Although it was always intended that the Latvian–Estonian Alliance should be cemented by the establishment of a customs union, this never materialised. But it was not only that the Baltic States failed to create a viable federation; they also failed to create viable federal states. Thus, nothing comparable to the Swiss or Belgian constitution was evolved in Estonia, Latvia or Lithuania.

Up to 1934 the Vilnius and Klaipeda/Memel disputes were the principal impediment to Baltic federation. If the Poles had not marched into Vilnius when they did, the Lithuanians might conceivably have been prepared to negotiate a compromise solution with the Germans. But as it was, they adopted an extremely rigid attitude on both fronts, which had an inhibiting effect on their two Baltic partners. Meanwhile, Latvian–Estonian collaboration was held up by particularist interests and psychological barriers. From 1934 onwards a new tripartite initiative would have been feasible in the cultural and educational spheres. Communal institutions – academies of art, technical colleges, etc. – could have been developed if the three communities had been able to agree on the adoption of a foreign language – German or English would have served equally well – as a common means of communication. Various attempts were made along these lines, but in 1934 time was running out, and at the end of the day those concerned had nothing to show for their labours.

By 1939 it was impossible for the Baltic States to keep out of the war. They could only have done so if the neutrality of the Baltic area had been guaranteed by the western powers back in 1936, i.e. before Hitler embarked on his aggressive eastern policy. And to have been truly certain of safeguarding the Baltic territories, France and England would have had to reach an agreement with the Soviet Union, for only then could they have prevented Moscow from bringing pressure to bear on Riga, Tallinn and Kaunas, and dissuaded Stalin from making a deal with Hitler. Clearly, the initiative lay with the great powers.

The incorporation of the three independent Baltic States into the Soviet Union in 1944-5 was symptomatic of the general post-war trend towards larger territorial groupings on the continent of Europe, which stood in such marked contrast to the disintegration process that set in following the First World War. In Western Europe, it is true, the movement towards unity was fitful, but in the whole of Eastern Europe, and in the eastern parts of Central Europe, Stalin drew every single country into his monolithic eastern bloc. In this process – in which the years 1948, 1956 and 1968 were the principal turning points – Stalin naturally had recourse to coercive measures. Nonetheless, ideological considerations also played an important part, just as economic and political considerations did in the west. And what emerged from the ideological struggle within the Communist world was the realisation that in future both the international Communist movement and the Soviet regime must take due account of the wishes of the East European peoples and the West European Communist parties. There can be no question of reverting to the Stalinist system of enforced integration; any attempt to do so would be doomed to failure in the long term.

But, of course, the Baltic States are in a somewhat different position from the satellite countries of Eastern Europe. Although the Kremlin has no doubt toyed with the idea of incorporating Poland, Czechoslovakia, Hungary, Rumania and Bulgaria into the U.S.S.R., this has never actually happened, with the result that these countries have remained outside the orbit of direct Soviet control. Of course, the Yugoslavs and Finns have acquired even greater freedom. The Baltic States, on the other hand, have acquired no freedom whatsoever, and it would be foolish to suppose that this situation is likely to change in the immediate future.

Yet despite their total subjugation – which led to the deportation of many of their citizens and the settlement in their territories of large numbers of foreign industrial workers – the Estonians, Latvians and Lithuanians have nonetheless retained a strong sense of their national identity and are still acutely aware of their national culture. Of course, the Baltic republics are nearer to Europe than the other territories of the U.S.S.R., and they have far more in common with the countries of the western world, which exerted a considerable influence on their historical, religious and cultural development. What is more, their peoples are aware of this close affinity, which they are determined to preserve at all costs. Factors of this kind operate at a very different level from ideological considerations.

Not that a Baltic Communist needs to be less of a Marxist–Leninist on account of this western orientation. But he will undoubtedly pay greater heed than his comrades in the Central Soviet republics to the kind of democratic demands pressed by the Yugoslavs and the Czechs. The memorandum composed by a group of Estonian technologists in response to the paper published by A. D. Sakharov, the Soviet atomic physicist, testifies to the perspicacity of the Baltic intelligentsia.

The Baltic peoples are now beginning to fulfil much the same kind of function within the Soviet Union as the Baltic Germans fulfilled in Russia in the eighteenth and nineteenth centuries. The plain fact of the matter is that the peoples of the U.S.S.R. still tend to regard the Baltic Soviet republics as an outcrop of Western Europe. One only needs to visit Tallinn or Riga with a party of Leningrad students to realise the fascination which these cities exert. It is, therefore, all the more regrettable – in view of the civilising effect which the Baltic territories are clearly capable of producing and which would undoubtedly help to improve interpersonal relations within the Soviet community – that Moscow is apparently still determined to undermine their ethnic and social structure.

Another problem that has to be considered is posed by the need to maintain communications between the Baltic peoples in the U.S.S.R. and their compatriots in exile, who now number over one million. (Some 115,000 Estonians and 180,000 Latvians – or about 10 per cent of the total population in each case – and nearly 800,000 Lithuanians – over 25 per cent of the total population – are living abroad.) The cultural and educational level of the emigrant communities is relatively high, which means that in both quantitative and qualitative terms it is imperative that contact be maintained with them. Of course, they too run the risk of being completely absorbed into their new communities, which makes it all the more necessary for positive links to be established across the iron – or any other – curtain. The existing postal and tourist services could be expanded; and sporting, artistic and scientific contacts could be maintained. Both sides would undoubtedly benefit from them.

The constitution of the U.S.S.R. does not encourage regional developments. On the contrary, any attempt to form special links between individual Soviet republics is frowned upon. In accordance with general Communist policy, the Kremlin is utterly opposed to the formation of anything remotely resembling a political bloc within its territory. But whether the Kremlin likes it or not, the three Baltic Soviet republics do in fact have special links with one another and constitute a specific region in the north-west of the country that is enthnically, historically, socially and educationally quite different from the neighbouring White Russian republic, the R.S.F.S.R. and the Union of Soviet republics. Even without official institutions, this region represents a political reality which cannot be denied and which could well become a focal point for future developments. After all, the monolithic eastern bloc of the Stalinist era has already started to disintegrate; and it is quite conceivable that changes in the international balance of power or the internal structure of the U.S.S.R. might produce a situation in which the Kremlin would consider it advisable to extend the constitutional rights granted to the Baltic peoples.

And if we take this hypothesis one step further, it is surely not altogether unreasonable to hope that in the long term the Kremlin might accord the Baltic republics the same kind of status as that enjoyed by the three Benelux countries in Western Europe. Such a gesture would undoubtedly be warmly welcomed in the west, and might well lead on to the conclusion of a general European peace settlement capable of allaying Soviet fears and providing firm guarantees for the security of the U.S.S.R.

APPENDIX A
BIBLIOGRAPHY

Introduction

Comprehensive Accounts

ESTONIA

H. Kruus, *Grundriß der Geschichte des estnischen Volkes*, Tartu 1932 (*Histoire de l'Estonie*, Paris 1935); *Eesti rahva ajalugu*, 1–3, Tartu 1932 ff., *Eesti ajalugu*, 1–3, Tartu 1935 ff.; M. Ojamaa *et al.*, *Eesti ajalugu*, Stockholm 1946; J. Parijõgi *et al.*, *Eesti ajalugu*, Stockholm 1954; E. Uustalu, *The History of the Estonian People*, London 1952; J. Uluots, *Grundzüge der Agrargeschichte Estlands*, Tartu 1935; Uustalu, E. (ed.), *Eesti Vabariik 1918–1940*, Lund 1968; G. Naan, *Eesti NSV Ajalugu*, Tallinn 1957.

LATVIA

A. Tentelis, Latvju vēsture, Riga 1934 ff.; A. Spekke, *History of Latvia: An Outline*, Stockholm 1957; A. Schwabe, *The Story of Latvija*, Stockholm 1950 (Histoire du peuple lettonien, Stockholm 1953)); A. Bilmanis, *A History of Latvia*, Princeton 1951; *Latvijas Werdegang*, Riga/Leipzig 1934; Ja. Zutis, *Istorija Latvijskoj SSR*, I, Riga 1952; K. Ja. Strazdiňš, *Istorija Latvijskoj SSR*, Riga 1955; A. Schwabe, *Histoire agraire de la Lettonie*, Riga 1929; F. Zālītis, *Latvijas vēsture*, edited and enlarged by E. Nagobads, Esslingen 1947; *Latvijas vēsture*, editions with contributions by E. Dunsdorf, A. Speeke, A. Švābe, E. Andersons, 1–4, Stockholm 1958 to 1967.

LITHUANIA

P. Klimas, *Der Werdegang des litauischen Staates*, Berlin 1919; C. R. Jurgela, *History of the Lithuanian nation*, New York 1948; A. Šapoka, *Lietuvos istorija*, Kaunas 1936; T. G. Chase, *The Story of Lithuania*, New York 1946; *Lietuvos TSR. Istorijos Šaltiniai*, documents ed. J. Žiugžda, Vilnius 1961, 1–4; V. Kapsukas, *Buržuazinė Lietuva*, Vilnius 1961; M. Hellmann, *Grundzüge der Geschichte Litauens*, Darmstadt 1966; J. Ochmański, *Historia Litwy*, Wrocław 1967; *Lietuvos TSR Istorija*, 3 vols., Vilnius 1965; Y. Niitemaa, *Baltian Historia*, Helsinki 1969.

ENCYCLOPAEDIAS AND BIBLIOGRAPHIES

Eesti entsüklopeedia, Tartu 1932–1937; *Latvju Enciklopēdija*, Stockholm 1950–5; *Lietuviu̯ enciklopedija*, New York 1951 ff., 1–34; H. Weiss, 'Baltische Bibliographie', *Zeitschrift für Ostforschung*, Marburg, 1954 ff.

GENERAL

H. Vitols, *La Mer Baltique et les Etats Baltes*, Paris 1935; A. Pullerits, *Estonia: Population, Cultural and Economic Life*, Tallinn 1953; A. Pullerits, *Estland. 20 Jahre Selbständigkeit*, Tallinn 1938; M. Walters, *Lettland: Seine Entwicklung zum Staat und die baltischen Fragen*, Rome 1923; R. Puaux, *Portrait de la Lettonie*, Paris 1937; *Latvia, Country and People*, ed. by J. Rutkis, Stockholm 1967; H. de Chambon, *La Lithuanie moderne*, Paris 1933; V. Jungfer, *Litauen, Antlitz eines Volkes*, Tübingen 1948.

V. Aschenbrenner *et al.*, (ed.) *Die Deutschen und ihre östlichen Nachbarn*, Frankfurt/M. 1968 (see esp. M. Hellmann, 'Die baltischen Völker', H. Weiss, 'Die Ostseefinnen').

STANDARD WORK FOR THE EARLY PERIOD

R. Wittram, *Baltische Geschichte. Die Ostseelande Livland, Estland, Kurland 1180–1918*, München 1954 (With a comprehensive bibliography). Reprint 1972.

THE POST-1918 PERIOD

Handwörterbuch des Grenz- und Auslanddeutschtums, 1936 ff. (See Articles: 'Deutschbalten', 'Estland', 'Lettland'); J. B. Duroselle, *Les frontières européennes de L'URSS 1917–1941*, Paris 1957 ('The Baltic States' by Stuart R. Schram).

THE BALTIC QUESTION AS AN INTERNATIONAL PROBLEM

H. Rothfels, 'The Baltic provinces: Some Historic Aspects and Perspectives', *Journal of Central European Affairs* 1944/2; H. Rothfels, 'Das Baltikum als Problem der internationalen Politik. Zur Geschichte und Problematik der Demokratie', *Festschrift H. Herzfeld*, Berlin 1958; A. Bilmanis, 'Grandeur and Decline of the German Balts', *Slavic Review* 1944/61.

Chapter I: 'Historical Background'

1. *The Baltic Peoples*

W. K. Matthews, 'Medieval Baltic Tribes', *Slavic Review*, 1949/2.

G. v. Rauch, *Der Deutsche Orden und die Einheit des baltischen Landes*, Hamburg 1961.

2. *The Emergence of Nationalism*

H. Rosenthal, *Kulturbestrebungen des estnischen Volkes während eines Menschenalters (1869–1900)*, Reval 1912; A. Taska, 'Die estnischen Sängerfeste', *Jahrbuch des baltischen Deutschtums*, Vol. 16, 1969; E. Nodel, *Estonia: Nation on the Anvil*, New York 1963.

L. Berzinš, *Latviešu literaturas vēsture*, Riga 1935; S. E. Page, 'Social and National Currents in Latvia 1860–1917', *The American Slavic and East European Review*, VIII, 1949; M. Lindemuth, 'K. Valdemars und A. Kronvalds', *Baltische Hefte*, 1967.

D. Alseika, *Lietuviu tautinė ideja istorijos šviesoje*, Vilnius 1924; M. Hellmann, 'Die litauische Nationalbewegung im 19. und 20. Jahrhundert' in *Zeitschrift für Ostforschung*, 1953/2.

The 1905 Revolution

H. Kruus, *Punased aastad* (Sources), Tallinn 1931; E. Blanks, *1905 g. revolucija*, Riga 1930; *Revoljucija 1905–1907 gg. v naciomal'nych rajonach Rossii*, Moscow 1955 (Estonia: G. J. Mosberg, Latvia: Ja. P. Krastyn', Lithuania: P. P. Girdzijauskese); *Istorič. Zapiski*, Vol. 45, 1954 (Articles by K. Ja. Strazdin' and Ju. J. Žjugžda); Ja. P. Krastyn', *Revoljucija 1905–1907 gg. v Latvii*, Moscow 1952; M. Yčas, *Atsiminimai*, 1–3, Kaunas 1935/6.

3. *The First World War and the Russian Revolution*

E. Laaman, *Eesti iseseisvuse sünd*, 1–4, Tartu 1936 ff. (Reprint Stockholm 1964); A. Rei, *Mälestusi tormiselt teelt*, Stockholm 1961; O. Rütli, *Mälestusi*, New York 1964. J. v. Hehn, H. v. Rimscha, H. Weiss, (eds.), *Von den Baltischen Provinzen zu den Baltischen Staaten, Beiträge zur Entstehung der Republiken Estland und Lettland 1917–1918*, Marburg 1971.

A. v. Taube, 'Nationale Demokratie, sozialistische Arbeiterkommune oder gesamtbaltischer Ständestaat?' *Baltische Hefte*, 1959/1.

U. Germanis, 'The Idea of Independent Latvia and its Development in 1917', *Res Baltica* (Memorial volume for A. Bilmanis) Leiden 1968; T. Ja. Draudin, *Boevoj put' latyšskoj strelkovoj divizii 1917–1920*, Riga 1960; S. W. Page, *The Formation of the Baltic States*, Cambridge, Mass. 1959; S. W. Page, 'Lenin and the Baltic States 1917–1919', *Slavic Review*, 1948/1; S. Paegle, *Kā Latvijas valsts tapa*, Riga 1923; J. Līgotnis, *Latvijas valsts dibinašana*, Riga 1925; J. Seskis, *Latvijas valsts izcelšanas*, Riga 1938; H. v. Rimscha, *Die Staatswerdung Lettlands und das baltische Deutschtum*, Riga 1939.

J. v. Hehn, 'Die Entstehung der Staaten Lettland und Estland. Der Bolschewismus und die Großmächte', *Forschungen zur Osteuropäischen Geschichte*, Vol. 4, Berlin 1956; H. Dopkewitsch, *Die Entwicklung des lettländischen Staatsgedankens bis 1918*, Berlin 1936; M. Lindemuth, 'Lenin und die lettische Sozialdemokratie', *Baltische Hefte*, 1968; *Latvijas vēsture*, Vol. 4 (1914–20: E. Andersons).

A. E. Senn, *The Emergence of Modern Lithuania*, New York 1959; G. Linde, *Die deutsche Politik in Litauen im I. Weltkrieg*, Wiesbaden 1965.

4. The German Occupation

GENERAL

E. v. Dellingshausen, *Im Dienste der Heimat*, Stuttgart 1930; C. Grimm, *Vor den Toren Europas 1918–1920. Geschichte der Baltischen Landeswehr*, Hamburg 1963 (reviewed by J. v. Hehn, *Zeitschrift für Ostforschung*, 1963/4); R. v. d. Goltz, *Meine Sendung in Finnland und im Baltikum*, Leipzig 1920 (New ed. 1936 entitled *Als politischer General im Osten*); A. Winnig, *Am Ausgang der deutschen Ostpolitik*, Berlin 1921; *Obrazovanie SSSR. Sbornik dokumentov 1917–1924*, Moscow 1949 (Proclamation in *Izvestija*, 25. 12. 1918); K. H. Janssen, 'A. v. Goßler und die deutsche Verwaltung im Baltikum 1915–1918' in *Historische Zeitschrift*, 1968/1; B. Mann, *Die baltischen Länder in der deutschen Kriegszielpublizistik 1914–1918*, Tübingen 1965; W. Basler, *Deutschlands Annexionspolitik in Polen und im Baltikum 1914–1918*, East Berlin 1962.

H. Laretei, 'Petrograd-esternas aktion för sitt hemlands frihet', in *Svio-Estonica*, N. F. 9, Lund 1967 (with the Memorandum of 25. 4. 1918); P. Vihalem, *Eesti kodanlus imperialistide teenistuses 1917–1920*, Tallinn 1960; K. R. Pusta, *Kehra metsast maailma . . . Mälestusi*, Stockholm 1960; A. Lossman, *Rahutus maailmas*, Stockholm 1961.

V. Sīpols, *Die ausländische Intervention in Lettland 1918–1920*, Berlin 1961; H. E. Volkmann, 'Probleme des deutschlettischen Verhältnisses zwischen Compiègne und Versailles', *Zeitschrift für Ostforschung*, 14, 1965; H. v. Rimscha, *Die Staatswerdung* . . . (see above).

A. N. Tarulis, *Soviet Policy toward the Baltic States 1918–1940*, Notre Dâme 1959; G. Linde (see above); A. E. Senn, 'Die bolschewistische Politik in Litauen 1917', *Forschungen zur Osteuropäischen Geschichte*, Vol. 5, 1957.

I*

246 THE BALTIC STATES

5. *The War of Liberation*

GENERAL

Documents on British Foreign Policy 1919–1939, Series I, 3, London 1947 *ff.*; *Papers relating to the Foreign Relations of the United States. Russia 1919; Peace Conference 1919*, Vol. 12; W. S. Churchill, *The World Crisis*, London 1923–31; D. Lloyd George, *War Memoirs*, London 1936, Vol. 5.

R. Ullman, *Britain and the Russian Civil War*, Princeton 1968; J. Bischoff, *Die letzte Front*, Berlin 1935; G. Bennet, *Cowans War: the Story of British Naval Operations in the Baltic 1918–1920*, London 1964; Sir Stephen Tallents, *Man and Boy*, London 1944; du Parquet *L'aventure allemande en Lettonie*, Paris 1926; E. Anderson, 'The British Policy toward the Baltic States 1918–1920', *Journal for Central European Affairs, 1959/19;* E. Anderson, 'An Undeclared Naval War: the British–Soviet Naval Struggle in the Baltic 1918–1919', *Journal for Central European Affairs*, 1962/3; W. E. Williams, 'Die Politik der Alliierten gegenüber den Freikorps im Baltikum 1918–1919', *Vierteljahrshefte für Zeitgeschichte*, 1964/2; R. Wittram, 'Zur Geschichte des Winters 1918–1919', *Baltische Lande*, Vol. 4, Leipzig 1939; G. v. Rauch, 'Die Rolle Amerikas im baltischen Freiheitskrieg', *Baltische Briefe*, 1962/6; H. v. Rimscha, 'Die baltische Mission des amerikanischen Oberstleutnants W. Greene im Jahre 1919', *Festschrift E. v. Sivers*, 1966; *Der Feldzug im Baltikum bis zur 2. Einnahme von Riga. Darstellungen aus den Nachkriegskämpfen deutscher Truppen und Freikorps*, Vol. 2, Berlin 1937; *Die Kämpfe im Baltikum nach der 2. Einnahme von Riga*, ibid., Vol. 3, Berlin 1938.

E. Laaman (see Ch. I/3); G. Naan (see Introduction); *Eesti Vabadussõda 1918–1920*, Tallinn 1937 ff.; J. Soots, *Eesti Vabadussõda*, Tallinn 1925; A. Rei, *Mälestusi* . . . (see Ch. I/3); A. Piip, *Tormine aasta*, Tallinn 1934 (Stockholm 1966); M. Martna, *Estland, die Esten und die estländische Frage*, Olten 1919; J. Poska, *Eesti iseseisvuse wõitluses*, Tallinn 1921; E. Laaman, *op. cit.*; A. v. Taube, *op. cit.*; W. Baron Wrangell, *Die Geschichte des Baltenregiments*, Hannover o. J. (Reprint of the 1st (1928) edition); C. v. Weiss, 'Mein strategischer Entschluß vom 17. 12. 1918', *Baltische Hefte*, 1958/1; H. Walter, 'Die Bolschewikenzeit in Dorpat', *Baltische Hefte*, 1968; J. M. Saat, 'Bor'ba V. Kingiseppa protiv buržuaznogo nacionalizma v. Estonii', *Istor. Zapiski*, Vol. 45, 1954; M. Penikis, *Latvijas armijas sākums un cīnas*, Riga 1932; M. Penikis, *Latvijas nacionālas armijas cīnas 1919 gada vasarā un rudeni*, Riga 1931; A. Niedra, *Kā tas lietas tika daritas*, Riga 1930; A. Niedra, *Tautas nodevēja atmiņas*, 1–3, Riga 1923–30; *Die Baltische Landeswehr. Ein Gedenkbuch*, Riga 1929;

M. Hunnius, *Bilder aus der Zeit der Bolschewikenherrschaft in Riga*, Heilbronn 1921; P. Stučka, *5 mesjacev Socialističeskoj Sovetskoj Latvii*, Moscow 1919; Ja. P. Krastyn', 'Amerikansko-anglijskaja intervencija v Latvii, v 1918–1920 gg', *Istor. Zapiski*, Vol. 35, 1954; *Očerki istorii kommunističeskoj partii Latvii*, 1–2, Riga 1965 ff.; V. Sīpols, op. cit.; *Militarismus gegen Sowjetmacht 1917–1919. Das Fiasko der ersten antisowjetischen Aggression des deutschen Militarismus.* Berlin 1967.

On Stučka, see D. Loeber, 'Unbewältigte Vergangenheit im sowjetischen Zivilrecht. Zur Auseinandersetzung um das wissenschaftliche Erbe von Peter I. Stučka', *Macht und Recht im Kommunistischen Herrschaftssystem*, Köln 1965.

A. Merkelis, *Antanas Smetona*, New York 1964; P. Ja. Šarmajtis, 'Intervencija anglo-amerikanskich imperialistov v Litve v 1918–1920 gg', *Istor. Zapiski*, Vol. 45, 1954.

6. The Peace Treaties

Dokumenty vnešnej politiki S.S.S.R., Vol. 102, Moscow 1958; for Lenin on the Peace of Tartu, see *Polnoe sobranie sočinenij*, Moscow 1963, Vol. 40, pp. 89–92 (2. 2. 20) and p. 123 (7. 2. 20).

For Peace of Tartu, see: E. Laaman, op. cit.; for the Bermondt Affair see: Fürst Awaloff-Bermondt, *Im Kampf gegen den Bolschewismus*, Hamburg 1925; R. Valande, *Avec le général Niessele n Prusse et en Lithuanie*, Paris 1922; du Parquet, *L'Aventure Allemande en Lettonie*, Paris 1926; A. Niessel, *L'Evacuation des Pays Baltiques par les Allemands*, Paris 1935; M. W. Graham, *The Diplomatic Recognition of the Border States*, Berkeley 1939.

Chapter II: The Early Stages of Independence

1. Constitutions and National Emblems

A. Mägi, *Das Staatsleben Estlands während seiner Selbständigkeit*, Stockholm 1967; S. v. Czekey, 'Die Verfassungsentwicklung Estlands 1918–1928', *Jahrbuch für Öffentliches Recht*, Vol. 16, 1928; W. Meder, 'Die Verfassungsentwicklung Estlands und Lettlands', *Jomsburg* 1937/38, 1; E. Hästad, *Den författningspolitiska utvecklingen i Balticum*, Stockholm 1943; B. Djušen, *Respubliki Pribaltiki*, Berlin 1921; G. Rutenberg, *Die baltischen Staaten und das Völkerrecht*, Riga 1928.

2. Demographic Developments and Nationalities

Handwörterbuch (see above); M. Valters (see above); A. Pullerits (op. cit); A. Bilmanis, *Baltic Essays*, Washington 1945. Deals *inter alia* with the Latvian minorities.

E. Blumfeldt, 'Estlands svenskarnas historia', *En bok om Estlands svenskar*, Stockholm, n.d.

A. v. Taube, 'Eibofolke im Schmelztiegel', *Baltische Briefe*, 1966, 1–3. H. Handrack, *Die Bevölkerungsentwicklung der deutschen Minderheit in Lettland*, Jena 1932; *Litauen und seine Deutschen*, Würzburg 1955; M. Hellmann, *Die Deutschen in Litauen*, Kitzingen, n.d.

3. Agrarian Reforms

Handwörterbuch (see above); *Das Estländische Agrargesetz*, Reval 1929; E. Kahn, *Die Agrarstuktur Lettlands bis 1939*, Königsberg 1942.

Contemporary Brochures: O. Bernmann, *Die Agrarfrage in Estland*, Berlin 1920 (?); E. Fromme, *Die Republik Estland und das Private-igentum*, Berlin 1922; A. Weller, *Die Agrarreform in Estland in juristischer Beleuchtung*, Berlin 1922; G. Bogdanoff, *Die Agrarreform: ein Mittel zur Unterdrückung der nationalen Minorität*, Berlin 1922.

Das Estländische Agrargesetz und das Entschädigungsgesetz, Reval 1929 (Speeches by Members of Parliament Bock, v. Stackelberg, v. Schilling, de Vries, Hasselblatt); H. v. Fölkersahm, *Die Entwicklung der Agrarverfassung Livlands und Kurlands und die Umwälzung der Agrarverhältnisse in der Republik Lettland*, Greifswald 1923.

4. The Political Parties

E. Laaman, *Erakonnad Eestis* (The Estonian Parties), Tartu 1934; A. Mägi, (see above); E. Laaman, *Uber die Verfassungsentwicklung in der Republik Estland*, Stockholm 1949; S. Klau, 'Zur politischen Ideologie des Estentums', *Baltische Monatshefte*, 1929; S. Klau, 'Die estnischen Sozialisten', ibid., 1930; S. Klau, 'Das Parteiwesen Estlands', ibid., 1931; A. Rei, *Mälestusi* (see above); E. Laaman, *K. Päts*, Stockholm 1949; *M. Raud, Kaks suurt* (Päts and Tõnisson) Toronto 1953; J. Tõnisson, *Koguteos*, Stockholm 1960 (Anthology on J.T.).

O. Rjästas, 'Die kommunistische Partei Estlands im Gefecht', *Die Kommunistische Internationale*, VI/1, 1925.

J. v. Hehn, *Lettland zwischen Demokratie und Diktatur. Zur Geschichte des lettländischen Staatsstreichs vom 15. 5. 1934*, München 1957 (see esp. the introductory chapters); G. v. Rauch, 'Zur Krise des

Parlamentarismus in Estland und Lettland in den 30er Jahren', *Die Krise des Parlementarismus in Ostmitteleuropa zwischen den beiden Weltkriegen.* ed. H. E. Volkmann, Marburg 1967 (see pp. 135–41); A. Zalts, *Die politischen Parteien Lettlansd*, Riga 1926. P. Stučka, 'Das "demokratische" Lettland', *Die Kommunistische Internationale*, V/33, 1924; P. Stučka, 'Der Kampf des Proletariats um die Annäherung Lettlands an die Sowjetunion', ibid., VIII/50, 1927.

5. *The Vilnius and Klaipeda (Memel) Questions*

E. A. Plieg, *Das Memelland 1920–1939*, Würzburg 1962; A. E. Senn, *The Great Powers, Lithuania and the Vilna Question 1920–1928*, Leiden 1966; G. Moresthe, *Vilna et le problème de l'Est d'Europe*, Paris 1922; *Conflit Polono-Lithuanien. Question de Vilna*, Kaunas 1924 (documents).

Chapter III: Baltic Politics in the 1920s

1. *Federation Politics after 1920*

K. R. Pusta, *Kehra metsast* (see above); K. R. Pusta, *Saadiku päevik*, New York 1964; H. Arumäe, *Za kulisami Baltüskogo sojusa 1920–1925*, Tallinn 1966; F. Cielens, *Laikmetu maina*, 1–3, Lidingö 1962–4.

G. v. Rauch, 'Die baltischen Staaten und Sowjetrußland 1919–1939', *Europa-Archiv*, 1954, 19, 20 and 21; Ch. Arumjae (= Arumäe), *Za kulisami baltijskogo sojuza*, Tallinn 1966.

2. *The Communist Putsch in Tallinn*

G. v. Rauch, 'Der Revaler Kommunistenputsch (1. 12. 1924)', *Baltische Hefte*, 1955/1; R. Liljedahl, 'Revalkuppen den 1. dec. 1942', *Svio-Estonica*, XVII/8, Lund 1964; V. Serge, *Memoirs of a Revolutionary 1901–1941*, London 1963, p. 177.

G. Naan (op. cit.); G. Pögelmann, 'Estland', *Die Kommunistische Internationale*, V/33, 1924; J. M. Saat, 'Bor'ba V. Kingiseppa protiv buržuaznogo nacionalizma v Estonii', *Istor. Zapiski 45, 1954*; J. M. Saat, *Vooruženoe vosstanie v Talline 1. dek. 1924 g.*, Doklady i Soobščenija Instituta Istorii, 1955/4.

3. *Moscow's Policy on Lithuania*

M. Hellmann, *Geschichte* (see above); M. Hellmann, *Litauen zwischen* . . . (see above); G. v. Rauch, *Zur Krise* . . . (see above).

Dokumenty vnešnej politiki S.S.S.R., Vol. 8; H. Laretei, *Birgiaad*, Stockholm 1962 (The Birk Affair); O. Mamers (= Öpik), *Kahe sõja vahel* (Between Two Wars), Stockholm 1957; K. V. Ozols, *Memuary poslannika*, Paris 1938.

A. Rūkas (ed.), *Mykolas Sleževičius*, Chicago 1954; W. Mickevicius-Kapsukas, 'Skizzen aus dem heutigen Litauen', *Die Kommunistische Internationale*, V/35, 1924; J. Paleckis, *Žiugsniai smėly. 1926 metai*, Vilnius 1968.

4. Developments in the Economy

A. Vendt, *Estnische Handelspolitik*, Emsdetten 1938; U. Kaur, *Wirtschaftsstruktur und Wirtschaftspolitik des Freistaates Estland 1918–1940*, Bonn 1962.

H. Zitron, *Außenhandel und Handelspolitik Lettlands und die Frage der baltischen Zollunion*, Riga 1935; P. Meyer, *Die Industrie Lettlands*, Riga 1925; A. Salts, *Lettlands Wirtschaft und Wirschaftspolitik*, Riga 1930.

5. Education and Culture

G. Ney, 'Das estnische Hochschulwesen', *Acta Baltica*, Vol. 3, Königstein 1963/64; L. Villecourt, *L'Université de Tartu*, Tartu 1932; A. v. Taube, 'Die Staatsuniversität Tartu 1919–1940 aus der Sicht deutsch-baltischer Studenten', *Jahrbuch für das baltische Deutschtum*, Vol. 12, 1965.

A. Namsons, 'Das lettische Hochschulwesen', *Acta Baltica* (see above); G. Klein, 'Die lettländische Universität zu Riga 1919–1940', *Jahrbuch für das baltische Deutschtum*, Vol. 13, 1966.

6. The Cultural Autonomy of the Minorities

R. Laun, 'Internationale Verträge für Minderheitenschutz', *Schriften über Minderheitenschutz*, Heft 2, Berlin 1920; E. Maddison, *Die nationalen Minderheiten Estlands und ihre Rechte*, Tallinn 1926; E. Maddison, 'Nationalpolitische Grundsätze der Estländischen Verfassung', *Nation und Staat*, 1927/28; K. Aun, *Der völkerrechtliche Schutz nationaler Minderheiten in Estland 1917–1940*, Hamburg 1951; O. Angelus, *Die Kulturautonomie in Estland*, Detmold 1951; H. Weiss, 'Das Volksgruppenrecht in Estland vor dem 2. Weltkriege', *ZfO*, 1952; H. Weiss, 'Der deutschbaltische Beitrag zur Lösung der Minderheitenfrage in der Zeit zwischen den beiden Weltkriegen', *Leistung und Schicksal*, ed. by E. G. Schulz, Köln 1967; W. Hasselblatt, 'Kulturautonomie', *Festschrift für R. Laun*, Hamburg 1948

(For information on Hasselblatt see *Jahrbuch für das baltische Deutschtum*, 1959, *Baltische Briefe*, 1958/2); For information on A. de Vries see *Jahrbuch für das baltische Deutschtum*, Vol. 11, 1964; M. Margulies, 'Die jüdischen Minderheiten', *Süddeutsche Monatshefte* 1927/28.

W. Wachtsmuth, *Von deutscher Arbeit in Lettland*, 1–3, Köln 1951–1953; W. Wachtsmuth, *Wege, Umwege, Weggenossen*, München 1952; see also F. W. Just, *Von deutscher Arbeit in Lettland 1919–1934*, I, 1–2, Riga 1938, II, 3–5, Riga 1939 typescript; P. Schiemann, *Die kulturellen Aufgaben der deutsch-baltischen Presse*, Riga 1928; H. v. Rimscha, 'P. Schiemann als Minderheitenpolitiker', *VfZG*, 1956/1; H. v. Rimscha, in P. Schiemann, Jahrbuch für die *Geschichte Osteuropas*, 1954, and in *ZfO*, 1956; *Baltische Köpfe*, ed. by H. Bosse *et al.*, Bovenden 1953 (article on P. Schiemann); W. v. Rüdiger, *Aus dem letzten Kapitel deutschbaltischer Geschichte in Lettland 1919–1945*, I, 1934, II, 1955.

F. Wertheimer, *Von deutschen Parteien und Parteiführern im Ausland*, Berlin 1930/2.

Chapter IV: New Developments in the 1930s

1. *The Parliamentary Crisis*

Die Krise des Parlamentarismus (see above, Hellmann, v. Rauch); E. Nolte, *Die faschistischen Bewegungen*, München 1966.

2. *Authoritarian Democracy in Estonia and Latvia*

V. Zinghaus, *Führende Köpfe in den baltischen Staaten*, Kaunas/Leipzig 1938.

W. Meder, *Die Verfassungsentwicklung Estlands und Lettlands*, Jomsburg 1937/1; W. Meder, 'Die Verfassung Estlands vom 17. 8. 1937', *Zeitschrift für Osteuropäisches Recht*, 1937/38, 4; E. Hästad, (op. cit., II, 1).

W. Meder, *Das Dekretrecht des Staatspräsidenten in Estland*, Dorpat 1936; *Põhiseadus ja Rahvuskogu*, Tallinn 1937; *Album koguetos 12. märtsi radadel*, ed. by v. H. Rahamägi *et al.*, Tallin 1936; A. Mägi, op. cit.; G. v. Knorring, 'Krisenjahre in Estland', *Baltische Hefte*, 1962/2; W. v. Wrangell, 'K. Päts', *Baltische Briefe*, 1964/4.

J. v. Hehn, *Lettland zwischen . . .* (see above); W. v. Knorre, *Wirtschaftspolitik Lettlands 1934–1939 während des autoritären Regimes* (unpubl.); H. Stegman, 'Aus meinen Erinnerungen', *Baltische Hefte*,

1961/2 ('Stadtverordneter in Riga') and 1961/3 ('Im sterbenden Parlament').

3. The Lithuanian Presidential Regime

R. J. Misiunas, 'Fascist Tendencies in Lithuania', *Slavonic and East European Review*, Jan. 1972; 'Faktai Kaltina', *Geležinas Vilkas*, Vilnius 1965; *Die Krise* (see above); M. Hellmann, *Geschichte* (see above); V. Zinghaus (see above).

4. Development of the Baltic German Community

Handwörterbuch, article 'Deutschbalten' (see above); R. Wittram, 'Rückblick auf den Strukturwandel der deutschbaltischen Volksgruppen im letzten Jahrzehnt vor der Umsiedlung', *Festschrift P. E. Schramm*, Vol. 2, Wiesbaden 1964; W. Wachtsmuth (op. cit.); F. Wertheimer (op. cit.).

E. Tatarin-Tarnheiden, *Die Enteignung des deutschen Domes zu Riga*, Breslau 1932; H. U. Scupin, *Die neuen lettländischen Wirtschaftsgesetze*, Hamburg 1939; H. v. Rimscha, 'Zur Gleichschaltung der deutschen Volksgruppen durch das Dritte Reich. Am Beispiel der deutschbaltischen Volksgruppe in Lettland', *Historische Zeitschrift*, 182/1, August 1956.

E. Kroeger, *Der Auszug aus .der alten Heimat. Die Umsiedlung der Balten-deutschen*, Tübingen 1967.

5. The International Status of the Baltic States from 1930 onwards

Dokumenty . . . (I, 4), Vol. 12, 13, 14 (up to 31. 12. 1931).

G. v. Rauch *Die baltischen Staaten* . . . (see above); A. N. Tarulis (op. cit.); F. Cielens (see above); G. Vigrabs, 'Die Stellungnahme der Westmächte und Deutschlands zu den baltischen Staaten im Frühling und Sommer 1939', *VfZG*, 1959/3; Duroselle (op. cit.); O. Sepre, *Zavisimost' buržuaznoj Estonii ot imperialističeskich stran*, Tallinn 1960.

6. The Baltic Entente

H. Zitron (op. cit.); the works listed under IV/5; For information on H. Munters, see *Osteuropa*, 1963/13; *Baltische Briefe*, 1967/3. E. Anderson, 'Toward the Baltic Entente', *Pro Baltica*, Stockholm 1965; E. Anderson, 'Toward the Baltic Union 1927–1934', *Lituanus*, 1967/1; E. Anderson, 'Die militärische Situation der baltischen Staaten', *Acta Baltica 1968* (1969).

Chapter V: The Baltic States and the two Great Power Blocs

1. Harbingers of the Storm

See IV/5.

E. Kirotar, 'Eesti Välisministeriumis', Eesti Riik ja Rahvas II. Maailmasõjas, Vol. 2, Stockholm 1955; A. Bilmanis, Latvian–Russian Relations, Washington 1944; A. Spekke, Latvia and the Baltic Problem, London 1952; L. Sabaliunas, Lithuania in Crisis 1939–1941, Bloomington, Ind., 1972.

B. Meissner, 'Die Großmächte und die Baltische Frage', Osteuropa, 1952/4; H. v. Rimscha, 'Die Baltikumpolitik der Großmächte', Historische Zeitschrift, 177/2, April 1954; B. Meissner, Die Sowjetunion, die Baltischen Staaten und das Völkerrecht, Köln 1956; A. Thulstrup, Aggressioner och allianser. Huvudlinier i europeisk storpolitik 1935–1939, Stockholm 1957; W. Baron Wrangell, 'Die deutsche Politik und die baltischen Staaten 1939', Baltische Hefte, 1959/4; E. Čeginskas, Die baltische Frage in den Großmächteverhandlungen 1939, Bonn 1967 (Commentationes Balticae XII/XIII, 2).

For the Zhdanov speech see Pravda 1. 12. 1936, and cf. Revaler Zeitung 1. and 2. 12. 1936, Schultheß Europäischer Geschichtskalender, N. F., Jg. 77, p. 448, and Osteuropa 1936/37, Heft 12, p. 264; also G. v. Rauch, Europa-Archiv, p. 6969 and 6972; B. Meissner in Osteuropa, 1952, Heft 1–2; and B. Meissner, Die Sowjetunion, die baltischen Staaten . . ., p. 14; M. Beloff, The Foreign Policy of Soviet Russia 1929–1941, Oxford 1947, Vol. 2, p. 78; A. Schwabe, Historie . . ., p. 216; E. Uustalu, Eesti . . ., p. 209.

2. Guarantees and Spheres of Interest

Akten zur Deutschen Auswärtigen Politik 1918–1945, Series D, Vol. V (June 1937–March 1939), Baden-Baden 1953; Vol. VI, (March–August 1939) 1956; Vol. VII (August–September 1939) 1956; Documents on British Foreign Policy 1919–1939, Series III, Vol. V–VII (1939), London 1952–4.

Eesti Riik ja Rahvas II. Maailmasõjas (The Estonian State and People in the Second World War), Stockholm 1954 ff., Vols. 1–5. G. Bonnet, Fin d'une Europe, Geneve 1948; L. B. Namier, Diplomatic Prelude 1938–1939, London 1948; L. Noël, L'Aggression allemande contre la Pologne, Paris 1946; G. Gafencu, Vorspiel zum Krieg im Osten (1939–1941), Zürich 1944; G. Hilger, Wir und der Kreml. Deutsch-sowjetische Beziehungen 1918–1941, Frankfurt, 1955.

For Hitler's Baltic policy see his *Mein Kampf* and *Tischgespräche* (Table Talk), the German Files (see above), and the memoirs of W. v. Blücher, E. v. Weizsäcker, R. Conlondre, J. E. Davies and G. Ciano. See also the articles by B. Meissner and H. v. Rimscha (op. cit.) in *Historische Zeitschrift*, 1954.

A. de Vries, *Aufzeichnungen über Gespräche mit K. Selter*, 17. 9. 1954 and 30. 1. 1955 (ms.).

On the Baltic German resettlement: W. v. Wrangell, 'Die Vorgeschichte der Umsiedlung der Deutschen aus Estlands', *Baltische Hefte*, 1958/3; H. Petersen, 'Der große Aufbruch. Die Umsiedlung und ihre politische Vorgeschichte', *Baltische Briefe*, 1964/11; H. v. Rimscha, *Die Umsiedlung der Deutschbalten aus Lettland im Jahre 1939*, Hannover n.d.; H. Weiss, 'Die Umsiedlung der Deutschen aus Estland', *Jahrbuch des baltischen Deutschtums*, 1964; W. Lenz, 'Die Umsiedlung der Deutschen aus Lettland', ibid.; E. v. Nottbeck, 'Organisation und Verlauf der Umsiedlung der Deutschen aus Estland', *Baltische Hefte*, 1971. Of special importance is the collection of documents by D. Loeber, *Diktierte Option. Die Umsiedlung der Deutsch-Balten aus Estland und Lettland 1939–1941*, Neumünster 1972.

3. The Attack on Baltic Sovereignty

J. J. Paleckis, 'V buržuazno-pomeščic'ej Litve', *Voprosy Istorii*, 1970/6–7; S. Raštikis, *Kovose del Lietuvos*, Los Angeles 1936/1–2.

Documents on German Foreign Policy, Series D, Vol. IX, Washington 1956.

See also A. Schwabe, *Histoire* . . . (see above); A. Rei, *Nazi-Soviet Conspiracy and the Baltic States*, London 1948; K. Selter, 'Die Sowjetpolitik und das Baltikum', *Monatshefte für Auswärtige Politik*, 1944; A. Bilmanis (op. cit.).

4. Final Attempts to Re-establish Baltic Independence

Tarulis (op. cit.); B. Meissner (op. cit.); J. A. Swettenham, *The Tragedy of the Baltic States*, London 1952; P. Olberg, *Die Tragödie des Baltikums*, Zürich 1941; A. Kristian, *The Right of Self-determination and the Soviet Union*, London 1952; M. Valters, *Das Verbrechen gegen die baltischen Staaten*, 1962.

Teheran, Jalta, Potsdam. Die sowjetischen Protokolle von den Kriegskonferenzen der Großen Drei, Ed. by A. Fischer, Cologne 1968; H. Weiss, 'Die baltischen Staaten', in Birke-Neumann, *Die Sowjetisierung Ostmitteleuropas*, Frankfurt/M 1959.

For an account of the military situation see: W. Haupt, *Baltikum 1941*, Neckargmünd 1964; Chr. Müller, 'Das militärische Drama im Baltikum 1944/1945', *Jahrbuch des baltischen Deutschtums*, Vol. 16, 1969; B. Kalninš, *De baltiska staternas frihetskamp*, Stockholm 1950; R. Bangerskis (Commander of the Latvian Legion in the Second World War) *Mana mūža atmiņas*, 1–4, Copenhagen 1958–60.

For an account of the liquidation of the Baltic Jews, see G. Reitlinger, *The Final Solution*, London 1953; For an account of the resettlement of the Estonian-Swedish community see: A. v. Taube (op. cit.).

O. Angelus, *Tuhande valitseja maa* (Memories of the German Occupation 1941–44), Stockholm 1956; A. Bilmanis, *Latvia under German Occupation*, 1–2, Washington 1942.

Eesti Riik ja Rahvas II. Maailmasõjas, 10 Lieferungen, Stockholm 1954 to 1962; A. Silgailis, *Latviešu legions*, Copenhagen 1964.

A. Kaelas, *Das sowjetisch besetzte Estland*, Stockholm 1958; *Die Deportationen im Baltikum*, ed. by The Information Bureau of the Estonian National Fund, Stockholm 1960; V. Stanley Vardys, 'Soviet Colonialism in the Baltic States 1940–1965', *Baltic Review*, 1965/29; V. Stanley Vardys, Lithuania under the Soviets, New York 1965; O. Angelus, 'Die Russifizierung Estlands', *Acta Baltica 1967*, 1968; V. Miller, *Sozdanie sovetskoj gosudarstvennosti v Latvii*, Riga 1967.

A. Grünbaum, 'Brücken von Volk zu Volk. Die baltische Emigration in Gegenwart und Zukunft', *Baltische Briefe*, 1967/4.

Chapter VI: Conclusion: the Past and the Future

Memorandum published by members of the Estonian technological intelligentsia: *Der aktuelle Osten*, Bonn 20. 1. 1969, no. 2; A. Küng, *Estland zum Beispiel: Nationale Minderheit und Supermacht*, Stuttgart 1973.

LISTS OF PRESIDENTS AND PREMIERS

ESTONIA

Presidents of the Republic	*Premiers*		
	K. Päts	24. 2. 1918	
		11. 11. 1918– 8. 5. 1919	
	O. Strandmann	8. 5. 1919–11. 11. 1919	
	J. Tõnisson	18. 11. 1919– 8. 10. 1920	
	A. Piip	26. 10. 1920– 4. 1. 1921	
	K. Päts	25. 1. 1921–24. 10. 1922	
	J. Kukk	21. 11. 1922– 4. 6. 1923	
	K. Päts	2. 8. 1923–10. 3. 1924	
	F. Akel	26. 3. 1924–16. 12. 1924	
	J. Jaakson	16. 12. 1924–25. 11. 1925	
	J. Teemant	15. 12. 1925–22. 11. 1927	
	J. Tõnisson	9. 12. 1927–13. 11. 1928	
	A. Rei	4. 12. 1928– 2. 7. 1929	
	O. Strandmann	9. 7. 1929– 3. 2. 1931	
	K. Päts	12. 2. 1931–29. 1. 1932	
	J. Teemant	19. 2. 1932–20. 6. 1932	
	K. Einbund	19. 7. 1932– 3. 10. 1932	
	K. Päts	7. 11. 1932–26. 4. 1933	
	J. Tõnisson	18. 5. 1933–17. 10. 1933	
	K. Päts	21. 10. 1933–24. 4. 1938	
K. Päts		*24. 4. 1938–21. 7. 1940*	
	K. Eenpalu (= Einbund)	24. 4. 1938–12. 10. 1939	
	J. Uluots	12. 10. 1939–21. 6. 1940	

LATVIA

Presidents of the Republic	Premiers		
	K. Ulmanis	18. 11. 1918–13.	7. 1919
	(A. Niedra	10. 5. 1919– 3.	7.1919)
	K. Ulmanis	14. 7. 1919–18.	6. 1921
	S. Meierovics	19. 6. 1921–26.	1. 1923
J. Čakste		*14. 11. 1922–14.*	*3. 1927*
	J. Pauļuks	27. 1. 1923–27.	6. 1923
	S. Meierovics	28. 6. 1923–26.	1. 1924
	V. Zāmuels	27. 1. 1924–18.	12. 1924
	H. Celmiņš	19. 12. 1924–23.	12. 1925
	K. Ulmanis	24. 12. 1925– 6.	5. 1926
	A. Alberings	7. 5. 1926–18.	12. 1926
	M. Skujenieks	19. 12. 1926–23.	1. 1928
G. Zemgals		*14. 3. 1927– 9.*	*4. 1930*
	P. Juraševskis	24. 1. 1928–30.	11. 1928
	H. Celmiņš	1. 12. 1928–26.	3. 1931
	K. Ulmanis	27. 3. 1931– 5.	12. 1931
A. Kviesis		*9. 4. 1930–11.*	*4. 1936*
	M. Skujenieks	6. 12. 1931–23.	3. 1933
	A. Bļodnieks	24. 3. 1933–16.	3. 1934
	K. Ulmanis	17. 3. 1934–19.	6. 1940
K. Ulmanis		*11. 4. 1936–21.*	*7. 1940*

LITHUANIA

Presidents of the Republic	Premiers		
(*A. Smetona*, President of the *Taryba*		*18. 9. 1917– 4. 2. 1919*)	
	A. Voldemaras	11. 11. 1918–26. 12. 1918	
	M. Sleževičius	26. 12. 1918–11. 3. 1919	
	P. Dovydaitis	12. 3. 1919–12. 4. 1919	
A. Smetona		*4. 4. 1919–19. 6. 1920*	
	M. Sleževičius	12. 4. 1919– 6. 10. 1919	
	E. Galvanauskas	7. 10. 1919–19. 6. 1920	
	K. Grinius	19. 6. 1920–18. 1. 1922	
A. Stulginskis		*19. 6. 1922– 7. 6. 1926*	
	E. Galvanauskas	2. 2. 1922–10. 6. 1924	
	A. Tumėnas	18. 6. 1924–27. 1. 1925	
	V. Petrulis	4. 2. 1925–19. 9. 1925	
	L. Bistras	25. 9. 1925–31. 5. 1926	
K. Grinius		*7. 6. 1926–17. 12. 1926*	
	M. Sleževičius	15. 6. 1926–17. 12. 1926	
A. Smetona		*17. 12. 1926–15. 6. 1940*	
	A. Voldemaras	18. 12. 1926–19. 9. 1929	
	J. Tūbelis	23. 9. 1929–24. 3. 1938	
	V. Mironas	24. 3. 1938–27. 3. 1939	
	J. Černius	28. 3. 1939–21. 11. 1939	
	A. Merkys	21. 11. 1939–17. 6. 1940	

BALTIC PLACE-NAMES AND THEIR EQUIVALENTS IN GERMAN/ INTERNATIONAL USAGE

Abrene/Pytalovo (Abrehenen)
Cēsis (Wenden)
R. Daugava (Düna)
Daugavpils (Dünaburg)
Emajõgi (Embach)
R. Gauja (Aa)
Haapsalu (Hapsal)
Helsinki (Helsingfors)
Hiiumaa (Dagö)
Jekabpils (Jakobstadt)
Jelgava (Mitau)
Jõhvi (Jewe)
Kaunas (Kovno)
Kingisepp (Arenburg)
Klaipeda (Memel)
Kuldiga (Goldingen)
Latgale (Lettgallen)
Liepaja (Libau)
Muhu (Moon)
R. Nemunas (Memel)
Paide (Weissenstein)

Pärnu (Pernau)
Lake Peipsi (Peipus)
Petseri/Pecory (Petschur)
Polanga (Polangen)
Pskov (Pleskau)
Rakvere (Wesenberg)
Rēzekne/Režica (Rositten)
Saaremaa (Ösel)
Šiauliai (Schaulen)
Tallinn (Reval)
Tartu (Dorpat)
Taurage (Tauroggen)
Tukums (Tuckum)
Valga/Valka (Walk)
Valmiera (Wolmar)
Venta (Windau)
Viljandi (Fellinn)
Vilnius (Wilna)
Vormsi (Worms)
Lake Võrts (Wirz)
Võru (Werro)

INDEX